Falling Towers

Falling Towers

The Trojan Imagination in
The Waste Land, The Dunciad, and
Speke Parott

J. A. Richardson

DELAWARE

Newark: University of Delaware Press
London and Toronto: Associated University Presses

Associated University Presses
440 Forsgate Drive
Cranbury, NJ 08512

Associated University Presses
25 Sicilian Avenue
London WC1A 2QH, England

Associated University Presses
P.O. Box 39, Clarkson Pstl. Stn.
Mississauga, Ontario,
L5J 3X9 Canada

The paper used in this publication meets the requirements of the American National Standard for Permanence of Paper for Printed Library Materials Z39.48-1984.

Library of Congress Cataloging-in-Publication Data

Richardson, J. A. (John A.), 1956–
    Falling towers : the Trojan imagination in The Waste Land, The Dunciad, and Speke Parott / J. A. Richardson.
        p.   cm.
    Includes bibliographical references and index.
    ISBN 0-87413-419-6 (alk. paper)
    1. English poetry—History and criticism—Theory, etc.   2. Eliot, T. S. (Thomas Stearns), 1888–1965.   Waste land.   3. Pope, Alexander, 1688–1744.   Dunciad.   4. Skelton, John, 1460?–1529.   Speke parott. 5. Regression (Civilization) in literature.   6. English poetry— Periodization.   7. Degeneration in literature.   8. Trojan War in literature.   9. Mortality in literature.   10. Old age in literature. 11. Cycles in literature.   I. Title.
PR502.R5   1992
821.009—dc20   90-50984
                                                                     CIP

PRINTED IN THE UNITED STATES OF AMERICA

For Fiona, Michael, and Sally

Contents

8   **Contents**

References and Abbreviations

References for the quotations from poems by Skelton, Pope, and Eliot are incorporated in the text, identified where necessary by short titles, and taken from the following sources:

John Skelton: The Complete English Poems. Edited by John Scattergood. Harmondsworth: Penguin, 1983.

The Twickenham Edition of the Poems of Alexander Pope. Edited by John Butt and others. 11 vols. London: Methuen, 1939–69.

The Complete Poems and Plays of T. S. Eliot. London: Faber and Faber, 1969.

Pope's poetry sometimes presents problems in ascribing short titles. Here, the titles *Epistle* and *Satire* refer always to the Horatian imitations. In giving references to *The Dunciad*, I have followed the Twickenham edition by denominating *The Dunciad Variorum* of 1729 as A, and *The Dunciad* of 1743 as B. Thus, the first line of the first book of the 1729 edition becomes A1 : 1, and so on.

The following abbreviations appear in the text:

Corr.	*The Correspondence of Alexander Pope.* Edited by George Sherburn. 5 vols. Oxford: Clarendon Press, 1956.
Poems	*The Twickenham Edition of the Poems of Alexander Pope.*
Prose	*The Prose Works of Alexander Pope.* Edited by Norman Ault and Rosemary Cowler. 2 vols. Oxford: Basil Blackwell, 1936 and 1986.
ASG	*After Strange Gods: A Primer of Modern Heresy.* London: Faber and Faber, 1934.
CC	*To Criticize the Critic and Other Writings.* London: Faber and Faber, 1965.
Facsimile	*"The Waste Land": A Facsimile and Transcript of the Original Drafts, Including the Annotations of Ezra Pound.* Edited by Valerie Eliot. London: Faber and Faber, 1971.
SW	*The Sacred Wood.* 1920. Reprint. London: Methuen, 1928.
SE	*Selected Essays.* 1932. Reprint. London: Faber and Faber, 1951.

Acknowledgments

Parts of Chapters Two and Three appeared in different form in *English* and *Neophilologus*. I am grateful to Faber and Faber and Harcourt, Brace, Jovanovitch for permission to reprint parts of *The Waste Land*.

Falling Towers

Part One
Trojans and Greeks

1

Introduction

The Trojan Imagination

"Nations," writes Johnson in the preface to his *Shakespeare,* "like individuals, have their infancy." It is, according to him, the infantile state of the nation in Shakespeare's time that explains both the general taste for "incredibility" and Shakespeare's bowing to that taste with representations of the marvelous and the fantastic.[1] Indeed, as Johnson remarks elsewhere, the genius of the age was such that a dramatic author could rely heavily upon agents, in this case supernatural agents, for which, in a more mature period, "he would be banished from the theatre to the nursery, and condemned to write fairy tales instead of tragedies."[2] There is much in these and similar comments of Johnson's that appears in the twentieth century to be narrow and misguided. The distaste for largeness of literary gesture betrays that constricted propriety, and the dismissal of the Elizabethans as barbarous that smugness, which we might still sometimes associate with a peculiarly limited eighteenth-century outlook. Moreover, the belief that the Middle Ages were sunk in a total, or to use Johnson's image, prenatal, darkness reflects a Renaissance view of history that has been unacceptable since the nineteenth century. Nevertheless, when these baser materials are removed, there remains in Johnson's conception of literary history a rich and largely unexploited seam of truth. If the late sixteenth and early seventeenth centuries cannot quite properly be seen in terms of the nation's infancy, the period does stand on the threshold of something, of what might be called, for want of better terms, a cultural epoch or a cultural tradition. Furthermore, it is this position on the threshold that accounts for some of the most distinctive features of that elusive but important phenomenon, the temper, or the spirit, of the age. The energy and excitement that seem to have been in the air during those decades, and that are everywhere evident in the literature produced then, are the energy and excitement of a people with a world all before them.

This book represents an attempt to pursue the approach to literary

history that underlies Johnson's account of the age of Shakespeare.
The assumptions behind it are, to rephrase Johnson, that cultural
traditions, like individuals, have their senescence, and that the imagination of an author writing during the senescence of a tradition is
likely to be shaped by the tradition's decay. While Elizabethan literature tends to be characterized by energy and excitement, the literature from the end of a tradition tends to be characterized by
restriction, defensiveness, and unease. This is a large claim, and, as so
often with large claims, it can best be advanced, at least in the initial
stages, by close and specific argument. Thus, the bulk of the book is
devoted to exploring in detail the affinities in imagination between
three poems—*Speke Parott, The Dunciad,* and *The Waste Land*—each
arguably the most important poem of its era, which stand at the end of
three different traditions. Each of the three poems, I maintain, engages in a similar conflict and betrays similar feelings of anxiety and
uncertainty about the future of the poet's tottering tradition, betrays,
that is, a kind of Trojan sensibility.

If nothing else, the study should achieve one of the aims that Anne
Wright proposes in her examination of *Howard's End, Heartbreak
House, Women in Love* and *The Waste Land,* namely, to propound "a
fresh configuration, and perhaps an alternative perspective" and to
"reproblematise" the literature it deals with.[3] However, just as Wright
wishes to do rather more than to establish a new grouping of writers
or to raise new problems, so I hope to suggest something beyond the
remarkable affinity between the three writers, and the three texts, I
deal with. What I should also like to advance, with a kind of cautious
confidence, is that one of the most essential qualities in the imagination of each of the three poets, what I have called the Trojan quality,
owes its existence to the decline of his tradition. Each of the three
poets stands, as I have said, at the end of a literary and cultural
tradition, at the end of the "medieval," the "Renaissance," and the
romantic traditions, respectively. Although the terms, especially the
first two, are highly unsatisfactory because of their vagueness, there
are none better. What I mean by each is a literary, more broadly a
cultural, tradition that, despite the wide range of authors within it, is
recognizable and fairly distinctive, producing works which bear some
family likeness to each other, looking back with respect to a group
(not really a canon in the Middle Ages) of accepted texts, and enshrin-
ing certain attitudes toward literature, authors, writing, and toward
human life in general. Skelton, Pope, and Eliot, I want to suggest,
shared a Trojan cast of mind because they each belonged to an end,
because their cultural traditions were showing that tendency of
cultural traditions to have, like individuals, their senescence.

If the three are in some essential respects alike, however, they do not, it hardly needs emphasizing, by any means form an obvious group. One problem with placing them together is that the later poets felt antagonism or indifference toward the earlier. Eliot took no part in the Skelton "revival" of the 1920s, and Pope's surviving comments about him label him "beastly" (*Epistle* 2.1.38) and describe his poetry as "all low and bad."[4] As for Eliot's attitude toward Pope, although he remarked in 1928 that "the man who cannot enjoy Pope as poetry probably understands no poetry,"[5] he offered no sustained critical comment on him, and his attempt at a pastiche of his style in the canceled Fresca passage of *The Waste Land* has generally been judged a failure. A further problem for comparison is the difference in stature between the three poets, for even after the rehabilitation of Skelton that has taken place in this century, he can hardly rank for most readers alongside Pope and Eliot. Despite these problems, however, a good case can be made for considering the three as a group. Even the disparity in stature is not too great a stumbling block, since Skelton is the major English poet of the first three decades of the sixteenth century and since the later eclipse of his reputation prefigures in an exaggerated way Pope's posthumous fortunes and what may turn out to be Eliot's fate. David B. Morris has remarked of Pope that "few major poets remain so unfailingly controversial,"[6] and there is at least some truth in David Ward's observation that "*The Waste Land's* reputation has fallen more rapidly since the Second World War than the public reputation of any major poem in any similar period."[7] Indeed, it may be characteristic of the poet from the end of a tradition that the reputation he enjoys during his life dwindles after death.

Reputation apart, the three poets are alike in their predilections for the mock-heroic and for learned poetry. There is perhaps no fourth major writer in English who sees the world so insistently from a mock-heroic perspective, and very few others who are so difficult. Furthermore, each of three appears in some of his poems as a conservative, even a reactionary, who sometimes indulges a radical or indecorous imagination. More striking than these similarities, though, are the similarities that exist between what is probably the major poem of each poet. It is a critical commonplace among Skelton scholars that *Speke Parott* is like *The Waste Land,* and several critics have drawn attention to the connections between *The Dunciad* and *The Waste Land.*[8] The grounds for comparison are clear enough. Each of the poems deals with, at least on one level, a cultural crisis, each envisages this partly in terms of a threat to a city, and each betrays what Grover Smith calls in reference to *The Waste Land* a "certain apocalyptic vibration."[9]

However, such affinities of theme and technique are less interesting than the way in which the three poems are built upon similar patterns of conflict and anxiety that manifest themselves in similar specific images and stratagems. These patterns reflect, I think, profoundly similar casts of the imagination, not necessarily conscious or recognized, in the three poets at the periods of composition. This might take us back to Johnson's comments on the Elizabethans. In discussing the "genius of the age," Johnson is less interested in reproducing the historical minutiae of prevailing opinions and ideas than in describing an essential human quality in the period, in characterizing the manner in which people responded, thought, and imagined. In a more limited sphere, I hope, by establishing the presence of similar underlying patterns in *Speke Parott, The Dunciad,* and *The Waste Land,* to demonstrate a fundamental resemblance in the imaginative responses of the three poets, and to suggest that the resemblance owes its existence to the periods in which they wrote. The first element in the pattern is that each poet presents his culture and himself as being threatened. The specific threats that I discuss in the body of this book are the threat posed by the young to the old and the threat posed to the conservative by large numbers of new ideas, new books, and new people. Secondly, each poet tries to counter the threat by asserting himself and his poetic authority. So, in the face of youth they insist upon their aged experience and wisdom, and in the face of the bewildering profusion of the new they insist upon their place in a strictly limited tradition. But importantly, these assertions are imagined in such a way that they appear to be defensive responses to a threat rather than expressions of real authority, with the result that the dominant mood of the poems is one of anxiety. The old man railing against youth is an insecure figure, as is the conservative desperately hanging on to his small canon of works.

This is what I mean by the "Trojan imagination," a way of perceiving the world, oneself, and one's relation to the world that is characteristic of the three poems and that is appropriate to a culture, like that of Troy, on the brink of destruction. The phrase itself was suggested by Skelton's position in the so-called Grammarians' War of 1519–21. As a supporter of the old teaching of Latin, he was a "Trojan," rather than a "Greek," a supporter of the new teaching of Greek. The appellation carries what was probably an unintentional irony, for while it deliberately characterizes the Trojans as conservative Latins, it also implies that they were fighting a losing battle. In a similar way, the three poets present themselves as Trojans in that they are fighting for the old ways, but they also imagine themselves as Trojans, with a degree of self-consciousness which varies both between the poets and within each poem, in that they appear to be insecure and heading for defeat. Interestingly, Troy itself, the model in European culture (along with the late preexilic Jerusalem) of the venerable civilization on the point of collapse, figures incidentally in each of the three poems. It is present in *Speke Parrot* through the references to the Grammarians' War, in *The Dunciad* through the connection between London and Troy and the allusions to the *Aeneid,* and in *The Waste Land* in the phrase "Falling towers" (373). But these distant echoes of the fall of Troy do not constitute my reason for using the epithet, "Trojan." That lies chiefly in the way that each poet imagines himself, at some profound level, as a kind of Priam, busy about the defense of his ancient city, while always knowing it cannot survive. Of course, this Trojan perspective is not peculiar to the three poems, but can also be found in other poems by the same poets, in the work of contemporaries, and occasionally in that of conservatives from other periods. Nevertheless, it is useful to isolate the poems as a group because the perspective is so crucial to each of them. In no other work is it quite so important that, while defending an old order with all the energy at his command, the poet also hints at the frailty of defenders and defenses and at the hopelessness of his own cherished cause.

The common Trojan cast of mind may, in a curious way, account for Pope's antagonism toward Skelton, and Eliot's indifference toward Pope. Skelton, as a beleaguered conservative, is in some ways aggressively medieval, even though the word *medieval* was not available to him and he would probably not have understood the idea. Nevertheless, even without quite appreciating what he was doing, he could strike medieval attitudes and adopt medieval positions in defiance of the rising new learning. To Pope, Skelton must have seemed the epitome of that millenium of dullness that he, as a late Renaissance poet, without possessing the word but with some sense of the idea, wanted to reject. Similarly, Pope himself, in fighting for his dying tradition, sought to defend those elements of it—decorum, rhetorical elegance, cultivated artistry, the respect for forms—for which the succeeding tradition had least sympathy. Consequently, Eliot, who for all his assertions of his own classicism and his occasional championing of Pope was essentially a romantic, seems to have felt the typically romantic antipathy for Pope and the Augustan, that age when, as he wrote, "poetry fell fast into a formalistic slumber."[10] The phrase, "formalistic slumber", is the language of romantic distaste for the defensively Renaissance attitudes of a poet like Pope.

Whether we can explain Pope's feelings for Skelton and Eliot's for Pope in this way or not, however, it remains true that the three poets faced a similar predicament. The similarity between their predicaments needs to be discussed further, and the third section of this chapter is devoted to that. First, though, it will be as well to turn to the poems themselves, in order to demonstrate more fully and more clearly the relationship between them and to face certain problems that arise in reading them. With *Speke Parott* and *The Waste Land,* in particular, the reader must struggle to identify the nature or the existence of the poetic speaker, and in addition, *The Waste Land* presents problems of categorization—it will not easily be reduced to type. Such difficulties should be dealt with, and the fundamental relationship between the three poems should be established at the outset of a long study like the present one.

Prophecy, Deluge, and Anxiety

In the world of *Speke Parott, The Dunciad,* or *The Waste Land,* those things the poet values most dearly are under threat. Later, I discuss in detail the deployment of images of youth and profusion to represent the threat, but here it is enough to say that in each poem a general modernity, or a new learning, or a widespread indifference, or a shift in taste, or a readjustment in social hierarchies, or an advance in technology, or a laxity of some kind, or a mixture of these, constitutes a potent danger to the civilization to which the poet belongs. In an effort to counter the threat, he makes himself a representative within the poem of his civilization, seeking to defend it by claiming with various devices a special authority and a special strength. So (to focus on one of these devices), Skelton, Pope, and Eliot all put on the prophet's mantle in order, so it seems, to acquire authority and to be able to prophesy their opponents' doom. In *Speke Parott,* Skelton rather demonstratively enters the prophet's role of excoriating and warning a collapsing society, and exploits the prophet's style of dense, allusive obscurity.[11] Perhaps the most strikingly prophetic moments in *The Dunciad* are the perverted vision of a new world in the third book, which harks back through *Messiah* to Isaiah (B3:241–48), and the coming of darkness at the end, which may be indebted to Jeremiah's vision of the earth "without form, and void" (Jer. 4:23).[12] In a similar manner, Eliot alludes to Ezekiel and Jeremiah, and his imagery of a land made waste and of water being withheld recalls the prophet's, particularly Jeremiah's, imagery of desert and drought as much as that of the Grail legends.[13] So, like Skelton and Pope, Eliot acquires a kind of weight for his words by associating them with Old Testament prophecy.

However, the important point is that each of the poets lacks, at least in these poems, both the prophet's faith in a surviving remnant and his confidence in his own calling. When Jeremiah, the prophet of the fall of Jerusalem, laments his suffering, God assures him of his safety with the promise "I will deliver thee out of the hands of the wicked" and of his truthfulness with the statement "if thou take forth the precious from the vile, thou shalt be as my mouth" (Jer. 15:19–21). In contrast, each of the three poets dramatizes his prophecies in such a way as to make them appear personally motivated, self-interested, and consequently, neither reliable predictions of his enemies' overthrow nor awe-inspiring expressions of his civilization's value. The anxiety inherent in all this explains my preference for describing the common cast of imagination of the three poets by reference to Troy rather than to Jerusalem. There is attaching even to the conquered Jerusalem the idea of a special value and an eventual restoration, whereas Troy provides us with the kind of image that hovers behind the anxiety of these poems, the image of a civilization on the brink of annihilation.

As well as through echoes of the Old Testament, the prophetic enters the poems through the recurrent allusions in each of them to the Flood. The motif deserves some attention because it is common to all the poems and because it shows, in particularly stark fashion, the poets indulging in dreams of triumph over their enemies. In *Speke Parott* the idea of deluge is present in the final invective's repeated references to "Dewcalyons flodde," a flood that Skelton identifies in *Phyllyp Sparowe* as being the same as Noah's (244–53), and in *The Dunciad*, in the large number of images connecting the dull with water, particularly with deep and spreading water.[14] There is also much in *The Waste Land* that suggests a flood. Madame Sosostris's warning of "death by water" is universalized when the prophetic voice of the fourth section enjoins his listeners to "Consider Phlebas" (321); the "unholy loves" of "The Fire Sermon" can recall those which precede Noah's flood as well as those of Saint Augustine's Carthage (Gen. 6:4; 307n); the repeated "afters" at the beginning of "What the Thunder said" and the changes they bring indicate the end of an epoch (322–30); the idea of a voice speaking in thunder is distinctly apocalyptic (Rev. 14:2); and even if the final paragraph has the speaker fishing with an "arid plain" behind him, the earlier thunder has come with "a damp gust / Bringing rain" (393–94). Although this is not the conventional interpretation of the poem's water images, the whole sense in it of a world in an end-phase makes the connection between coming rain and a terminal and purging flood quite as obvious as that between rain and rebirth.[15]

The idea of flood works partly as an image of the problem facing the poet's civilization, as when Martin Scriblerus complains that "a deluge

of authors cover'd the land" (*Poems* 5:49), but it is also, in true
prophetic fashion, a warning and a threat. The threat of flood is quite
a common part of the Old Testament prophet's rhetorical armory, so
Jeremiah, for example, prophesies against the Philistines.

> Behold, waters rise up out of the north, and shall be an overflowing flood,
> and shall overflow the land, and all that is therein; the city, and them that
> dwell therein: then the men shall cry, and all the inhabitants of the land
> shall howl. (Jer. 47:2)

Similarly, Isaiah foretells the overthrow of Israel by Assyria in terms of
an overflowing Euphrates passing through Judah (Isa. 8:6–8);
Ezekiel deals with the fall of Tyre as a sinking in the sea (Ezek. 26:3–
5); Nahum considers Jehovah's vengeance as "an overrunning flood"
(Nah. 1:8); and Amos calls on judgment to "run down as waters, and
righteousness as a mighty stream" (Amos 5:24). More generally, the
threat of flood carries within it the hint of the end of the world.
Although the biblical deluge ends with God's promise that it shall not
be repeated, there is a strong link between it and the Last Judgment,
between the flood which has destroyed and the fire which shall destroy
the earth. So, the flood is both the decisive end to one phase of human
history and a kind of rehearsal for the end of history itself.

Skelton exploits the threat in the final invective of *Speke Parott*. His
claim that things have not been so bad since the flood contains within
it the memory of God's response to the evil then and the expectation
of the same kind of response now. A period so similar to that of the
last days before the flood, it is implied, must come to a similar end.[16]
Although Eliot is less literal than Skelton in his use of the myth, he
also plays upon the idea of the flood as punishment. Both his decayed
prophetess and his more authoritative prophetic voice of the fourth
section warn of water, and the thunder that dominates the fifth section
with its "reverberation," its black clouds, and its loud voice is decidedly threatening. More important still, the way that the thunder
presents criteria by which the speaker and his generation should live,
and by which they fail to live, places it in the role of a judge, with
implicitly a judge's power to condemn. The thunder's only instru-
ments for executing sentence are lightning and, of course, rain. The
apocalyptic elements in *The Dunciad* are slightly different from those
in *Speke Parott* or *The Waste Land*, and generally more complex than
them. Among the most direct sources for books 3 and 4, the more
apocalyptic books, are *Messiah* and the passages of Isaiah that Pope
imitates in the poem. *Messiah* provides models for the raptured bard in
the third book, the repeated imperative "see," which is so important to

its structure, and a number of details of the new kingdom, as well as models for the arrival of the nations in book 4 and the final vision of consuming darkness.[17] What Pope does in these books is to develop a mock-prophetic parallel (and one quite as important as the mock-heroic parallel between Colley and Aeneas) between the triumph of Dullness and the triumph of Jesus at the Last Judgment, and by means of the comparison and contrast involved in the mock-prophetic, he intensifies his ridicule of the dull. But the introduction of these images, however ironically done, also gives a genuinely apocalyptic tenor to the poem, albeit an imaginative rather than a literal one. In the context of this sense of a coming Judgment, the darkness and confusion of Dullness's empire grow to resemble the darkness and confusion of the days before the end, and the images of flood recall and foreshadow God's punishment.

The threat of flood in the three poems is directed particularly at contemporary evildoers and opponents of the poets. Skelton is warning Wolsey that the Judgment may literally be close at hand, while Pope and Eliot are warning, in a more figurative way, that the present course of the world could lead to catastrophe. But in addition to this, the flood allows the poets to imagine, more or less covertly, a wholesale destruction, and there is considerable triumph and imaginative satisfaction in the fancied picture of (to mix metaphors) such a holocaust. When Parrot in the early part of the poem hints darkly about the approaching Judgment or when he later speaks out more plainly about it, Skelton is clearly relishing delivering his enemies up to God's wrath, and something similar is at work in Pope's imagination of the dunces buried in the darkness of their own dullness. This kind of imaginative relish is also quite marked in Eliot's warning to the "handsome and tall" at the end of "Death by Water."

> Gentile or Jew
> O you who turn the wheel and look to windward,
> Consider Phlebas, who was once handsome and tall as you.
>
> (319–21)

Behind the deliberate heightening of the second line and the slight obscurity of the third, the reader can sense the pleasure in warning us all, especially the young, that we will lose beauty and strength and go the way of Phlebas. The image of the deluge is particularly well suited to affording such pleasure, for while it preserves the writer's pose of righteousness, it also allows him to indulge in the imagination of his enemies' utter annihilation and of a world reduced from its confusing and threatening complexity to nothing.

Unfortunately for the poet, the imaginative triumph is, as I have already said, never secure, but is constantly subverted by the dramatic contexts in which it is set. In order to discuss dramatization in *Speke Parott,* it is necessary first to consider the kind of persona Skelton has created in Parrot. David Lawton distinguishes between two kinds of persona, the "closed," dramatic persona that draws attention to itself, and the "open," rhetorical persona that draws attention to a moral question, and he goes on to argue that Parrot, though highly fictionalized and placed in a specific setting, is essentially an open persona.[18] In this, he agrees with some of the most influential commentators on the poem but is at odds with S. E. Fish, who sees the "focal point" of *Speke Parott* as "the psychology of the speaker."[19] My view is that while Skelton probably consciously intended Parrot to be an open persona, his imagination created a character too complex and too fully realized to be taken just as a rhetorical device, and he placed him a situation too redolent with other human possibilities to be taken just as allegory. These "extra" elements in the poem seem to have risen, unbidden, and unrecognized, out of Skelton's own state of mind and feeling. So, for example, in his presentation of a wise creature with an urgent message turned into the plaything of trifling women, Skelton is apparently figuring forth his discontent at his powerlessness and lack of influence. Certainly, to ignore the implications of entrapment and frustration that the situation of Parrot among the ladies carries is to ignore part of the meaning of the poem.

With this in mind we can turn back to the dramatization of Parrot as prophet. Perhaps the most striking aspects of his situation are that it is dangerous and that the danger has a specific source (Wolsey), while its most marked effect on Parrot is to make him afraid. Fear is apparent in the most characteristic aspects of his behavior. He hides his denunciations timorously in brief, obscure phrases; when the ladies warn him to "ware the cat" or "ware ryot" (if these injunctions are from the ladies and not from his own fears), he changes the subject of conversation (99–102); he asks for defense against detraction (360–62); and when he finally speaks out plain, his plainness is marred by the fact that what he offers is less a specific condemnation than a general, conventional account of the evil times. None of this quite makes Parrot one of the "causeless cowardes" he complains of toward the end (390), but it does make him something different from the fearless prophet. What is more, there is always the possibility with someone who is both frightened and aggressive that the aggression is a result of the fear, in this case, that Parrot, with Skelton behind him, indulges in dreams of destruction in order to compensate for his terror. Further doubts about motive are made possible by Parrot's character. He is boastful about both his mind and his body (25–26, 15–18); he is trivially playful (106–9); he is ambitious to be set above others (112); and he is sexually suggestive in his talk with his ladies (105). By all this, I do not wish to suggest that Skelton deliberately created an equivocal figure in Parrot, or that he wished to subvert his bird's prophecy. Rather, in predicting the end of his enemies, Skelton imaginatively, and largely unconsciously, placed the prediction in a dramatic context in which it can appear to be self-interested and unauthoritative. The result is that the poem resonates with an anxiety that concerns not simply the present evil and the coming Judgment but also the poet's authority and his expectations of his enemies' defeat. At heart, Skelton is not quite so sure that he is right, that Wolsey will soon get his just deserts, or that the wicked generally are about to be soundly punished.

The Dunciad is different from *Speke Parott* in that it provides no specific dramatic setting in which the poet, or a representative of the poet, is shown in relation to his enemies. However, as Dustin Griffin has pointed out, the apparatus of prefatory essays, notes, and appendixes "permits Pope to establish his presence clearly and openly in the poem."[20] The reader who becomes aware of this presence, and few readers can remain unaware of it for long, sees Pope in battle with the dunces and can take all his rhetorical stratagems, as many readers have taken them, to be devices for exalting himself and belittling his enemies. So, Pope's veiled threats of flood and apocalypse can be interpreted, like Skelton's more open threats, as arising not from some special knowledge or insight but from his situation and needs. Of course, Pope did not want to be interpreted in this way. But since such interpretations are invited by the dramatic context that his imagination created, they and their attendant doubts must have originated in him and his (probably unacknowledged) anxieties.

There is also a further element in *The Dunciad* that brings out the uncertainty inherent in its implied dramatic situation, and that is Pope's discomfort with the prophetic role. The underestimation by most scholars of the importance of prophecy to *The Dunciad* is readily explained by the fact that Pope himself did not draw attention to it. While the notes gloss many allusions to Vergil and even to Milton, they ignore those to the Bible, with the exception of the echo of the fourth beatitude toward the beginning of book 1, which is annotated with an attack by Edmund Curll on Pope's profanity, followed by a passage from Lewis Theobald citing some of Shakespeare's biblical borrowings (A1:48n). There are two connected reasons that Pope might choose to ignore his own scriptural references. Firstly, the mantle of the Hebrew prophet sits rather awkwardly on the Augustan gentleman, as is evident from *The Narrative of Dr. John Norris,* in which Pope makes a mad John Dennis exclaim:

O Destruction! Perdition! *Opera! Opera!* As Poetry once rais'd a City, so when Poetry fails, Cities are overturn'd, and the World is no more. (*Prose* 1:162)

Dennis is supposed to be absurd for striking the prophet's pose and predicting the end, but the irony is that later Pope himself would express, more politely and subtly, no doubt, the same feelings about opera and the same fears about the future.[21] The silence of the notes at those points where he approaches closest to prophecy reflects, and alerts the reader to, Pope's uneasiness about behaving like an undignified Dennis. The second probable reason that Pope left his biblical references unannotated is that, although one of Warburton's notes maintains it is "a common and foolish mistake, that a ludicrous parody of a grave and celebrated passage is a ridicule of that passage" (B2:405n), ridicule of the borrowed, ancient source is an effect of the mock-heroic and the mock-prophetic. So, when Pope has Colley taking on Moses' role in climbing his Mount Pisgah (B3:67–72; Deut. 34:1–4), or when he describes the new world of Dullness in terms close to those of Isaiah (B3:241; Isa. 65:17), he not only reduces his victims but he also reduces Scripture by using it flippantly and placing it in an inappropriate context. The disrespect for Scripture suggested in the humorous use of it casts doubt on Pope's validity as a prophet, and this returns us to the comparison with Skelton. It seems that in writing, Pope's imagination released a different, more subversive side of the poet from the official one, just as Skelton's imagination released his boastful, threatened bird. The subversive Pope (and, I could add, the uneasy Pope) undermines the prophetic Pope, and in the tension between the two, the reader can sense the poet's anxiety about his own authority.

Finally, Eliot undercuts his own prophecy in *The Waste Land,* partly deliberately (in that his prophets are of rather dubious character) and partly, it seems, unintentionally. Before turning to that, though, we must pause to consider the status of the poem's speaker or speakers, and the nature of the poem. Some critics deny the existence of a single speaker, preferring to see the poem, with Marianne Thormählen, as a "mosaic of voices," or to argue, with David Spurr, that "Eliot's persona and poetic form, as if cracking under the strain of some inner turbulence, literally break apart into a variety of voices and meters."[22] However, while it is impossible to know with every line whether it belongs to the speaker or to someone else, the presence of a dominant speaker seems fairly certain.[23] The deciding factor is tone. There is a similar tone of despondent, tired, and often condemnatory meditation in many of *The Waste Land*'s most important passages, passages such as the opening reflections on spring and winter, the questions in the desert, the description of the hyacinth girl, the silent responses to the neurotic woman in "A Game of Chess," the opening of "The Fire Sermon," the account of Phlebas's disintegration, and the answers to the thunder at the end. The closeness in tone implies that these passages at least are spoken by one speaker. What is more, those parts of the poem which do not reproduce the same tone provide glimpses or, more precisely, echoes of an existence that might account for the recurring speaker's despondency. Incidents such as the failure in the hyacinth garden and the seduction of the typist, and characters such as Madame Sosostris, the neurotic lady, Mr Eugenides, and the Thames-daughters, all suggest the kind of world the despondent speaker would be likely to inhabit or to perceive and the kind of people he would mimic. So, although the poem gives the reader few clues as to the exact relation between the recurring speaker and the other characters, it implies that they constitute his world. Put another way, the most coherent (and, it seems to me, the most natural) reading is that which recognizes a dominant speaker who observes people, remembers incidents, imagines possibilities, and mimics voices from a world he finds depressingly and shamefully inadequate.

Since the speaker of *The Waste Land* judges as well as laments, the poem may be defined as a satire of sorts. C. K. Stead has objected to any such definition.

> Eliot set out in *The Waste Land* to imitate Dryden and Pope and to castigate his age, but without quite knowing what he was about he passed beyond his satiric intention into a new depth and a new freedom.[24]

Stead wishes to save Eliot from the label of "satirist" because of his own romantic assumptions that satire is a limited, prosaic genre, involving wit and judgment perhaps, but lacking, in his words, a certain "depth" and "freedom." The same assumptions are at work, although leading to quite the opposite conclusion about Eliot, in Yeats's remark that "I think of him as a satirist rather than poet."[25] Yet the most essential feature of satire is not its intellect or its wit or its concern with superficial manners, but its dramatic situation of conflict. As Irvin Ehrenpreis puts it, "one man, the reader, is listening with pleasure to abuse or ridicule which a second man, the author, is dropping upon a third man, the object of satire."[26] The situation offers a number of "poetic" possibilities, not all of them having anything to do with wit or reform, or reflecting the limitations implied by Stead and Yeats. With this kind of definition in mind, it is easy to see that *The Waste Land* rests upon satiric conflict and is a kind of satire. It may only, as Grover Smith says, be "impure satire" in that it lacks any real hope of change, but it is satire all the same.[27]

There still remains a question as to the identity of the poem's satiric speaker. One possibility is that Tiresias is the speaker, since he is, according to Eliot's famous note, "the most important personage in the poem, uniting all the rest" (218n). However, to hear the ancient prophet's voice in all those passages I have mentioned is to find in the poem the kind of sustained, consistent, and limited fiction that it seems to lack. In fact, the obscure hint in the note that Tiresias provides a unifying consciousness is probably one of those red herrings that the evasive Eliot was so apt to use. A more convincing approach to the whole question of the speaker is to regard Tiresias as closely related in mind and attitude to a dominant speaker, and the dominant speaker as a version of the poet himself. Since the passages of meditative gloom reflect so closely the mood of the whole poem, and since we know that Eliot was in a depressed state when he wrote *The Waste Land,* it seems sensible to take the gloomy, accusing meditations as the poet's own. Even so, some distinction between speaker and poet should be retained, for, while the speaker experiences his gloom within a context, the poet imagines the speaker inside his context from without. The imaginative situation can be compared, as can that of most satires, to a play with a dominant central character whose consciousness reflects that of the whole play. Assuming the author has identified strongly with the character in the process of writing, the audience is invited to do likewise while watching, but both author and audience have a slightly different perspective from the character because they see him in context.

It is, to return to the main concern here, the speaker's context that produces what I see as the unintentional subversion of the poem's prophetic ambitions. Although the speaker who warns us to "Consider Phlebas" is not placed in any specific setting or situation, the reader can extrapolate something of his relation to the world from how he appears in the rest of the poem. The speaker is presumably the same person as the one whose most notable memory concerns a sexual failure in the hyacinth garden (35–41), who withdraws into silence when faced with a neurotic woman (lover or wife) (111–38), and who walks by the Thames thinking of other people making love there (173–86). In the last two examples in particular, Eliot's imagination seems to be working in a way that is not fully deliberate. The speaker's gloomy, allusive, and obscurely profound meditations in the middle of "A Game of Chess" and in the opening of "The Fire Sermon" appear to be meant, at least on one level, to indicate that, for all his misery, he is erudite, perceptive, and, implicitly, superior to his neurotic companion or to the vacuous nymphs and city heirs. The scenes in which he is placed, however, afford the reader a different perspective, from which the assertions of superiority (poet's and speaker's) can be regarded as the self-protective tactics of someone who is sexually frustrated and lonely and who has great difficulty in adjusting to other people. Seen in the context of scenes like these, then, the threat to the "handsome and tall" appears partly to be a defensive response to those who, with their stature and beauty, fit more easily into the world. Similarly, the covert warning of rain and destruction in the final part comes from a speaker who, as well as being disinterestedly concerned about society and himself, is almost pathologically melancholy. The effect is close to those of *Speke Parott* and *The Dunciad*. The reader can easily suspect that, in making his prophetic utterance, the speaker is personally motivated and, further, that the dramatic situations which invite such suspicions reflect a deeply anxious imagination in the poet.

It should be emphasized that the anxiety in *Speke Parott, The Dunciad*, and *The Waste Land* includes both the poet's tradition and the poet himself. What happens is that each of the poets, by taking on the role of the prophet or of some other authoritative spokesman of the old way, makes himself the defender and the representative of his tradition, so that in the poems, the tradition and the poet are very closely identified with each other. To return to the imagery of Troy, the poet fashions himself or his speaker into a kind of composite of Hector, on whom the city relies for valor, and Priam, in whom the ancient values are invested. Consequently, the exposure of the poet's weaknesses, of his questionable motivation, his crankiness, his fears, implies corresponding weaknesses in his tradition. A more disturbing effect is that the weaknesses, reflecting as they do flaws in the poet's personality and cracks in his integrity, cast doubt on the value of the tradition. They raise the question of why the tradition, if it is so precious, should be defended by such a dubious representative, and this in turn reflects on the poet's role as defender. In short, each of the poems, while attempting to defend the tradition in which it stands, reverberates with anxieties about the future of the tradition, the tradition itself, and the poet.

The Trojan Predicament

The affinities between the ways of imagining in the three poems have their source ultimately, as I have said, in affinities between the cultural conditions under which the three poets wrote. Each stood at the end of a tradition, at the point where his tradition became exhausted within and threatened without. T. E. Hulme, writing in the second decade of this century, believed that romanticism was nearing its end, and explained his belief with an account of the nature of traditions.

> A particular convention or attitude in art has a strict analogy to the phenomena of organic life. It grows old and decays. It has a definite period of life and must die. All the possible tunes get played on it and then it is exhausted; moreover its best period is its youngest. Take the case of the extraordinary efflorescence of verse in the Elizabethan period.[28]

There is much to object against in this account. If traditions do tend to grow old and decay, that does not necessarily mean that they have "a strict analogy to organic life," since machines and buildings also grow old and decay. What is more, the best period of a tradition is not its youngest, and Elizabethan verse does not represent the earliest work of the tradition that produced it. Nevertheless, Hulme is surely right in his general idea that traditions grow old, and in his implicit argument (which reflects Johnson's) that a writer's place in his tradition, his position relative to its development, is probably as important for his work as the nature of his tradition itself. This second consideration is usually neglected by criticism. When we talk of Pope as a late-Renaissance poet, we tend to emphasize the Renaissance rather than the late, but his lateness is crucial. It is his lateness that leads to his fighting a desperate rear-guard action in defense of his tradition and to his entertaining, only half acknowledged to himself, fears about the nature and the outcome of his fight. Indeed, it is his lateness that makes him in some respects closer to the unlikely figure of Skelton than to the far more obvious Dryden.

The argument in the preceding paragraph raises a host of problems, and the bulk of this section will have to be given to the consideration, if not the resolution, of some of them. Perhaps the most obvious problem is that to treat the medieval, the Renaissance, and the romantic as like represents a distortion, since the words signify, or can in some of their meanings signify, very different phenomena. This is partly a problem of terminology, which can be avoided to some extent by emphasizing that each of the words is used here to denote a literary and cultural tradition of a certain duration and its attendant attitudes and assumptions.[29] Even then, it might be argued that the medieval, the Renaissance, and the romantic should not be regarded as such separate, distinctive groupings. Exceptions can be found to puncture any definition of them, and relationships can be established between writers who are supposed to belong to different traditions. Nevertheless, as rough generalizations, they work, and it is fair to assume, without hazarding any unsatisfactory definitions, that students of English literature recognize the three categories.

A further problem lies in the fact that the medieval, the Renaissance, and the romantic are not simply different traditions but are in some respects different kinds of tradition as well. In particular, they differ in the degree to which writers and readers within them were aware of a distinctive tradition. Romanticism was a reasonably well defined (at least compared with the two others) literary and intellectual movement, within which there was a strong sense of the age. If Eliot was, as I believe, somewhat muddled about his own attitudes toward romanticism, and the relation of his poetry to it, he at least knew more or less what it was. The Renaissance was less well defined, but still, the assumption was available for Pope that European culture had flowered again in the three-and-a-half centuries before him, and in looking back at English poetry, he had a clear idea of a tradition going in an unbroken line back to Spenser, with Chaucer as a kind of unaccountable prelude from the Dark Ages. Skelton lacked this kind of perspective altogether, for there was little sense either of literary traditions or of literary periods in the late Middle Ages. If he had thought in terms of periods at all, these would have been the seven ages of man, not of literature, and he would have believed himself to have been living in the last age, after Christ and before the Judgment. Such differences in awareness, though real, are incidental to my argument. My concern is with the feeling in the three poems that something valuable is being lost, and with the connection between this feeling and the decline in the poet's tradition. A poet need not be distinctly aware of his tradition as a tradition or of his place within it in order to cherish its works, share its values, or suspect its danger from unfamiliar and incomprehensible new forces.

There remains one important problem, that of identifying the tradition in which each of the three poets belongs. Pope is the least awkward of my examples in this respect. Not only do his attitudes concerning literature reflect Renaissance attitudes quite clearly, but his version of the English literary tradition envisages, as I have said, a straight line from himself to Spenser. Skelton is rather more problematic than Pope, since the question of his connections to the Middle Ages and the Renaissance used to be a prime debating point among scholars. So, F. M. Salter and H. L. R. Edwards could attack the notion of his being a medieval poet by adducing the large number of words for which his work provides the first reference as proof of his "humanistic zeal,"[30] while Ian Gordon could strike the compromise by calling him "Mr. Facing Both-Ways."[31] More recently, though, as Skelton has come to be more thoroughly understood, the current of opinion has moved toward regarding him as essentially medieval. A. C. Spearing, for example, characterizes him as "thoroughly, and indeed combatively, a man of the medieval world," and F. W. Brownlow describes *Speke Parott* as a "typical mediaeval work of art in that the system of ideas on which it is based is external to it."[32] This seems to be the correct view. Although Skelton might sometimes show an aggressive individuality that appears to belong to the Renaissance, he was opposed to those elements in his own day which represented the beginnings of the English Renaissance, and his poetry for the most part relies upon medieval approaches, ideas, referents, and forms.

Eliot is perhaps even more problematic than Skelton, largely because he himself declared his classicism, and early critics like F. R. Leavis, taking their cue from Eliot's and Pound's own pronouncements and propaganda, wrote of the new poets as representing a "decisive reordering of the tradition of English poetry."[33] Recently, however, growing numbers of critics have come to realize, with Louis Menand, that "the nineteenth-century cultural values he [Eliot] made such a show of discrediting can be read, so to speak, beneath the modernist ones he made a show of declaring."[34] The point can be quickly made. Eliot's poetry is lyrical and idiosyncratic, his theory of the "objective correlative" treats poetry, as M. H. Abrams points out, as the expression of emotion,[35] and his canon of authors is essentially romantic. Donne was not, as we sometimes think, the discovery of Grierson and Eliot but rather of Coleridge,[36] and Dante enters the pantheon of European literature, so E. R. Curtius remarks, only with romanticism.[37] Even Eliot grew to see his early poetry in terms of the ending of an era, for looking back in 1939 on his editorship of *The Criterion,* he wrote:

> Only from about the year 1926 did the features of the post-war world begin clearly to emerge—and not only in the sphere of politics. From about that date one began slowly to realize that the intellectual and artistic output of the previous seven years had been rather the last efforts of an old world, than the first struggles of a new.[38]

Although Eliot does not associate these "last efforts" with romanticism, that was the dominant cultural tradition of the era up to the Great War, of the "old world" he mentions. He implies, then, what literary historians of the future might (I would guess) take as a given, that the third decade of this century saw the death throes of a tradition, the death throes of the romanticism to which Eliot (without ever admitting it) owed allegiance.

What I want to suggest is that *Speke Parott, The Dunciad,* and *The Waste Land* each represents, in Eliot's phrase, "the last efforts of an old world." Moreover, the nature of the poems is largely determined by this. Skelton, Pope, and Eliot imagined and wrote, and presumably thought and felt, like Trojans because they were, at least in terms of their culture, in the position of Trojans, the position, that is, of defenders who are fighting a losing battle. Other contemporary poems and poets may have been influenced in similar ways, but the remarkable thing about these poems is the extent to which they are shaped by the cultural conditions under which they were written. Each of the three addresses the crisis of its times directly and is, in turn, profoundly affected by it. Such an argument is not meant to turn the poems into cultural documents, interesting only insofar as they give accurate accounts of historical conditions. Rather, it should emphasize how intimate the connection can be between a poet's cultural situation and his imagination, feeling, and sense of himself. The anxiety I analyze is both personal and profound. Having allied himself with a tradition and having founded a good part of his identity on the alliance, each of the poets fights, in defense of his tradition, to protect something that is essential to himself. What is more, his failures in this fight, those revelations of self-interested motive which subvert his authority and foreshadow his defeat, are all personal failures. So, far from being dry documents, these poems resonate with an intense personal anxiety, a personal anxiety that arises, at least in part, from the larger cultural situation.

Part Two
Old Poets and New Men

2
Youth and Age

The Youthful World

In *Speke Parott, The Dunciad,* and *The Waste Land,* each of the poets imagines the contemporary world as one that is growing increasingly degenerate and inhospitable. The degeneracy is figured forth through a number of different images, and very often these suggest at once an evil that the poet is called upon to oppose and a threat to his values and to himself. Madness is present in *Speke Parott,* for example, both as the modern tendency against which the sanely learned poet pits himself and as the condition into which he appears to be falling. In the same way, the image of youth, which is common to all the poems and central to each of them, implies the present folly of the world and its danger for the poet. Both implications become particularly clear when they are seen in relation to the poems' speakers. Each of the poets, whether fully consciously or not, casts his poem in the voice of an old man, a voice that allows considerable scope for the expression of superior scorn concerning the folly of juniors. The attitude of age toward youth is rarely the simple one of assured judgment, however, and beneath the old man's outwardly confident scorn it is often possible to detect fear and insecurity. The element of anxiety, which is principally present in the poems through the implied tensions of the dramatic conflict between old poet and young world, is the subject of the following chapter. Here, I concentrate on the more straightforward aspects of the opposition of age to youth, on the ways in which each poet characterizes the world of his poem in terms of youthful folly while also claiming for himself or his speaker the authority of venerable age.

Of the three poems I am dealing with, it is perhaps *The Waste Land* in which the motif of youth is most obvious and, taken on its own away from the context of the poem's aged speakers and observers, the least complex. The world of the poem, in terms both of what is remembered in the past and of what is seen in the present, is dominated by youth. Of course, it is populated with the old as much as

37

with the young, for many of the characters are old, and Eliot annotates his description of the crowds in the "Unreal City" with a reference to Baudelaire's "Les Sept Vieillards" (60n). Nevertheless, while the old figures in the poem do very little beyond watching, remembering, and being unhappy, it is the young who act and whose actions determine that individual lives will be unfulfilled and that society as a whole will be degenerate. By their actions, which are chiefly characterized by irresponsible sexual behavior, the young, so to speak, make the world. So, when the old look back on their lives, it is especially the incidents of youth that they recall, a reflex which is evident in the apparently aged speaker's first reply to the thunder. He and his friend have, he admits, only "existed" through the dubious pleasure of a moment of youthful abandon, through the "awful daring of a moment's surrender" (402–6). Perhaps more importantly, the actions of youth dominate the present world of the poem, as can be seen most clearly in "The Fire Sermon." The section moves from the gloomy meditations on the nymphs and heirs to Sweeney and a bawdy popular song, its singers ironically identified as "ces voix d'enfants" (202); to Mr. Eugenides of no certain age; to Tiresias's observations of the clerk and typist; to the twenty-seven-year-old Elizabeth on her barge with Robert Dudley; to the Thames-daughters; and finally, to the reflections of two holy men on misspent youth. The picture that emerges from all this, and to a slightly lesser extent from the other parts of the poem, is of a world of young people in which copulation thrives.

Images of youth, though equally important to the poem, are rather less conspicuous in *Speke Parott* than in *The Waste Land*. Both their presence and their implications, though, become clearer when seen in the context of other works by Skelton, and one work in particular that casts light on the poem's imagery of youth is the play of a few years earlier, *Magnyfycence*. Since *Magnyfycence* figures quite largely in my analysis of *Speke Parott*, it is as well to say something about it here. Although scholars differ as to whether both works attack Wolsey,[1] there is a close relationship between the play and the poem, which can be seen, for example, in their common interest in busy meddling and in excess.[2] More interesting than this, however, and more illuminating for a reading of *Speke Parott*, is the fact that while Skelton follows the conventional morality format of representing a fall into vice and a subsequent rescue by virtue, he also adopts a less common approach in making his vices young and his rescuing virtues old. The youth of the vices appears both through their references to themselves and through their behavior. Fancy, who reveals his immaturity when he says, "ye se but fewe wyse men of myne age" (289), admits later,

Somtyme I wepe for a gew gaw;
Somtyme I laughe at waggynge of a straw,

(1013–14)

Folly is the same age as Fancy, since they are old school friends (1065), and Crafty Conveyance describes himself, Fancy, and Counterfeit Countenance as "thre galauntes" (511). "Am not I a joly rutter?" asks Courtly Abusion (752), and he exemplifies the youthfulness of the description in his carefree song, "Rutty bully, joly rutterkyn, heyda!" (747). Of all the vices in the play, the only grave one is Cloaked Collusion, and he abandons his gravity once Magnificence has fallen (2160–2197). Finally, Liberty who, though not exactly a vice, is associated with them in Magnificence's downfall, is described as leaping and running (133). The sense in all this that Magnificence falls because of youthful failings is reinforced by the discussions in the play of the dangers of too much freedom for young people. Adversity comments on the negligent tolerance of parents (1920–30), and Liberty explains that he himself must be restrained,

As evydently in retchlesse youth ye may se
Howe many come to myschefe for to moche lyberte;

(2133–34)

The case of Magnificence is just that—he falls into trouble because of the recklessness of youth.

Needless to say, he escapes Mischief in the end, but he has to undergo the trials of Adversity and Poverty before he is restored to prosperity. These figures are less vices than images of experience, and they both have a connection with age. As soon as he meets Magnificence, Adversity addresses him as "Vyle velyarde," as if the difficulties he represents have aged the prince (1878), and when Poverty asks of himself "where is youth that was wont for to skyppe," he indicates that he personifies age (1957). What is more, when the vices encounter Magnificence after his fall, they bestow on him toothache, boneache, and gout (2253–55). It is only having gone through these difficulties and having met Despair and Mischief that Magnificence discovers his virtues. The age of these is not explicit, but the way that Good Hope addresses Magnificence as "dere sone" (2325), their general gravity (2476), and the fact that Magnificence comes to them through experience all suggest that they belong with age. Indeed, the whole dramatic action of *Magnyfycence* is, like that of the slightly earlier interlude *Mundus et Infans,* an action that reflects the growing maturity of the protagonist. *Speke Parott*, of course, does not share the same kind of action, but it does share the same general concern with the dangers of youthful folly as well as a number of more specific attitudes.

The idea of youth is present in the poem both in the satirist's deliberate hints of his butts' immaturity and in apparently less deliberate associations, and the two elements combine to make a controlling image of considerable complexity and force. The world of the court, particularly the female part of it, is purposely characterized by Skelton as foolishly infantile. This can be seen from the court ladies' language, because their unsophisticated sentence structure, their use of phrases like "pus catt" (24), and their communication with Parrot through diminutive endearments all indicate immaturity. They even go in for some of the specific kinds of baby talk, which appear in other poems by Skelton. In *Phyllyp Sparowe*, Jane, who is "but a yong mayd" (770),[3] calls her sparrow "so prety a fole" (115), just as one of the ladies addresses Parrot as "My propyr Parott, my lytell pratye fole" (20). Moreover, one of the demands for a kiss, "'Bas me, swete Parrot, bas me, swete swete'" (104), recalls the "'Ba, ba, ba', and 'bas, bas, bas,'" of the mock-lullaby of *Dyvers Balettys and Dyties Solacyous* (1:8), where a lady coddles her lover to sleep in order to beguile him "lyke a chylde" (1:1). The same kind of deliberate reduction of an object through an implication of immaturity is at work in the section of the poem where Parrot focuses his attention most directly on the new learning (142–82). Early in this section, when Parrot claims of the newly learned, "Ye go about to amende, and ye mare all" (154), his charge echoes the boast of the infantile Fancy in *Magnyfycence*, who says "All that I make forthwith I marre" (1036). Later, an account of the prevailing vandalism in the world of learning is capped by the line, "Prisians hed broken now, handy-dandy" (171), in which "handy-dandy," a description of the methods of academic vandals, is the name of a children's game. Finally, Skelton's complaint in the last stanza of the section that children are now being encouraged to "reherse" Plautus and to "medyll" with Quintilian implies a kind of youths' invasion of learning (176–79).

The general condition of England is also characterized by two qualities that seem to have been associated in Skelton's mind with youth: recklessness and excess. The quality of recklessness is evident in the way that modern self-will casts caution to the winds and in the final invective. Although this closing section is often compared with such commentaries on the evil times as William Dunbar's *A General Satyre* and the anonymous "Now is England Perished,"[4] it differs from them in not relying chiefly on a cumulative effect. Rather, Skelton uses a good deal of antithesis of the kind found in such lines as

"So many morall maters, and so lytell usyd" (449) and "So myche nobyll prechyng, and so lytell amendment" (452). The effect of such lines is to suggest less that England is being buried under an ever-increasing mountain of evil than that the English are persistently refusing to listen to good advice. Such a reckless unwillingness to heed caution appears earlier in Skelton in the refusal of Magnificence to obey Measure, and later in the "rechelesse youthe" of the two young heretics of *A Replycacion*.[5] To turn to madness, this has been identified by one critic as "the central vice at which the satire takes aim."[6] That is probably to overstate the case, but certainly madness is important, as can be seen when Parrot sums up the state of English folly by saying, "Frantiknes dothe rule and all thynge commaunde" (420). "Frantic," Skelton's preferred word for "mad," seems to have carried con-notations of childishness and arrested youth for him. In *Magnyfycence*, Fancy's full name is "Frantyke Fansy-Servyce" (1023), or, as Folly calls him, "frantyke Fansy" (1300), and Folly earlier accuses him of being

> so feble-fantastycall,
> And so braynsyke therwithall,
> And thy wyt wanderynge here and there,
> That thou cannyst not growe out of thy boyes gere;
>
> (1072–75)

To be frantic or mad is in Skelton's terms to be fixed in childhood, and the specific nature of the contemporary madness of English society is that of a kind of general arrested development.

In *Speke Parott*, the principal source of the madness is Wolsey, and Skelton also associates the cardinal with youthful folly, though the association is neither always very obvious nor, I suspect, fully deliber-ate. One way in which Skelton may be half-consciously accusing Wolsey, a man only twelve or thirteen years his junior, of childishness is through the appellation "bull-calf." This is the insulting term he applies most frequently to the cardinal, different versions of it appear-ing seven times in the poem (59, 348, 352, 378–80, 484). The phrase, which recalls both the golden calf of the Old Testament and Wolsey's butcher father, may also connote empty-headed youth in the way that "puppy" does. Although there is no *Oxford English Dictionary* reference for such a meaning, it occurs in proverbs. Certainly, Skelton knew that calves were proverbially stupid, for he uses the ironic "As wyse as Waltoms calfe" in *Collyn Clout* (809), and he may also have known the childish calves of the proverbs, "as wanton as calves" and "as wanton and toying as a young Calfe."[7] At the beginning of the next century, Jonson uses another calf proverb to comment on the long-standing relationship of Mill, my lady's woman, with the steward, hoping she will "First bearing him a calfe, beare him a bull."[8] The calf here refers to her youthful failings, the bull to those of a riper age. Finally, Shakespeare in *Love's Labour's Lost,* without the support of any proverb, can have Katherine call Longaville "a fair lord calf" in mockery of his youthful greenness (5.2.246–55). "Calf," then, seems once to have had something of the weight that "puppy" acquired later, and given that, Skelton's use of the word (though this is to anticipate the subject of the following chapter) probably reflects anxiety as much as scorn. People who call other people "puppies," as Mrs. Elton does in *Emma,* are usually indulging a very self-defensive kind of aggression and thereby exposing their own insecurity.

As well as through the word "calf," the immaturity of Wolsey might be inferred from one his most striking characteristics, his willfulness.

> *Moderata juvant* but *toto* dothe exede;
> Dyscrecion ys modyr of nobyll vertues all;
> *Myden agan* in Grekys tonge we rede,
> But reason and wytte wantythe theyr provynciall,
> When wylfulnes ys vicar generall.
>
> (50–54)

It is clear from *Magnyfycence* that Skelton associated this kind of self-will that sweeps away reason and moderation with youth. When the prince decides to transfer his favor from Measure to the gallant vices, Courtly Abusion, his new adviser, suggests:

> By waywarde wylfulnes let eche thynge be convayed;
> What so ever ye do, folowe your owne wyll,
>
> (1594–95)

This is, of course, a young man's advice, and it is significant how closely the recommendation of "wylfulnes" parallels the description of Wolsey. Later, Liberty, who is himself "so lusty to loke on" (2145), connects *"totum in toto"* (excess) with "to moche lyberte" (2099–2100). So, the excess that is connected with Wolsey in the poem, and that is indicated by the same word, *"toto,"* has a distinctly immature quality in the play. The immaturity of Wolsey's excessive willfulness shows itself in *Speke Parott* in his assaults on the impossible and in his liking for trifles. The wish to rule alone is as senseless as trying "To bryng all the see into a cheryston pytte" (331), and the allusion to the dissolution of an abbey with a watermill as the exchange of a "A trym-tram for an horse-myll" implies childish concerns (128). But the horrifying thing is that the overgrown child, Wolsey, is the second most powerful man in England, and that his kind of childishness reflects the general condition of the whole country.

Like Skelton in *Speke Parott,* Pope in *The Dunciad* deploys the image of immaturity for satiric effect, though Pope's use of the image appears to be more deliberate than Skelton's and it achieves its complexity in different ways. In the first book, he identifies the infancy of the works of Dullness when she sees in her Chaos

> How hints, like spawn, scarce quick in embryo lie,
> How new-born nonsense first is taught to cry,
> Maggots half-form'd in rhyme exactly meet,
> And learn to crawl upon poetic feet.
>
> (B1 : 59–62)

By presenting Dullness in the perversely divine position of beholding Chaos, this description emphasizes her evil, uncreating side, but at the same time, her newborn, half-formed, crying, crawling nonsense is decidedly childish. The same idea occurs later in the first book, and interestingly, it receives far greater emphasis in the 1743 than in the 1729 version. While Tibbald in 1729 addresses his books as "my children" (A1 : 197), Colley in 1743 speaks at much greater length to his books as a father to his infants (B1 : 225–42). In the second book, the childishness of the dunces' productions is matched by the dunces themselves as they compete in games that in their abandoned enjoyment of movement, sensation, noise, and dirt are highly reminiscent of the junior school playground.[9] Then, in the third book, Settle foresees the triumph of Dullness.

> Proceed, great days! 'till Learning fly the shore,
> 'Till Birch shall blush with noble blood no more,
> 'Till Thames see Eaton's sons for ever play,
> 'Till Westminster's whole year be holiday;
>
> (B3 : 333–36)

This image of a world at play, which comes as the culmination of the book's vision of approaching Dullness, brings out the immaturity implicit in that. The new theater, the chief agent in Dullness's conquest, is closely related to the puppet theater (B3 : 299) and is presided over by John Rich, about forty-seven even in 1729 and still described as a "matchless Youth" (B3 : 255). What is more, the image, like that of Dullness before Chaos, manages to combine associations of folly and of greater evil. Coming just before the description of lights going out in the 1729 version and ushering in the fourth book in the 1743 version, it suggests both the demonically threatening and the youthfully foolish.[10]

The details I have mentioned so far serve to delineate the world of *The Dunciad* as one dominated, like the worlds of *Speke Parott* and *The Waste Land,* by youthful folly. However, Pope differs from Skelton and Eliot in that he also focuses upon the part played by the old in creating the anarchically youthful world, and he develops the whole idea of generations with considerable subtlety. In the first three books, the responsibility of the old is particularly clear in the third, with Old Bavius dipping the souls of unborn poets in Lethe (B3:23–24) and Settle appearing as Colley's poetic father (B3:42), and in the first. Since Dullness is introduced as being the daughter of senile parents, her idiocy is implicitly a kind of arrested development brought on by physical weakness (B1:13). More centrally, she herself is presented as the mother of the dunces, a role that is given greater emphasis in the 1743 version than in the 1729. Not only are the opening words changed from "BOOKS and the Man" to "THE Mighty Mother, and her Son," but a new passage outlines exactly the kind of mother Dullness sets out to be.[11]

> O! when shall rise a Monarch all our own,
> And I, a Nursing-mother, rock the throne,
> 'Twixt Prince and People close the Curtain draw,
> Shade him from Light, and cover him from Law;
> Fatten the Courtier, starve the learned band,
> And suckle Armies, and dry-nurse the land:
> 'Till Senates nod to Lullabies divine,
> And all be sleep, as at an Ode of thine.
>
> (B1:311–18)

While these images are appropriate for the relations of a mother to her children, they also serve to convey the sense of a country where the most august individuals and institutions are rocked, sheltered, and sung to sleep like babies. Under Dullness's care, the whole country will be a nursery and no one will ever grow up. Like Dullness, Colley (and, again, this appears only in 1743) is introduced first in relation to his father and brainless brothers (B1:31–32), then later as a father himself. In the later instance, he is both the metaphorical father of his books and the "real" father of Cibber's real daughter, Charlotte, who is alluded to as one of the books' "smutty sisters" walking the streets (B1:230).[12] He fails as both kinds of father, and it is significant that he bids his intended sacrifice of books to remain in "infant state" (B1:237). Anticipating his queen, Colley as a parent wants simply to keep his children young.

The theme of false guardianship that is implied in these examples is the central theme of the fourth book.[13] The idea is introduced early in the picture of Dullness's throne, to which Morality is drawn by her "false Guardians" to be tied up there and killed (B4:27–30), and it continues as the book's series of guardians proceeds to kill the good qualities of their charges. It is most obvious in the three teachers, Busby, Bentley, and the "lac'd Governor," but is also important with the other figures. Annius is a cheat who sees his task in terms of the deception of youth (B4:359–60), and eventually he and Mummius confederate in duping the implicitly youthful Pollio (B4:395–96). Although the botanist and lepidopterist pursue their interests for their own pleasure, Dullness recommends to them the care of our "sleeping friends," those identified earlier as the "lazy, lolling sort" of young court gentlemen (B4:439–40, 337–46). So, they too are given the responsibility of guardianship. The "gloomy Clerk's" resolution to spread atheism (B4:459), though not explicitly an act of false guardianship, takes on something of that significance from its placing. He accepts the task just after Dullness has been recommending the "sleeping friends" to the botanist and lepidopterist, and his speech both mentions Silenus approvingly and immediately precedes his appearance. Silenus, of course, is very much the guardian as he presents Dullness with the finished product of a dull education (B4:498). Finally, the "WIZARD OLD" leads the children (the word is used four times in the closing passages of the book) to be initiated in the greater mysteries of Dullness.

The important point in all this is that each guardian leaves his charge or charges as childish as before, and when Silenus proudly presents the "finish'd Son" of Dullness, "child and man the same," he could be providing the motto for the whole book (B4:500–502). Busby's educational system, with all its ferocity, is designed to arrest his pupils' development, as is evident from his great series of containment images and his boast of the effect of rhyming mnemonics.

> A Poet the first day, he dips his quill;
> And what the last? a very Poet still.
>
> (B4:163–64)

The method is to fix the pupils at the jingling stage and make their writing, and their character, as childish in age as in infancy. In the same way, Bentley brags that a student of his might show his paces but "not a step advance" (B4:266), and he defies anyone to develop the mind or discover the man in one of his graduates (B4:269). The case of the representative member of the "gay embroider'd race" is slightly

more obscure because the young wastrel is so unnatural he "ne'er was
Boy, nor Man" (B4:288). Nevertheless, like the others, he ends as he
began. He belongs to Dullness from birth (B4:283), and the effect of
his upbringing and education is to preserve the qualities he already
possessed as "A dauntless infant! never scar'd with God" (B4:284).
The figures who follow this (Annius, Mummius, the botanist, lepidopterist, and clerk) are all concerned with the sleeping court fops,
and their task, as Dullness makes clear, is to provide them with narrow
distractions when they awake (B4:445–58). The fops, then, are to be
prevented from growing out of trifles and toys. Finally, the finished
children of Dullness are initiated in her mysteries, and she sends them
out into the world.

> The Judge to dance his brother Sergeant call;
> The Senator at Cricket urge the Ball;
>
> . . . .
> Others import yet nobler arts from France,
> Teach Kings to fiddle, and make Senates dance.
>
> (B4:591–98)

The lines recall Settle's rapturous welcome of the great, approaching
days when Eton's sons will "for ever play," and they suggest that the
duncely guardians have done their work so well that England has
become a country of children's amusements and games.

One interesting aspect of Pope's representation of his irresponsible,
older dunces is the way in which he manages to invest them, despite
their age, with a good degree of childishness. The best example of this
is Colley. The real Cibber was seventy-two in 1743, and there are a
number of references to his age in the prefatory essay about the hero,
in the poem itself, and in the notes. He is made even older by Ricardus
Aristarchus, who calls him "fourscore" (*Poems* 5:258), is compared to
Priam in book 1 (B1:255), is described as in "doting age" in book 3
(B3:304), and has his own words about his "Old age" quoted back at
him in a note to book 4 (B4:20n). Yet, just as the real Cibber
continued to take youthful roles such as Tom in *The Conscious Lovers*
into the 1720s, the elderly Colley shows himself to be a true son of
Dullness by preserving his immaturity intact, or in Ricardus
Aristarchus's words (using the same quotation from Horace as Cibber
applies to himself in his *Apology*[14]) by

> continuing to the very *dregs,* the same he was from the beginning,
> ——*Servetur ad* IMUM
> *Qualis ab incepto processerat*——
>
> (*Poems* 5:259)

This quality is apparent in the poem in the decisive couplet where Dullness's gaze first falls on Colley.

> Dulness with transport eyes the lively Dunce,
> Remembring she herself was Pertness once.
>
> (B1:111–12)

"Lively" and "Pertness" are the key words here, and perhaps the latter is the more important. Pope indicates twice that he is using it on the authority of a letter Cibber wrote to him in which he insists he is "pert" as well as "dull" (*Poems* 5:261; B1:109n), but there may be a further, less open, and more uncomfortable reason for its use. Cibber applies the word to Pope at the climactic moment of *A Letter from Mr. Cibber*'s scurrilous description of the young Pope's visit to a prostitute, in which Cibber bursts into the bedroom to find "this little hasty Hero, like a terrible *Tom Tit*, pertly perching upon the Mount of Love."[15] It seems likely that Pope's characterization of Colley as "Pertness" is an attempt to fling the insult back, an insult that in *The Dunciad*, as in general usage, carries strong connotations of impudent youth. It is used in book 2 for the three "Templars" who help read the dunces to sleep (B2:379), and the fact that Dullness "was Pertness once" places the quality back in her childhood. This, along with his briskness, brazenness, and debauchery, marks Colley as being, like the Silenus of *Vertumnus and Pomona*, "youthful in Decay" (24).

The description could also apply to the other old dunces of book 4. Since it is Silenus who presents the final product of a dull education to Dullness, he becomes the epitome of all the guardians and teachers, and he is "Rosy and rev'rend," a "bowzy Sire" (B4:493–96). While one word of each description signals his age, the other indicates that he maintains an unnatural youthfulness in it. Of those who precede him, the university teachers are drunken, sporting, and apt to be "lulled" to sleep (B4:200), the "lac'd Governor" debauches his pupil's mistress, and there are strong sexual, sometimes homosexual, implications surrounding Annius, Mummius, the botanist, and the lepidopterist. Even Busby, the least youthful of all the guardians, is tarred with a childish brush by his character as the genius of a place where the chief labor is to ensure that the boys will always be boys. Finally, Walpole appears twice in the closing section of the fourth book. The first instance is:

> With that, a WIZARD OLD his *Cup* extends;
> Which whoso tastes, forgets his former friends,
> Sire, Ancestors, Himself. One casts his eyes

Up to a *Star,* and like Endymion dies;
. . . .
Lost is his God, his Country, ev'ry thing;
And nothing left but Homage to a King!

(B4:517–24)

The power possessed by this wizard, his corrupting use of it, his
connection with court honors (the star), and his closeness to the king
all make it hard to avoid associating him with the recently fallen First
Minister. Later, Dullness, sending her children out into the world,
looks forward to one of them soaring above princes to become a
"Tyrant supreme" (B4:604), and again the allusion is unmistakably to
Walpole. He is, then, a curiously protean figure in these closing
sections, at one moment an old wizard, at the next a child of Dullness,
and his movement between age and youth perhaps reflects the tendency of the old dunces to be youthfully aged, to wear a silly young
head on their reverend old shoulders.

Pope's complex satiric representation of his older dunces as false
guardians who themselves remain immature is a far cry from Skelton's
taunts at Wolsey and further still from Eliot's general picture of a
young world of misdirected sexuality. Yet the fundamental similarity
remains, that in *Speke Parott, The Dunciad,* and *The Waste Land* each
poet imagines his degraded world as one dominated by youth. Moreover, the similarity becomes still more interesting when it is remembered that each of the poets chooses to present the youthful world
from a similar perspective, that of an aged speaker. Before going on to
discuss the aged speakers in the three poems, however, it will be useful
to turn briefly to the general tendency of each poet to adopt an aged
voice and to consider the position occupied by each in a literary
tradition. In the case of Pope (and this also applies to a lesser extent to
Skelton), the habitual presentation of himself as an old poet contrib-
utes toward the voice of *The Dunciad;* in the cases of all three poets,
the habit seems to reveal that the aged voice is no simple rhetorical
device but a reflection of a whole aged state of mind. That this state of
mind owes something at least to the cultural conditions under which
the poets were writing is suggested by the tendency among contemporaries to think in the same way.

The Aged Voice and the Three Poets

Both Skelton and Pope were writing for quite limited and intimate
audiences and the presentation of the personae of *Speke Parott* and *The*

Dunciad relies to some extent upon the reader's recognition of a known poetic character. Several years before *Speke Parott*, Skelton had declared in *Calliope* that "I waxe olde / And somdele sere" (15–16), and the readers among whom the satire circulated in manuscript would have known the poet, or known of him, as an old man and a supporter of old ways.[16] This kind of reliance upon an established character is clearer, chiefly perhaps because there is more material available, in *The Dunciad* than in *Speke Parott*. The 1743 version of the poem echoes, often in ironic and distorted ways, the voice that Pope carefully cultivates for himself in the imitations of the 1730s and that he repeatedly returns to, the voice of the world-weary old man, out of step and out of sympathy with the emerging new society. In *The Second Epistle of the Second Book of Horace,* for example, he expands upon Horace's lines dealing with the way that the years steal and he alters Milton's "suttle theef of youth" to "subtle Thief of Life" (72–79).[17] The last of the imitations, published a year after this, has Pope talking of "the Sabbath of my days" (*Epistle* 1.1.3), hoping to "hide my Age" (5) and looking forward to death (22). Death is implied again at the end of the second *Epilogue to the Satires,* also published in 1738, when he imagines himself falling in the battle for freedom (253). Some of the most distinctive characteristics of the Pope in these poems also serve to emphasize his age. So, in the last of the imitations, he presents himself as someone who is preparing for death, turning away from verse in order to give all his attention to the right, the true, and the fit, ready for his final day (*Epistle* 1.1.17–22). A second important characteristic is that of Pope as a member of the old guard of wits and politicians, all now retired and out of place in the young Whig world. In the first of the imitations, he shows himself at home, talking and drinking with Bolingbroke and gardening with Peterborough (*Satire* 2.1.127–30); in the last, he remarks on the retirement of Cibber from acting and of "Our Gen'rals" to their estates (*Epistle* 1.1.6–7). The cumulative effect of references such as these is that anyone who reads the later poems together cannot escape the image of the decaying poet, of the veteran who lags superfluous upon the stage.

The recurrent hints about the poet's age in Pope's late poetry suggest that the figure of the venerable poet reflects something of the real man's state of mind. The same might also be said of Skelton, for he frequently emphasizes his own age in the later satires. In *A Replycacion* and *Why Come Ye Nat to Courte?* he writes in his own person as the poet in his sixties sadly observing his country's decline. The result is that *A Replycacion*'s repeated contemptuous references to the youth of its two objects take much of their force from the implied reverend age of their author, something that is true even where there are no explicit references to youth. Having cited Saints Gregory and Ambrose as authorities, for example, Skelton sneers, "Ye have reed them, I suppose," with all the animus of the old against the ignorance of the young (276). In the same way, toward the beginning of *Why Come Ye Nat to Courte?* he gives one reason for his absence.

> For age is a page
> For the courte full unmete;
> For age can nat rage,
> Nor basse her swete swete.
>
> (32–35)

Skelton's age here does not make him unfit for courtly service in the way that it potentially could in *Calliope,* but rather the vicious youthful games of the modern court make it no fit place for one of his gravity and wisdom. The speaker of *Collyn Cloute,* a disguised version of Skelton, is also angry and old. In the opening lines he speaks wearily of the futility of satire as one who has written much in vain (1–12), and a little later he describes himself as a "hagge" (52), his verse as "rayne-beaten, / Rusty and mothe-eaten" (55–56), all epithets that suggest age as well as rusticity. The closing lines have Colin heading his ship for "the porte salue / Of our Savyoure Jesu" (1260–61), and the voyage away from the world and toward Jesus has the ring of someone abandoning public effort in order to see to his soul, perhaps in preparation for death. As with the other two speakers, Colin is an aging, weary representative of the old ways, out of place in the new world.

Like Skelton and Pope, Eliot often adopts an aged voice in his poetry, but the tendency in him is complicated, and made psychologically very curious, by the fact that he acquired the habit in youth, something that is, as we shall see, also partially true of Pope. Of course, some of the early work is appropriately youthful. Reflecting on vers libre in 1917, he argues that the absence of a tradition can lead artists to court theory and adopt polemic.

> This is bad for the artist and his school, who may become circumscribed by their theory and narrowed by their polemic; but the artist can always console himself for his errors in his old age by considering that if he had not fought nothing would have been accomplished. (*CC, 184*)

The second part of the sentence is all the more convincing because of its casual air, and its assumption is that the innovative artist, indeed any artist, will be young and out there fighting. The kind of youthful challenge this suggests is present in some of Eliot's poetry, as well as in a good deal of his criticism. Thus, the difficulties of "The Love Song of J. Alfred Prufrock" led one reviewer to talk of the author's "premature decrepitude" and another to characterize him as "one of those clever young men who find it amusing to pull the leg of a sober reviewer."[18] The fictional personae of the poems are also quite young. The speaker of "Portrait of a Lady" is identified in the second section as possessing youth, and the nocturnal wanderer of "Rhapsody on a Windy Night" seems to be adolescent. Even Prufrock is only middle-aged, and behind his lament, "I grow old . . . I grow old . . . ," one can perhaps sense the luxurious weariness and disillusionment of the poet in his early twenties.

Nevertheless, if Prufrock may betray something of his creator's youth, he still stands as the first of a long line of aging or aged speakers in Eliot's poetry. Old Possum adopts an old voice so often that it becomes one of his most distinctive features as a poet. The major poem of the second volume is "Gerontion," whose speaker's cryptic utterances seem sometimes to border on senility. The age of the scarecrows in *The Hollow Men* is not given, but their "dried" voices sound old, and Eliot provides the epigraph, "A penny for the Old Guy." This is significant, since the traditional demand of British children is simply "a penny for the guy," and by 1925 Eliot had been in England long enough to know that. The change draws attention to the age of the hollow men and, possibly also by shifting to American usage, to the "old guy" (all of thirty-six) who wrote the poem. *Ash Wednesday* is the poem of an "aged eagle," and finally, the second section of each of the last three quartets presents the speaker (Eliot) as old or as becoming old and deals with this in some detail. Eliot, then, is like Skelton and Pope in that his poetic voice is characteristically old, though it might be added that his gloomy meditations upon decay and death are rather different from Skelton's exuberantly violent attacks on folly and from Pope's pose of the old philosopher watching the foolish world from his garden.

The curious tendency of even the young Eliot to cast his poems in the voice of an old man can also be detected in Pope's early writing. Needless to say, some of it bears the stamp of youth. There is in his letters to Wycherley, as Pope himself admits, "a juvenile ambition of Wit,"[19] and the same ambition appears in "A Farewell to London," in which he boasts that his absence from town will allow the harlots to "sleep at ease" (4). In more considerable works as well, Pope seems to be young—he appears at the end of *The Temple of Fame,* for example, as the "fond Youth," eager for praise and looking forward to his life

ahead (500–502). Given this, though, there is still often an aged note
even in the early works. When young, Pope was more at home with
older company, and he was later to remark to Swift that at sixteen he
found the seventy-year-old Wycherley "Not grave enough or consistent enough for me" (*Corr.* 3:80). His own gravity is present in the
measured, judicious couplets of *An Essay on Criticism* and in his desire
for contemplative retreat in *Windsor Forest*. In that poem, he passes on
from the "vig'rous Swains" (93) and "bold Youth" (155) out on their
hunting expeditions to another of his aged friends, Sir William
Trumbull. Trumbull is praised for his retirement of "Successive Study,
Exercise, and Ease" (240), and Pope seems to wish to emulate that
himself when he demands to be borne to "sequester'd Scenes" (261).
Indeed, he even writes in the character of a kind of Trumbull in one of
his *Spectator* essays (*Prose* 1:51). The pull toward the old appears in a
different way in *Eloisa to Abelard*. The "argument" gives the occasion
of the poem as Heloise's receipt of the *Historia Calimatatum,* which
probably occurred when she was about thirty-two,[20] but in the poem
she seems to be older than this. The heat of her heart is "long-
forgotten" (6), her tears have been "for ages, taught to flow in vain"
(28), and a number of passages deal in some detail with her approaching death. It is perhaps indicative of the way that Pope generally
regarded his own poetic persona that Eloisa should finish her lament
with an address to the "future Bard" who "shall join / In sad similitude
of griefs to mine" (259–60). Pope's similitude to Eloisa, which lay
partly in their comparably unfulfilled sexual positions, may also have
lain in a comparably melancholy and prematurely old cast of mind.

Traditions of the Satirist

If the characteristic adoption of an aged voice reflects an aged
mental outlook, that outlook seems to owe a good deal to the writer's
position in a cultural tradition. This can be seen especially clearly with
Skelton and Pope, since they were writing in reasonably well-defined
traditions of satire, which had within them quite specific expectations
about the character and age of the attacking satirist figure. What is
interesting is that contemporary expectations about the age of this
figure match Skelton's and Pope's, while earlier and later expectations
do not. It is not to stretch a point too far to suggest that the general
tendencies in different periods to regard the satirist as old or young
owe something to the qualities of the periods themselves.

Since the attacking speaker of a satire is nearly always a version of
the author, one might expect his age usually to match his author's,

with a youthful author exploiting the energy and freedom of youth, an older one the gravity and wisdom of age. To some extent this is the case, and even with a prematurely aged poet like Pope, the sense of a venerable author is much stronger in the later poetry than in the earlier. The congruence between the ages of real author and satiric persona can be seen in other satirists as well. Horace recognizes it when he comments on the way that Lucilius's satires present the whole course of his life, implying that its different stages are captured in different poems.[21] In line with this, Horace's own satires follow his aging and development, from the crude vigor of the second satire of the first book to the mature sagacity of the epistles. Similarly, Swift's satiric career reflects his life. The "apology" for *A Tale of a Tub*, published six years after the original edition, explains with repetitive emphasis that any faults of the book are those of youth. It is a typically double-edged retraction.

> *He was then a young Gentleman much in the World, and wrote to the Tast of those who were like himself; therefore in order to allure them, he gave a Liberty to his Pen, which might not suit with maturer Years, or graver Characters*[22]

Swift's still-youthful invention ironically undercuts "maturer" and "graver," and as the passage develops, these characters become hardly distinguishable from *"the Sour, the Envious, the Stupid, and the Tastless,"* who have also attacked his book. Later in his life, he turned aged despair to satiric effect. This is best seen in some of the Irish tracts, and above all in the greatest of those, *A Modest Proposal*. At the heart of the grim joke is the rejection of the "other Expedients" passage, the list of measures for Ireland that Swift has been putting forward, in vain, for years.

> THEREFORE I repeat, let no Man talk to me of these and the like Expedients; till he hath, at least, a Glimpse of Hope, that there will ever be some hearty and sincere Attempt to put *them in Practice.*[23]

The imagination here that forces the reader ("let no Man talk to me . . .") back to the possibility of cannibalism is the imagination of one whose long experience has taught him the impossibility of better solutions.[24]

However, if satires sometimes reflect the age of their authors at different stages of their lives, theorists or traditions of satire can come to typify the genre as appropriate to authors of a particular age—the muse of satire can be regarded as stuck in her twenties, her forties, or her sixties. George Gascoigne attempts such a characterization in his

poem of 1576, *The Steele Glas*. Developing a parallel with the myth of
Tereus and Philomel, he creates his own myth of the way that Satyra
learns to sing bitter songs after rape and mutilation. She arrives at
satire through experience, and practices it only when she is old, when
"pride of youth is past."[25] This sense of satire as a genre of maturity
can also be found in the Roman tradition. Although Horace sees
Lucilius's whole life in his work, he calls his master in satire "senex,"
and he seems himself to breathe a sigh of relief when, in the first
epistle, he can finally adopt the air of the aged philosopher.[26] A
fragment of Ennius indicates that he writes satire only when rheu-
matic while Juvenal in his first satire hints, with a reference to past
youth, at what becomes explicit in his eleventh, that he writes as an
old man.[27] Even Persius, who writes as a young man, tries to tap the
authority of age in three of his six satires. *Satires* three and four involve
dialogues in which a youth, in three apparently Persius himself, is
rebuked by an older man, and *Satire* five begins with a lengthy
acknowledgment of the debt Persius owes to his elder and teacher,
Cornutus. Resting on the assumed connection between age and
wisdom, these devices imply that Persius is wise despite his years.

The idea of the aged satirist is prominent also in sixteenth-century
satire, at least in that which was written before the upsurge of the
1590s, when the changed cultural conditions of the Renaissance
produced a changed satiric voice. The notion of satire that existed
before the upsurge is summed up in Gasgoigne's myth in *The Steele
Glas*. There, Satyra's age is reinforced by some of the prefatory materials: by his own "epistle dedicatoire," which mentions how "the
crowes foote is growen under mine eye," and by Nicholas Bowyer's
commendatory sonnet, which contrasts the "loving ryme" fit for youth
with the "workes of worth" intended to delight the "gravest."[28] The
comments reflect expectations about satire, expectations that can also
be found in the earlier part of the century, particularly in Skelton and
Alexander Barclay. If Colin is, as I have suggested, an aging rustic
satirist, Skelton may have borrowed the idea from Barclay, four of
whose five eclogues employ old shepherds to castigate vices. In the
first three, Cornix, a former courtier, "well aged and with lockes hore
and gray," explains the evils of court life to Coridon, who is "like vnto
the same" in everything except that he has spent his life in the fields.[29]
In the fourth, Minalcas asks Codrus to "Succoure my age, regarde my
heares gray," and it is only in the fifth that the two "herdes" are both
"freshe of age."[30] Like Barclay's shepherds, Colin is old and knowing,
and he uses these advantages to denounce the world around him.
Finally, Thomas Wyatt strikes a similar note. Although there is no
specific evidence of age in his satires, and although they were probably

written before he was forty, his general air of weariness has led one critic to write that "the poet is urbane, older and wiser than the society that is contemporary with him."[31]

The satire of the 1590s produced, as I have said, a different kind of satiric voice from this, and satire came to be thought of, in the phrase John Weever applies to his epigrams, as "yong mens Rhetoricke."[32] Weever's remark typifies the attitude of the Elizabethan satirists. John Marston talks of "my young Satyrick vaine" and introduces himself at the beginning of the second of *Certaine Satyres:*

> I That euen now lisp'd like an Amorist,
> Am turn'd into a snaphaunce Satyrist.[33]

This is not like Gascoigne quitting love after long years of hard experience, but it is the sudden, wayward change of youth. Similarly, Donne, while he does not announce his age so obviously, appears in the first satire as the friend of a "fondling motley humorist," who eventually runs off after his lover and becomes involved in a brawl.[34] Joseph Hall is explicit about his youth:

> Al these & more, derserue some blood-drawne lines:
> But my six Cords beene of too loose a twine.
> Stay till my beard shall sweepe myne aged brest,
> The shall I seeme an awfull *Satyrist:*
> While now my rimes relish of the Ferule still,
> Some nose-wise *Pedant* saith; whose deepe-sene skil
> Hath three times construed either Flaccus ore,
> And thrise rehears'd them in his Triuiall floare,
> So let them taxe mee for my hote-bloodes rage,
> Rather than say I doted in my age.[35]

The passage shows a self-conscious satirist reacting against one element of the earlier tradition of English and Roman satire. Hall concedes that great age might be a necessary qualification for an "awfull *Satyrist*," and he half concedes that he is still wet behind the ears; but then he immediately turns on one aged figure of authority, the pedant, and he ends his poem by vigorously asserting his preference for the "hote-bloodes rage" of youth over any kind of dotage. Both the violence and the youth of this rage are part of the Elizabethan conception of the satirist as a furious, aggressive character.[36]

Later English satire is often more dignified than Elizabethan, but it remains associated with the young. In the Restoration Rochester, the least dignified of my examples here, begins *Satyr* [*Timon*] with a friend's question.

> *A*. What *Timon* does old Age begin t'approach
> That thus thou droop'st under a Nights debauch?[37]

Timon, who is another Rochester, quickly replies that it is not long years but long hours with a "dull dining *Sot*" which have caused his indisposition, and he goes on to describe his entertainment. The satiric joke is that a man of Timon's strength and vigor can be made to droop only by someone of even stronger and more vigorous dullness. Although the Dryden of *Absalom and Achitophel* is a much older and soberer figure than Rochester, he echoes something of this version of the satirist in his opening.

> IN pious times, e'r Priest-craft did begin,
> Before *Polygamy* was made a sin;
> When man, on many, multiply'd his kind,
> E'r one to one was, cursedly, confin'd:[38]

The lines partly draw a parallel with Restoration England (which leads onto a compliment to Charles's virility) and partly project an image of the author, with the "cursedly" implying his approving complicity with the gang of courtly libertines. In a later period and a different satiric vein, Johnson still pictures the satirist as youthful. In *London,* he not only includes a reference to his own "Youth, and Health," which marks one change from his Juvenalian model, but he also, and more importantly, makes the departing friend, the poem's chief satirist, much younger than Juvenal's.[39] While Juvenal's Umbricius describes himself as being in the first stage of old age and talks of his lengthy period of service, Johnson's Thales declares that "Life still vig'rous revels in my Veins" and makes no mention of a long career.[40] Johnson has altered the situation, so that instead of one old man reminding another of the decline of Rome, an energetic man of uncertain age addresses a youngster about London. The alteration reflects the English tradition of satire from the Elizabethans onward as "yong mens Rhetoricke," a tradition, moreover, that continues down through Charles Churchill and Byron to Roy Campbell.[41]

The major exceptions to this rule are all contemporaries or near contemporaries of Pope, and this seems to indicate that the aged voice reflects a frame of mind appropriate to that time. I have mentioned already how Swift exploits aged despair for rhetorical effect in the Irish pamphlets of the 1720s, and when Gulliver returns from his voyage as a raging misanthrope, he is in his middle or late fifties.[42] To Swift may be added Edward Young. His second *Epistle to Mr. Pope* begins by presenting its credentials as a weighty poem, "Serious should be an author's final views," and at the end of the earlier second satire of *Love of Fame*, Young considers his own need to learn wisdom: "Be wise with speed; / A fool at forty is a fool indeed."[43] Similarly, Johnson, with *London* out of his system, catches in *The Vanity of Human Wishes*, published when he was not yet forty, the tone of mature wisdom that was to become a feature of the *Rambler* essays.[44]

Although it is not possible to place Eliot in a contemporary tradition of aged voices in the way that it is with Skelton and Pope, Yeats provides one parallel case. Even before he was forty-five, Yeats could write of himself as "being grey" and express the wish that he might "wither into truth,"[45] and the withered poet is central to his later poems. If he uses this to explore ideas and areas of feeling different from those of Skelton, Pope, and Eliot, he also appears in a role similar to theirs, the role of his seven sages in the poem of that title, "old men . . . massed against the world." Curiously enough, Yeats's aged voice is in some ways closer to those of Skelton and Pope than to that of Eliot. Though more skillfully crafted than Skelton's, some of the later poems capture a tone of energetic violence or sexuality that is reminiscent of *Agenst Garnesche* or *Phyllyp Sparowe*. Perhaps more striking still is the way that in poems like "The Municipal Gallery Revisited" and "Beautiful Lofty Things," Yeats enumerates old friends, just as Pope does in his Horatian poems. Of course, the two poets are very different in many respects, but this reflex of dwelling on a lost past and of presenting oneself as just about the last survivor from that past, and as someone consequently doomed to live in an uncongenial present, is the same in both. Pope's implication, like Yeats's in "Beautiful Lofty Things," is that he writes of and has known "All the Olympians: a thing never known again." Besides Yeats and Eliot, however, few modernist poets speak as old men, and the aged voice cannot be said to be a feature of modernist poetry.

The Aged Voice in the Three Poems

The nature and the function of the aged voice in *Speke Parott* are perhaps more straightforward than those of the voices in *The Dunciad* or *The Waste Land*. What Skelton does in the poem is to create a fabulous speaker who, by virtue of his wisdom and his age, can comment authoritatively on the present unfortunate drift of society. Parrot's birth in Paradise, which is mentioned in the first line, makes him about five-and-a-half-thousand years old, and Skelton deliberately exploits this sense of a very old creature, at least in the early part of the poem,[46] in order to contrast past and present, and to protest about what has been, and is being, lost. Parrot complains:

> My lady mastres, Dame Phylology,
> Gave me a gyfte in my neste when I lay,
> To lerne all langage and hyt to speke aptlye.
> Now *pandes mory,* wax frantycke som men sey;
> Phronessys for frenessys may not hold her way.
>
> (43–47)

The "now" introduces a sharp contrast between the way that Parrot learned to speak "aptlye" in his nest and the madness that characterizes learning and destroys understanding ("phronessys") in these modern days. It is a contrast that can be made only because Parrot hails from an earlier, better time, and it both relies upon and emphasizes his age. In much the same way, when Parrot draws a comparison between the old days in Paradise and his present need to seek refuge "*in valle Ebron,*" he simultaneously draws attention to his venerable years (186–88). Even the cryptic line "In Popering grew peres, whan Parrot was an eg" (70) has something of this burden. The first clause contains, as annotators point out, a number of puns that allude to Wolsey's intriques in France and his general attempt to become Henry's peer ("pere"). The line, then, that might be paraphrased as meaning "evils of this kind have existed since before Parrot was born" would make sense only if before Parrot was born was a very long time ago.

In the second part of the poem, Parrot's birth and age are not explicitly mentioned but they are implied in the references to his food. The opening stanza of the whole poem links Parrot's diet with his birth in Paradise. There, he was "dyetyd with dyvers delycate spyce," and consequently, when he comes to England, he must have "an almon or a date" (3–7). The same connection occurs later in the first part. Immediately after describing his early language learning, Parrot demands an almond (48), and another request for food precedes the allusion to the pleasures of Paradise and the assertion "Nowe *in valle Ebron* Parrot is fayne to fede" (188). So, when Galathea in the second part promises Parrot a date and when Parrot demands one (416, 439), the nature of the food recalls the nature of the bird, his birthplace, and age. But the date is also more important than that. Parrot makes a final pun before he speaks out plain in the closing invective: "Yet the date of Owur Lord / And the date of the Devyll dothe shurewlye accord" (444–45). The date for which Parrot has been impatiently waiting since the seventh line of the poem is an appointed time as well as a piece of food, and the description suggests the Judgment.[47] The approach of that time allows Parrot to denounce the world's being more evil now than at any time since Deucalion's flood, that is, he finally has the "lyberte to speke," without interruption, which he has been demanding throughout the poem.[48] His denunciation has a peculiar weight as he is, with his great age, a link between the beginning and the end of the world.

In addition to giving him a unique perspective on world history, Parrot's age enables him to speak with authority about the youthful folly of the present world. In order to emphasize this authority, Skelton attaches to Parrot the same accepted attributes of aged wisdom as those possessed by the virtuous counselors of *Magnyfycence*. At the end of the play, Magnificence has learned the conventional lesson that "the welthe of this worlde can not indure" (2558, 2565), just as Parrot pronounces:

> Pompe, pryde, honour, ryches and worldly lust,
> Parrot sayth playnly, shall tourne all to dust
>
> (223–24)

More centrally, the virtues underpin the moral of the play, that "Measure is treasure" (125), when Circumspection instructs Magnificence, "Measure of your lustys must have the oversyght" (2491). Parrot, too, is the spokesman of moderation as both his whole opposition to excess and his citation of the same proverb, "In mesure is tresure" (62), show. He follows the proverb with the phrase *"cum sensu maturato."* This is the important point—despite his chattering and his joking, Parrot possesses a mature judgment that, like that of the venerable virtues in *Magnyfycence,* imposes upon him the duty to advise, and like that of Skelton himself in *Why Come Ye Nat to Courte?* and *A Replycacion,* gives him the authority to condemn. He is the embodiment of an ancient wisdom, ancient in terms both of the age of the wisdom itself and of the age of its possessor, which is being recklessly discarded by the young representatives of the new society.

The aged voice in *The Dunciad* achieves a slightly different tone from that in *Speke Parott,* largely because the voice belongs not to a fictional persona but to an ironic version of Pope.[49] As I have already argued, much of the reader's impression of the age of the voice comes through knowledge of Pope's self-projections in his earlier poetry,[50] and to the poetry may be added the correspondence. The way for publication in 1742 of the new fourth book was prepared by the appearance of the Swift-Pope letters in the previous year. It is useful to read these letters as a group, since the self-portrait as an old man that Pope presented to his public in 1741 can be obscured in larger collections of letters. Although Swift quite frequently (and to Pope it must have been irritatingly) refers to their difference in years and to his friend's relative youth, Pope is constantly harping on his age. As early as 1729, having mentioned his mother's deteriorating health, he remarks:

> I look upon myself to be many years older in two years since you saw me: The natural imbecillity of my body, join'd now to this acquir'd old age of the mind, makes me at least as old as you, and we are the fitter to crawl down the hill together; I only desire I may be able to keep pace with you. (*Corr.* 3:80)

This letter is particularly interesting since it is one in which Pope's consciousness of an audience other than Swift is very marked. Before the quotation above, he has been smiling to think of their letters in the hands of Curll, and shortly after it, he imagines this letter being copied at the post office and printed (3:79–80). So, this is how Pope would have liked to have been seen, almost competing with Swift for the title of oldest and weakest. Elsewhere in the letters, there are other references to his frailty and approaching death. In 1729 he prophesies that he will not live to be very old (3:57); in 1733 he thinks of nothing "more than mortality" and is "tired of this life" (3:347, 383); in 1736 he talks of winter coming in a clear allusion to his own death (*Corr.* 4:5); and in 1737, in the last letter of the series, he finds himself approaching "that period of life which is to be labour and sorrow" (4:63). Taken together, then, the Swift-Pope letters almost invite Hervey's public assertion that Pope's versifying skill is "from Age and Rust entirely lost," or William Shenstone's private dismissal of *The New Dunciad* as "Mr Pope's dotage."[51]

Contemporary readers, coming to the new fourth book almost straight from this volume of correspondence, would have been in no doubt about the meaning of the opening lines.

> YET, yet a moment, one dim Ray of Light
> Indulge, dread Chaos, and eternal Night!
> Of darkness visible so much be lent,
> As half to shew, half veil the deep Intent.
> Ye Pow'rs! whose Mysteries restor'd I sing,
> To whom Time bears me on his rapid wing,
> Suspend a while your Force inertly strong,
> Then take at once the Poet and the Song.

(B4:1–8)

Although these lines have a general thematic significance, their main import is personal in way that the earlier invocation is not,[52] and the implication of approaching death in the lines is taken up again toward the end, when nature nods and Pope asks, "What Mortal can resist the yawn of Gods?" (B4:606). The question, which has no parallel in the descriptions of sleep in the earlier books, suggests, as does the phrase "all-composing Hour" (B4:627), that Pope, too, is about to be swallowed in a vast, dark yawn. The sandwiching of the main part of the book between these passages of self-revelation has an effect on the voice there. Every line of book 4, with the force of darkness suspended behind it, seems snatched from the jaws of death, and the undoubted energy exists always in the context of time running out. This takes us back to the contrast in tone with *Speke Parott:* the intimations in the final *Dunciad* of Pope's own approaching death add a distinct note of melancholy and lament to the old man's censures on his youthfully foolish society.

As well as in its hints of death, the voice of the fourth book is aged in its limited range of reference. The ironic praiser of dullness through whom Pope speaks is a grotesque version of the Pope of the imitations in his insistent allusions to the people of earlier eras. From the beginning, a great majority of the minor figures are either dead or relics of the past, and of the fourteen men incidentally mentioned in the first two-hundred lines, only three were younger than Pope. The more important figures also generally hail from the past. Richard Busby, the seventeenth-century schoolmaster, rises as a "Spectre" to give his thoughts on education (B4:139), while Richard Bentley, the representative university teacher, belongs with the literary quarrels of the late seventeenth and early eighteenth centuries. If Annius is meant to represent Sir Andrew Fountaine, he would have been sixty-six in 1742, and if the "gloomy Clerk" is Samuel Clarke, he would have been thirteen years dead. The botanist and lepidopterist identify their period by their allegorical involvement in the destruction of the dead Queen Caroline, and Walpole, the "WIZARD OLD," whose grip had been slipping for some years, fell from power in 1742. But if Pope seems almost to parody the imitations in the fourth book by ironically identifying himself through his choice of examples with an old guard of dunces, there is also an important difference in the way that he presents these figures. Whereas the Bolingbrokes and Peterboroughs of the imitations are in philosophical retreat, these somewhat superannuated dunces are hard at work making other people as dull as themselves, an active influence that justifies Pope's account of them. He is not just an irrelevant old man always talking of the past but is rather exploiting his position as a member of the older generation in order to identify and to attack the ancestors and the origins of modern folly.

The culmination of modern folly is ultimately the triumph of Queen Dullness herself, and the sense of that triumph, both in the fourth book and in the fully reworked *Dunciad* of 1743, also relies upon and gives expression to the aged voice. The "argument" of the fourth book, which describes its subject as "*the* Completion *of the* Prophecies *mention'd at the end of the former*" (*Poems* 5 : 337), implicitly calls attention to the relation between the earlier *Dunciad*s and this new book. Pope, who has warned his public of impending catastrophe in the past, must now tell them it has occurred despite his warnings. Since the whole book bears this message, it reminds the reader throughout of the time between the prophecy and its completion, the years in which the dunces triumphed while Pope grew old and defeated. What is more, the relationship between the first three books and the fourth in the four-book *Dunciad* of 1743 encapsulates that period of aging and defeat within the one poem. The effect is further to reinforce the aged air and, as with the references to death, to invest that air with a certain melancholy.

The Waste Land presents problems different from those of *Speke Parott* and *The Dunciad,* since, as with so much of the poem, the age of the speaker is neither made explicit nor is even very obviously implied. Nevertheless, there is sufficient evidence to conclude that the speaker is old, and moreover, Eliot's own recognition of the aged quality of the poem's voice can be seen in his idea at one time of prefixing "Gerontion" to it.[53] Evidence for the speaker's age can be found both in the general cast of his mind and in more specific allusions and links. Two of the most characteristic reflexes of his mind are to look forward to approaching death and back to past life. The first intimation of death is the invitation to enter "the shadow of this red rock" (26), and it is taken up by the speaker in the middle of "A Game of Chess" who waits "for a knock upon the door" (138). The river walker at the beginning of "The Fire Sermon" hears a "chuckle spread from ear to ear" (186), the fisher's obsession with bones and bodies indicates a mortuary imagination (193–94), and the speaker at the beginning of "What the Thunder said" states that "We who were living are now dying" (329). At the same time as there is this looking forward to death, the speaker also displays a highly retrospective cast of mind. The idea of memory is introduced in the second line, and the poem soon goes on to exemplify it in the apparently remembered Marie incident. But the operation of memory becomes most marked at the end. The use of past tenses to reply to the thunder gives the impression that this life is nearly over, an impression strengthened by some of the details of the replies.

> By this, and this only, we have existed
> Which is not to be found in our obituaries
> Or in memories draped by the beneficent spider
> Or under seals broken by the lean solicitor
> In our empty rooms

(405–9)

Approaching death is present throughout these lines in the obituaries, the spider's drapery, and the empty rooms, and it gives extra point to the memory of how the speaker existed. The same sense of termination is carried in the thunder-response structure of the section. The recollection of specific instances in earlier life in response to a set of criteria for living suggests the attempt to evaluate a life already largely lived, an occupation appropriate to its end. Although the evaluation is less explicit earlier, the whole poem is imbued with the sense of a consciousness at a final stage looking back on what has gone.

As well as from this general air, the age of the speaker can be inferred from a number of specific details. The passage from Ecclesiastes alluded to in the second paragraph is an account of old age (23n), while the winter journey south mentioned at the end of the first is an old person's expedient, as the discussion of it by Amy's graying sisters in *The Family Reunion* shows (1.1). Perhaps the most telling details of this kind, though, occur in the opening paragraphs of "The Fire Sermon." In the first of fourteen lines, the speaker repeats variations of Spenser's line "Sweete *Themmes* runne softly, till I end my song" three times. The allusion partly provides a contrast between the wedding that Spenser celebrates in *Prothalamion* and the illicit affairs of Eliot's nymphs and city heirs, but it also reflects upon the situation of the speaker. Spenser begins his poem on a calm day.

> When I whom sullein care,
> Through discontent of my long fruitlesse stay
> In Princes Court, and expectation vayne
> Of idle hopes, which still doe fly away,
> Like empty shaddowes, did aflict my brayne,
> Walkt forth to ease my payne[54]

The lines set Spenser's own neglected condition and disconsolate mood against the happiness of his vision for most of the rest of the poem, and the phrase "long fruitlesse stay" suggests he has grown old (he was about forty-four) in courtly service. The melancholy note is sustained in the supplication of the refrain (the line Eliot borrowed) for softness, and there is even the elegaic implication that the end of his song might be the end of his singing. All this has a bearing on Eliot's speaker. Like Spenser, he presents himself walking by the Thames in melancholy mood, and his melancholy takes on an aged color from his use of Spenser's line.

The second paragraph of "The Fire Sermon" is equally revealing. The speaker's fishing (189) links him with the Fisher King, on the subject of whom Jessie Weston (allowing that his age varies in different versions of the legends) draws attention "to the significant fact that in no case is the Fisher King a youthful character."[55] When the speaker refers to his fishing again in the last paragraph of the whole poem (424), it is a prelude to the series of fragments, and to the reference to "my ruins," another image connoting age (430). What is more, the Fisher King is, according to Weston, a version of the drowned god, Tammuz or Adonis,[56] so Eliot's fisher has some relation to Phlebas the Phoenician. Since Phlebas passes in death "the stages of his age and youth" (317), he must have died old, and his earthly self may well have been the "garçon délabré," the "vieux lubrique" of the earlier poem "Dans le Restaurant," where the lines concerning Phlebas, with only slight differences beyond their being French, first appear. Another interesting, though highly puzzling, line is the one that alludes to Ferdinand in *The Tempest:* "Musing upon the king my brother's wreck" (191). Whatever this means exactly, it clearly makes the speaker a contemporary ("my brother") of Alonso, Ferdinand's wrecked father, rather than of Ferdinand himself. The line also catches echoes from other parts of *The Waste Land*. The visitor to Madame Sosostris seems to interject (the sentence could conceivably be hers) a line from the song by Ariel, which comes immediately after Ferdinand's speech (48). The use of such related allusions suggests that the fisher of "The Fire Sermon" and Madame Sosostris's visitor are the same person, and again the visitor is linked with Alonso and with Phlebas through his predicted "death by water" (55).[57]

The Waste Land, then, is like *Speke Parott* and *The Dunciad* in that it comments on the contemporary situation through the medium of an aged voice. Of course, Eliot generally speaks more in sorrow than in anger, and his poem is in some respects more personal than Skelton's or Pope's. However, like them, he uses his aged voice to condemn the youthful world around him. Tiresias watching the clerk and typist provides the paradigmatic situation. Tiresias has done everything, knows it all, has even experienced the ultimate in degradation when walking among "the lowest of the dead" (246). Consequently, he can pass weary judgment on the futile amours of the clerk and typist, and there is a similar tone to this in those parts of the poem that belong to the dominant speaker. At the beginning of "The Fire Sermon," he knows the heirs will have left no addresses, a gloomy knowledge that implies both authority (because he knows) and condemnation (because he is gloomy). The world-weariness that opens the poem casts its doleful shadow on the Marie incident and provides a context in which it must be judged. Even the attempted evaluation of a past life at the end is conducted in terms of superior experience. The person who meditates that an age of prudence cannot retract a moment's surrender, nor can the key turn again in the lock, is someone who has passed through youthful folly. He has reached the mature, unhappy knowledge that, it is implied throughout *The Waste Land*, belongs to the speaker.

3

Intimations of Mortality

Old Fools

The habit of taking on an aged poetic voice reflects a wish to construct a position of venerable reverence from which to view the world, and its most obvious rhetorical function is to claim a kind of authority. However, the habit also seems to reflect, as I mention in the previous chapter, a more wholesale adoption of an aged cast of mind, a cast of mind that is only in part authoritative and assured. Something of the equivocal nature of the old man's psychology can be seen in "Geron- tion." In that poem, Eliot deliberately creates an aged speaker who is confused, incoherent, and rather peevish, "a dry brain in a dry season." Similarly dubious characteristics of the old, though often apparently less deliberately included, can be found in other poems by Eliot, Skelton, and Pope, and they have an especially important place in *Speke Parott, The Dunciad,* and *The Waste Land.* The presence of such characteristics in the poems alongside the more respectable attributes of age tends to work against, to subvert, the claims to authority. So, while Gerontion's age and experience command for him a certain right to speak and to be heard, his obvious bad temper detracts from the compulsion of what he has to say. In the same way, the betrayal by the speaker of *Speke Parrot, The Dunciad,* or *The Waste Land* of spleen, of personal crankiness, or of some other dishonorable motive for opposing the current of the world, works to undermine the apparently weighty revelations of contemporary folly. The betrayal also suggests a degree of insecurity and anxiety in the poet about his role as a moral censor. It is as if one part of his imagination constructs the reassuring figure of the ancient sage while another (remembering that the old man has vices as well as virtues) gives whispering voice to doubts and fears about the substance and integrity of this figure.

The vices of age are thrown into particularly sharp relief when the aged speakers of the poems are shown in dramatic confrontations with youth. Each of the poets seems to have been unable to maintain the pose of reverence when imagining, in however implicit a manner, his opposition to a world of youthful folly. Moreover, it is in the context of the old man's struggle with the youthful world that the betrayal of peevishness, envy, or self-interest serves most to expose anxiety and insecurity, this being the context in which the poet needs his wished-for authority most. Although dramatic presentations of such a conflict might seem at first simply to show the wise ancient's disinterested denunciation of folly, they often also suggest the old man's personally motivated attack on the young and his half-acknowledged, nervous awareness of his own failings. The nervousness is further compounded by the implied knowledge of weakness and impotence. Say what he will, the ancient must shortly leave the world to his young adversaries, and his opposition to youth is doomed to failure because he himself is doomed soon to die. The implied sense of that inevitable failure adds another element to the complex feeling of anxiety which haunts each of the three poems, an element again which is generated by the opposition between age and youth. The bulk of this chapter will be devoted to examining this opposition, but before going on to that, I will look briefly at some instances where each poet exposes aged folly outside the context of generational conflict.

The guilt of Eliot's aged speaker in *The Waste Land* is more pronounced than that which emerges in *Speke Parott* or which lies below the surface of *The Dunciad*. His relation to the Fisher King saddles him with a very large share of blame, since it is the Fisher King's failure that has laid the land waste. More importantly, the old characters in general seem to have been guilty of culpable sexual behavior in their youth. Tiresias's foresuffering all does not simply mean that he has experienced sexual intercourse as both a man and a woman but that he has experienced couplings as sterile as that of the typist and her young man (243). Likewise, Lil, who, though only thirty-one (very slightly younger than Eliot himself), already looks antique (156–57), tells through the narrator/rival of her seduction by Albert, mentioning in the process such sexually suggestive details as the "hot gammon" that first tempted her (166–67).[1] The speaker, too, has a guilty past. The third recollection in reply to the thunder recalls, at least potentially, the adventures of the Thames-daughters, and the word "gaily" does little to lessen the sense of a man exploiting a woman. Similarly, the episode in the hyacinth garden, cryptic and puzzling though it is, involves an unsatisfactory encounter and some kind of failure (35–41).

Although none of Skelton's speakers is quite as markedly guilty as Eliot's, his wise old men are still very often in danger of becoming old fools. While Colin's frequent claims that he is repeating only what he has heard people say serve to confer authority on his opinions,[2] they also lead into the problem of the poem, the speaker's simultaneous defense and subversion of the Church. In a central passage, Colin turns on the people.

> For it maketh me sad
> Howe the people are glad
> The churche to deprave.

(511–13)

He himself is, of course, depraving the Church, and this makes him something far more difficult than a simple voice of authority. Elsewhere, Skelton touches upon some of the problems of aging. The attitude of the mature poet toward Jane Scrope in *Phyllyp Sparowe* is not in the least, as C. S. Lewis says, "like an affectionate uncle or even a grandfather."[3] In his imaginative journeys under Jane's clothes (1194–1203), Skelton is exposing the unrealizable and illegitimate desires of an aging man, and all the passages of violent self-defense manage only, whether this is an intentional effect or not, to highlight his awkwardness and guilt. Some such suspect old figure is perhaps also important in poems that neither handle the theme of maturity nor make reference to the speaker's age. The five flyting poems, *Agenst Garnesche*, were written, as Skelton tells us, "Be the kynges most noble commandement" (1:43) and were clearly very public affairs. In them, Skelton insists on his dignity as laureate (3:14), as a priest (3:89), and as one whose degree was conferred by the king (5:80), while he attacks Garnesche as so ugly "Thy myrrour may be the devyllys ars" (5:18), as so foul of breath "He wyl cause yow caste your crawes" (3:155), and as so infatuated with Mistress Audelby "Ye wolde have bassyd hyr bumme" (3:62). It seems likely that some of the pleasure this kind of poetry offered Henry's boisterous court, and much of the power of the vituperation, must have arisen from the fact that Skelton was old, and should have been wise. Henry and his friends must have relished the unedifying spectacle of the foulmouthed old priest verbally assaulting one of their number.

Parrot, too, in addition to his wisdom, possesses other aged characteristics, some of which are at odds with wisdom, and which seem therefore to have been less deliberately intended by Skelton. It is possible only to speculate in such matters, but the creative process may have been the following: in fashioning an ancient creature through which to speak his own opinions and in working within a tradition of riddling verse prophecies,[4] Skelton may have given his imagination the rein, with the unforeseen result that his own insecurities about himself came into play and his parrot ended up talking not only like a sage or a prophet but also like a garrulous, petulant, and lecherous old man. Certainly, whatever the cause, Parrot possesses these features, and they are all traditionally associated with old men. He can hardly stop talking, and Aristotle in his *Rhetoric* points to the "loquacity" of the old, to the way that they are "incessantly talking of the past."[5] His bad temper is anticipated in *Phyllyp Sparowe*, where Skelton describes envy as an old man, complete with dry cheeks, wan face, cracking bones, lean figure, and rusty gums (909–14), and this old man's character is highly choleric, "His tong never styll / For to say yll" (941–42). Such churlishness is also associated with parrots in *Agenst Garnesche* (3:167), and although Parrot denies that he is a "churlish chowgh" (204), his account of the state of England in the later parts of the poem betrays a good deal of the old man's, or the parrot's, irascibility. Finally, by boasting that "Parrot hath a blacke beard and a fayre grene tayle" (84), and by punning "To dwell amonge ladyes, Parrot, is mete" (105),[6] Parrot is exposing the old man's lechery and sexual braggadocio. The boast of the black beard and green tail may allude to Chaucer's Reeve's argument that all old men wish to have "an hoor head and a grene tayl" a wish which is only a wish and which exists "thogh oure myght be goon."[7] The same idea appears elsewhere in Chaucer. January of "The Merchant's Tale" brags that his "lymes been as grene / As laurer thurgh the yeer," but (even though Chaucer withholds all the details) his lovemaking seems to be less than energetic. On his wedding night, he excuses himself from working hastily, and on another occasion, having kissed his wife "ful ofte," he falls asleep, "and that anon."[8] For all his playing, kissing, and talking, January is probably pretty much in the position of the wife of Bath's first three husbands, of being scarcely able to carry out his conjugal duties.[9] Parrot is curiously similar to January in that he thinks a lot about sexual matters and talks a lot about them, but he does not (and, of course, as a bird he cannot) engage in any sexual activity with the ladies.

Pope's aged voice in his late poems, like that of Skelton in his, is primarily intended to confer authority on the poet. In general, this authority is firmer than Skelton's, as Pope fashions out of himself a venerable, dignified public figure whose allegiance to virtue, philosophy, and the values of the past allows him to see and to judge the decadence of the present. However, Pope's poetry of old age is not always as straightforward as that, and in particular, *Sober Advice* unleashes similar complex energies to those of Skelton. The relation of the imitator to the original author is very interesting in this poem. Horace's vigorously scandalous satire on sexual excess is a young man's outburst, as is clear from its position as the second poem of his first book of satires, the first poem of that book being described later as belonging to his earliest muse.[10] Pope's title for the first anonymous edition of his imitation, on the other hand, *Sober Advice from Horace, to the Young Gentlemen about Town,* implies with the word "sober" that the poem is to be an old man's counsel to the young. The age of the imitator is further suggested by the subtitle, "Imitated in the Manner of Mr. POPE," and the prefatory letter to Pope, which states that the imitation is "in your own Manner" (*Poems* 4:73).[11] The joke is that although a young man's salacious gossip is transformed when repeated, or adapted, by an old man, it is not transformed into "sober advice." Rather, it becomes prurient, envious, and voyeuristic. This element is perhaps clearest in the sexually explicit reference to the misdemeanors of Pope's near contemporary (she was four years older than he) Viscountess Hillsborough. Having alluded to her *"hoary Shrine"* (*Sermon* 1.2.46), he draws the reader's attention in a note to his strange translation, which while it finds a euphemism for "cunni" (carefully capitalized in the Latin text) misapplies "hoary" to pubic hair instead of to dress (Latin text, line 36n). In effect, Pope, in indicating to the reader the way that his imagination works and the details on which it feeds, is making fun of his own prurience, but it is dangerous fun involving sensitive areas of feeling. The same areas of feeling, though usually without the protection of self-conscious joking, come into play in *The Dunciad,* particularly in the oppositions between Pope and the dunces.

Contexts and Conflicts

As I have already remarked, the fallibility of the old becomes especially conspicuous when the various aged speakers of the poems are seen in relation to the young in dramatic contexts. The most direct dramatic confrontation in *The Waste Land,* and one of the most illuminating from any of the poems, occurs in the lines in which Tiresias perceives the scene between clerk and typist, where the implied purpose is to expose a degraded sexuality. The clipped quatrains suggest that Tiresias is safely removed from the maddeningly complacent young man, his grubby advances, and his lover's bored submission. Tiresias's experience is also important, for having done it all before, he can watch with seeming indifference and report, and judge, with icy accuracy.[12] However, his apparent disinterest is belied by the nature of the dramatic situation. Tiresias is a man, now at least, watching another man making love, and the success of the clerk, however qualified and deflated, poses a threat to the impotent observer.[13] The defensive antagonism provoked by this threat is unmistakable in the original version of the event, in which Tiresias (or Eliot) is clearly out to get the clerk. In lines that Pound deleted for being "probaly [*sic*] over the mark," for example, the clerk is described as urinating and spitting (*Facsimile,* 47). Although there is no such open aggression in the final version, the dramatic situation makes it easy to detect a covert aggression lurking beneath the cold description.

This situation is further complicated by the presence of Eliot behind Tiresias. If Tiresias is not the speaker of the poem, he is the character closest to him, as the scope and nature of his perception, his central position, and Eliot's famous note all indicate. Consequently, he can be seen as a mask for the evasive poet to hide behind, or a mechanism for dealing with a perceived threat, since his presence allows Eliot to observe and describe the scene at one extra remove.[14] The reader who spots this evasion will only be the more aware of the atmosphere of threat, an atmosphere that is further heightened by the evasiveness of Eliot's note. The note declares that what "Tiresias *sees,* in fact, is the substance of the poem" (218n), but what Tiresias sees is not even the substance of this incident. As with any dramatic scene, the substance lies in the relations between a set of people in a set of circumstances and in what those relations create. In this scene, the relations between the three people involved (four, if we count Eliot) chiefly create anxieties and uncertainties, only half contained by contempt, for the observer. While those relations and anxieties do not quite form the substance of *The Waste Land,* they and similar situations and sentiments are closer to it than anything Tiresias simply sees.

Like Tiresias, Parrot is sometimes shown in fairly direct confrontation with the youthful world, most notably in the dramatic situation of the pet bird among the court ladies. When their childish phrase "bas me, swete swete" (104) appears again in the later poem, *Why Come Ye Nat to Courte?* it casts considerable light on Parrot's predicament among the ladies. Skelton, speaking more or less in his own person, explains why he feels he must stay away from court.

> For age is a page
> For the courte full unmete;
> For age can nat rage,
> Nor basse her swete swete.
>
> (32–35)

With a certain degree of bravado and pride, he proclaims that the foolish and childish triviality of the court make it an unfit place for one of his gravity and years. But Parrot is in a more difficult position than this, and it may be one that reflects something closer to Skelton's real position than the pose he strikes in *Why Come Ye Nat to Courte?* Parrot, a special bird with special knowledge, must stay at court, must please the ladies, must "basse her, swete swete," and must expect to have his gravest utterances ignored, misunderstood, or silenced. Instead of his weighty thoughts, the ladies want entertainment, and Parrot obliges with verbal pyrotechnics, chatter, sexual innuendo, and reeling to and fro "Lyke a wanton" (109). Skelton may have felt that his own place in the England of Wolsey and in the youthful court of Henry VIII was not so very different from this. Several years earlier, he had engaged in the coarse flyting match with Garnesche, and a few years later he would picture himself allegorically and retrospectively in *Garlande or Chapelet of Laurell* producing poetry for a little court of ladies. Even with works as serious as *Speke Parott*, Skelton may have felt that his voice, a voice that he was to insist later in *A Replycacion* was inspired by the Holy Ghost (383), was destined to be ignored in favor of the voices of timeservers and hypocrites. So, in creating a parrot who is caged in court and treated with less respect than he deserves by his audience, Skelton may have been representing his own frustrations. Whether this was the case or not, it remains true that the image of the ancient, wise bird turned into the pet of silly young women is one that is loaded with implications of constraint and frustration.

Most of the dramatic confrontations between age and youth in the poems are less explicit than the two I have discussed so far. Rather than being directly presented, the confrontation is implied in the conflict that the reader observes between satirist and world, and our sense of the speaker's aged fallibility depends upon our sense of his age and his world's youth. The importance of the implied age of the satirist who chooses to vilify the youth of his butts can be emphasized by looking at a contrastive example. Marston, as I have said, writes as a young man, and in one poem he sneers at a fop's ruff.

> Nay he doth weare an Embleme bout his necke.
> For vnder that fayre Ruffe so sprucely set
> Appeares a fall, a falling-band forsooth.
> O dapper, rare, compleat, sweet nittie youth![15]

Like Skelton, Pope, and Eliot, Marston is using his butt's tender years as a stick to beat him with, yet the satire is quite different from theirs. The difference arises largely from the implied context of a conflict between one young man and another young man, a context that determines much of the nature of the aggression and rivalry. In particular, the word "youth" can have few of the complex associations of irritation, fear, envy, and regret in the mouth of a young man that it has in the mouth of an old. Thus, while Marston's satire on youth is youthfully rough and energetic, that of Skelton, Pope, and Eliot is agedly anxious and splenetic.

Parrot's (and behind Parrot's, Skelton's) anxiety and spleen can be detected throughout the poem in the vehemence of feeling that the poem's language repeatedly betrays. The taunting of Wolsey with the epithet "bull-calf," for example, suggests not the speaker's confident superiority and contempt but his desire to be superior and contemptuous, and his secret fear that he is not. Similar feelings are at work in the last of the stanzas dealing with the errors of the new learning.

> Plautus in his comedies a chyld shall now reherse,
> And medyll with Quintylyan in his *Declamacyons,*
> That *Pety Caton* can scantly construe a verse,
> With, *"Aveto"* in *Greco,* and such solempne salutacyons,
> Can skantly the tensis of his conjugacyons;
> Settyng theyr myndys so moche of eloquens,
> That of theyr scole maters lost is the hole sentens.
>
> (176–82)

The subject of these lines is straightforward enough. Parrot is complaining that new methods of teaching, while providing children with what he considers to be inappropriate texts such as Quintilian and Plautus, do not give them any solid grounding in Latin grammar. But there is more going on in the stanza than simply a reasoned critique of a new kind of learning. Firstly, the young scholars are presented not merely as passive recipients of education but are rather active in the way that they meddle with Quintilian, offer "solempne salutacyons," and insist on their right to practice eloquence. This activity suggests their encroachment, or the fear of their encroachment, upon the world of learning, the preserve of Skelton and other old men like him. Secondly, Skelton's rhetoric for dealing with the young is somewhat excessive. The exasperated repetition of "can skantly" and the aggressive sneer that the young ignoramuses mistake the Latin *"Aveto"* for Greek expose something of the powerless, threatened anger of the decaying man against the vigorous rise of the young.

The nature of the conflict between Pope and both the young and the youthfully old is slightly more difficult to pin down than the nature of the conflict in *Speke Parott.* Because Pope's elusive personality is largely hidden behind the elaborate constructions of the mock-encomium and the mock-epic, there is little of the fairly open confrontation that takes place between Skelton and his butts or, on occasion, between Eliot and his. Nevertheless, the conflict is there in *The Dunciad.* At its most obvious and official, it involves the opposition of the mature, cultured Pope (implicitly present in every balanced, allusive, controlled couplet) to the disorderly freedom of the infantile dunces.[16] But the poem also contains more personal and complex energies than that.[17] In particular, it carries a strong implied sense of the old man's frightened, envious fascination with the untrammeled ebullience of the young and of his immature contemporaries.[18]

The mixture of envy and fear in Pope is perhaps most marked in the passages that employ sexual images. His own sexual character comes into play in such passages, a character defined by physical deformity and frailty and, in his last years, by the added weakness of age.[19] He was, at his public knew, extremely sensitive on this subject, and the two attacks on him that elicited the most vigorous poetic replies both made liberal reference to it. In *Verses Address'd to the Imitator of Horace* (1733), Lady Mary Wortley Montagu asks

> But how should'st thou by Beauty's Force be mov'd,
> No more for loving made, than to be lov'd?[20]

To this charge of a physical matched by an inner ugliness, Cibber adds the imputation in *A Letter* that Pope possesses only diminutive sexual prowess.

> his Lordship's Frolick propos'd was to slip his little *Homer,* as he call'd him, at a Girl of the Game, that he might see what sort of Figure a Man of his Size, Sobriety, and Vigour (in Verse) would make, when the frail Fit of Love had got into him;[21]

The references to size and vigor, emphasized by subsequent parentheses, imply that Pope is no great lover and has a small penis. As if in rebuttal, or anticipation, of such attacks, Pope seems almost to protest his own sexual normality in some parts of the imitations. In the closing passage of *Sober Advice,* a passage much expanded from Horace's original, he advises sexual moderation:

> Give me a willing Nymph! 'tis all I care,
> Extremely clean, and tolerably fair,
> Her Shape her own, whatever Shape she have,
> And just that White and Red which Nature gave.
>
> (*Sermon* 1.2.161–64)

As well as offering advice, Pope is presenting himself here, and the hidden declaration is that he is as fit for, and as capable of, enjoying a "tight, neat Girl" as the next man. The later imitation of the Venus ode is still more self-revelatory. The poem's concern is less with its elegant compliment to William Murray than with its expression, behind the shield of Horace's original, of Pope's condition, and like *Sober Advice*, it presents that as unexceptional. Having directed Venus and her doves toward Murray, Pope laments, "With me, alas! those joys are o'er," with the clear implication that his own youth was spent as healthily and vigorously as his friend's (*Ode* 4.1.31). But it is important that these joys are now over, while the unrealizable dream of them remains tormentingly alive. The aging poet of the ode is in the position Pope must always have occupied to some extent, stuck on the sidelines, conscious of his own frustrated sexual feelings, and enviously aware of the activity of others.

This sensitivity informs a number of the most striking images of youthful dunces in the early books. The first of the new duncely generation to whom Settle draws attention in book 3 is Theophilus Cibber.

> Mark first that Youth who takes the foremost place,
> And thrusts his person full into your face.
>
> (B3 : 139–40)

The fact the "person" connotes genitals as well as the body in general gives the image a specifically sexual coloring.[22] In part, this adds an extra menace to the sense of threatening physical proximity, while it also possibly suggests a degree of suppressed envy at such uninhibited, energetic exhibitionism. But perhaps the most important example of the complex relations between Pope and the young dunces is to be found in the portrait of the "young Aeneas" in the fourth book. In all the long analysis of false guardianship, this young man is the only ward who is portrayed in any detail, and consequently, he becomes a central figure in the book. It is significant that his character is that of the rake—in Europe he,

> The Stews and Palace equally explor'd,
> Intrigu'd with glory, and with spirit whor'd;
>
> (B4 : 315–16)

The personal animus betrayed in the sarcasm of these lines makes them less than successful in writing off the youth's behavior. However much Pope may sneer, he cannot annul the rake's spirit in whoring or glory in intrigue, both of which stand in contrast to his own exploits.

His whoring days, probably never very spirited, were long over by 1742, and his most glorious rumored intrigue had collapsed ignominiously years earlier in Lady Mary's reported laughter.

The sexual is also important in the attacks on those of a similar age to Pope. The portrait of Colley in the poem, grafted as it is onto the original Tibbald, is so engrossed with his sleepiness that it does not emphasize his character as an old debauchee. The prefatory essay concerning the hero of the poem, on the other hand, dwells upon this aspect of the real Cibber, likening him to "an *old, dull, debauched, buffoon Cyclops*" (*Poems* 5:256), quipping that the lust of old age "becometh a standing ornament to the little Epic" (5:258), and asserting that the "man is sure enough a Hero, who has his Lady at fourscore" (5:258). The official purpose of these ironies, to place Cibber in reprehensible contrast to the dignified old Pope, is overshadowed by their expression of the frightened, fascinated awareness that at eighty (actually a few years less), Cibber's masculinity is unimpaired. Instead of simply reducing Cibber, they bring into play the anxiety, interest, and distaste of one old man faced with another whose lust remains, with appropriate sexual innuendo, as ever "a standing ornament." A similar mixture of attitudes is present in the fourth book in relation to the sexual excesses of the old guardians, and especially in the representative figure of Silenus. Something of Pope's partial and equivocal affinity with Silenus may be contained in the familiar, false, and (in Pope's day) already exploded etymology of "satire" as deriving from "satyr."[23] The name of the muse under Dullness's throne is "Satyr" rather than Pope's more usual "satire" (B4:42), which, together with her femininity, might characterize Pope himself, the poem's satirist, as a frustrated Silenus. But that is only curious speculation. What is certain is that Silenus boasts of the rakishness of the "finish'd Son," and with his red cheeks, large, naked belly, stroking gestures, and familiar air is a formidably potent figure (B4:495–98). In creating this epitome of senile debauchery, the aged, philosophical, of necessity celibate, Pope not only surrounds him with proper disapproval but conjures up along with that more disturbing jealousies and fears.

Such feelings, however covert they might be, suggest an alternative character for the old poet, a character that in its partiality and passion works powerfully to subvert the more open character of the ancient sage. As with Skelton and to a lesser extent with Eliot, Pope seems to have begun with the intention of constructing for himself an impressive and authoritative poetic speaker. But in imagining the confrontations between this speaker and the youthfully foolish world, he apparently accorded to his voice much less impressive and authoritative attributes. Their effect is to expose the flaws in the speaker and to imply Pope's unacknowledged or half-acknowledged doubts about his own position and role in relation to the world.

The Waste Land's speaker's responses to youth are somewhat more complex than those of Parrot and even than those of Pope. The attitude that emerges most openly from him is the complementary assertion of others' youthful blindness and his own superior knowledge, an assertion closely related both to Tiresias's description of the clerk as "One of the low" (233) and to the attempt by all three poets to establish authority. The opening of "The Fire Sermon" creates the kind of landscape in which significant questions are asked. The clutching of the leaves and the brownness of the land recall the desert of the second paragraph of "The Burial of the Dead," where the heightened colloquy between (apparently) prophet and God takes place (173–75, 19–20). But these significant landscapes are, significantly, empty, with the wind crossing the later one "unheard." In fact, the wind is not entirely unheard, since the speaker hears it, which indicates the difference between him and the nymphs and city heirs. While they have visited the place only in crowded summer, he makes his solitary way through it in winter. His isolation, though no doubt a burden, helps mark him as the kind of man who perceives the real nature of things, and implicitly marks them as the kind of people who do not. Again, he laments toward the end of the paragraph, "By the waters of Leman I sat down and wept" (182). If this echoes the psalmist's "By the rivers of Babylon, there we sat down, yea, we wept, when we remembered Zion" (Ps. 137:1), it is noteworthy that the pronoun has shifted from plural to singular. In Eliot's version, only the speaker weeps, the others presumably being too blind to realize that there is cause for weeping. There is a similar attitude elsewhere in the poem. The quotation from *Hamlet* at the end of the pub scene, those from Saint Augustine and the Buddha which follow the songs of the Thames-daughters and the knowledge of Phlebas's fate, all give the speaker an edge of ironic insight over other people.

The speaker's pose of superiority often develops into a veiled warning, something that is perhaps most obvious in "Death by Water."

> Gentile or Jew
> O you who turn the wheel and look to windward,
> Consider Phlebas, who was once handsome and tall as you.
>
> (319–21)

The identity of those addressed here is not quite clear, as the first line suggests a rather broad reference, while the second seems to point specifically to an earlier passage of an earlier version. In that, the sailor is described as a "concentrated will against the tempest and the tide" and as retaining a dignity even through visiting prostitutes, getting drunk, and contracting gonorrhea (*Facsimile*, 55). Yet despite this confusion, it appears that the passage is directed chiefly at the young, at those who are still "handsome and tall." The injunction that they consider Phlebas warns that they, too, will be reduced to bones, and it carries, beneath the prophetic afflatus, a vindictive triumph at their downfall. The same warning appears by implication at the end of the first paragraph of "The Fire Sermon." When the speaker hears "The rattle of the bones, and chuckle spread from ear to ear" (186), he is foreseeing not only his own death but also those of the nymphs and heirs. The allusion to Marvell's account of the death of lovers establishes this, and the linking of "White bodies naked" and "bones" a few lines later reinforces the idea (193–94). As in the Phlebas passage, the warning, with its sardonically enjoyable description of the cadaverous chuckle, is heavily laced with triumph. Finally, the echo of Ophelia at the end of "A Game of Chess" operates in much the same way (172). The irony of the line is partly that Lil and the pub gossip are less than sweet and less pathetic than Ophelia, and partly also that their time, like hers, will one day be up, a point that is rather ponderously emphasized by the barman's repeated calls. Since they remain apparently unaware of their mortality, the speaker (as well as the reader) is afforded a moment's glory over their ignorance and their approaching death.

If, however, the speaker indulges in assertions of superiority and triumph, there is a strong sense in *The Waste Land* that these are defensive responses to a threat. Perhaps this comes across most clearly through the avoidance of confrontation with its subject, which is so marked a feature of the poem's imagination. Eliot seems constantly to be placing distance and barriers between himself, or his speaker, and the young people he observes. The speaker's isolation at the beginning of "The Fire Sermon" implies not only that he is in some respect superior to the nymphs and city heirs but also that he has kept well out of their way. What is more, their summer activities, though these haunt the scene, are chiefly imagined indirectly through the debris, the now-disappeared empty bottles, and so on, which they must have left (177–79). So, the scene presents us with the imagination of the clues to past summer nights, and the nights themselves are kept safely several steps away. Similarly, the rape of Philomel is perceived from a distance.

> Above the antique mantel was displayed
> As though a window gave upon the sylvan scene

The change of Philomel, by the barbarous king
So rudely forced;

(97–100)

Again, the event takes place in the past, and here it has the added separation from immediate reality conferred by myth. Further, the sense of distance that is created by its existing only in pictorial, and specifically decorative, representation is emphasized by the image of a window, which suggests an observer watching outward from a building. Lastly, the language retreats by adopting an archaic and inadequate adverb ("rudely") to describe the rape. Elsewhere, Eliot puts on in the same way a kind of protective style or persona when he approaches youthful sexuality. The best example of persona is Tiresias, but the two other fairly explicit accounts of couplings are also given secondhand. Lil's seduction, another past event, is described by her friend, and the first Thames-daughter's story is told through the character of the Thames-daughter herself. As for style, Eliot slips at some crucial moments into the inflatedly prophetic (the injunction to "Consider Phlebas") or the incomprehensibly cryptic. The most important moment in the speaker's own youth, the hyacinth garden episode, is conveyed in a very unspecific way, "Looking into the heart of light, the silence" (41). The obscurity of the phrase, like the other distancing devices, exposes the attempt to evade and, beyond that, the fear that prompts the attempt.

As a complement to this fear, the speaker displays a strong fascination with the subject that also repels him. If his meditations on the nymphs and heirs at the beginning of the "The Fire Sermon" are appropriately oblique, it is important that he does think about them and their summer behavior. What is happening in the passage is that an old man is walking by the river and thinking, in however indirect a way, of the fornications that went on there among the young during the previous summer. There is something similar at work when Eliot uses a persona to imagine an act of intercourse.

Trams and dusty trees.
Highbury bore me. Richmond and Kew
Undid me. By Richmond I raised my knees
Supine on the floor of the narrow canoe.

(292–95)

No amount of formal analysis should obscure the reader's knowledge that it was a man, specifically a young man with an outlook prematurely old, who created these lines. More importantly still, the woman speaker, whose lover is not even identified by a pronoun, is quite separate from any human context except that of her relationship with her creator. So, Eliot appears to be exploiting this female figure in order to dwell upon such details as her undoing (in both the moral and the button senses), her raised knees, and her supine position. The conclusion to the account of the rape of Philomel states that "still the world pursues, / 'Jug Jug' to dirty ears" (102–3). Throughout *The Waste Land* it is Eliot who pursues in imagination the ravishings of Philomel, Lil, the typist, and the Thames-daughters, revealing in the pursuit his own dirty ears, his half-unwilling fascination with his subject.

The exposure of the poet's "dirty ears" in *The Waste Land* has a similar effect to that of the exposure of aggression in *Speke Parott* or of anxious sexuality in *The Dunciad*. It works against the authority sought in the pose of maturity. Thus, while the speaker seems to comment with all the knowledge of experience on the errant generation that has taken over the world, his commentary is simultaneously being shown to be far from disinterested or objective or necessarily truthful. The revelation affects adversely the status of both commentary and commentator, and it hints, as it does so, at the poet's own insecurity. What is left in the poem is less a weighty pronouncement against an erring generation than a powerful mood of doubt and anxiety.

The End of It All

The anxiety that, so to say, lurks in the exposure of the aged speaker's own frailties is complemented by a (usually more open) feeling in each of the poems of the poet's impotence and inevitable defeat. The feeling has both a personal dimension, in that it is connected with the old man's approaching death, and a more general dimension, in that it reflects a disinterested sorrow at the course of the world. Pope's revised introduction to the magnificent closing lines of *The Dunciad* betrays the feeling, in both its dimensions, very clearly. Originally, the vision of Dullness's triumph ended the third book and was introduced by the rather bland couplet.

> Signs following signs lead on the Mighty Year;
> See! the dull stars roll round and re-appear.
>
> (A3 : 335–36)[24]

In the fully reworked *Dunciad* of 1743 (though not in the separately published fourth book, *The New Dunciad,* of the previous year) this becomes:

> In vain, in vain,—the all-composing Hour
> Resistless falls: The Muse obeys the Pow'r.
>
> (B4:627–28)

In the context created by the opening invocation of the book, by Pope's declining health and by his public's knowledge of it, these lines acquire the poignant personal significance that the poet is soon to die and can do nothing about it. There is also, however, the more general significance of the triumph of Dullness, the poet's horrified dismay at this triumph being strongly colored by the impotence of one approaching death. All he can do is watch and lament. The feeling here is rather different from the antagonism, competitiveness, and envy that are present in the conflict between Pope and the dunces in other parts of the poem, and its presence adds another element to the poem's complex responses to the conditions it addresses.

A similarly complex response is evident in the final paragraph of *The Waste Land,* in which the situation of the ancient faced with youth is again implied and important. The fact that the speaker's age is a central part of his consciousness and his conception of himself is to be inferred from his reference to fishing and from the way that so many of the literary fragments which echo in his mind are associated with the old or the dying or the dead. He remembers Arnaut Daniel suffering in Purgatory because of youthful follies, and Gerard de Nerval's "El Desdichado," a poem written two years before the poet's death and gathering evocations of his past. He links himself with old Hieronimo, with the poet of *Pervigilium Veneris,* who suddenly reveals that he is cut off from springtime lovemaking and asks, "when is my spring coming? / When shall I be as the swallow?"[25] and probably with an aged Philomel looking back at her youth in the half-line "O swallow swallow" (428). Although this is usually traced to Tennyson's *The Princess,* a more likely source is Swinburne's "Itylus." It is true that there is no precise verbal echo, but Swinburne's poem does employ a large number of variations on "O swallow" and "O sister swallow," and one would not necessarily expect precision from a poem written like "What the Thunder said" in a kind of trance.[26] Most importantly, "Itylus" is supposed to be the song of Philomel to her sister, Procne, a long time ("a thousand summers") after her rape and the slaying of Itys, a song in which she rebukes her sister for forgetfulness and meditates in memory on the horrible events of all those years ago. Both Philomel's position as the speaker of "Itylus" and her retrospective cast of mind make the poem far more relevant to *The Waste Land,* and a far more convincing source for the half-line, than the prince's song from *The Princess.* Finally, Eliot's speaker shows a consciousness of age in his final, "Shantih shantih shantih," which in context may be taken as connoting approaching death.[27]

The aged speaker of the final paragraph regards youth with mixed feelings. The retrospective cast of mind implied by the allusions to "El Desdichado" and "Itylus" suggests a regret for things past, while the allusion to *Pervigilium Veneris* evokes the envious sadness of one who sees the joys of others and knows he cannot share them. A different attitude toward youth is evident when the weighty question "Shall I at least set my lands in order?" is ironically answered by a nursery rhyme whose cheerful tune denies its gloomy subject, "London Bridge is falling down falling down falling down" (425–26). The implication here is that the young people of the waste land, like the nymphs and city heirs of earlier, are still failing to see the seriousness of their condition. But now the speaker betrays no personal animus against the young and he makes no attempt to distinguish himself from them or to appear superior. Instead, the guilt implied in his question and the melancholy of the whole paragraph define his attitude as one of genuine and disinterested sadness at the folly of youth. The only point at which the antagonism of "The Fire Sermon" returns is in the line that quotes from *The Spanish Tragedy,* "Why then Ile fit you. Hieronymo's mad againe" (431). But although the speaker seems to associate himself with Hieronimo and his plans for revenge on his young enemies here, the effect is different from earlier, since the conscious association of himself with a mad old man suggests a self-knowing irony that is absent from the malicious delight at, for instance, imagining heirs turned to bones. This is the crucial point about the final paragraph. The dramatic context, developing out of the self-examination involved in answering the thunder, is one in which the old man looks at himself and his world honestly. Without the evasion, the self-defensive aggression, and the triumph of earlier, the lines become expressive of the ancient's sorrow before his own weakness, his own coming death, and the destruction of all he values.

Although the fear of the poet's or his speaker's death has no part in *Speke Parott,* the poem does contain a comparable sense of powerlessness and grief. Shortly after claiming that "Frantiknes dothe rule," Parrot describes English behavior in more detail.

> To jumbyll, to stombyll, to tumbyll down lyke folys;
> To lowre, to droupe, to knele, to stowpe and to play cowche-quale;
> To fysshe afore the nette and to drawe polys.
> He maketh them to bere babylles, and to bere a lowe sayle;
> He caryeth a kyng in hys sleve, yf all the worlde fayle;

(425–29)

The first four lines indicate how the tyranny of Wolsey has forced courtiers into a series of undignified and humiliating activities, and they achieve their effect through two sets of comparisons. The courtiers are compared to their own fools in the way that they perform acrobatics and carry baubles, and they are like children in their tumbling, their games, and their liking for toys. But it is the final line I quote that shows how serious this all is, for the ominous aside "yf all the worlde fayle" can only mean, in a poem so full of hints of the coming Judgment, that the world may be about to end. According to Skelton, his contemporaries are either playing while destruction comes or playing their way to destruction. The idea takes on even more force when we remember that it belongs to an old man. Because of his age, Skelton, like Parrot, is out of place in this world, unrespected by it, and can only expect, again like Parrot, to have his warnings slighted or ignored by the dominant young. Rendered powerless by age, Skelton and Parrot can observe and condemn, but they must recognize that their words will have no effect.

In his biography of Skelton, Maurice Pollet argues that his satire is "akin to ecclesiastical censures and to the chastisement administered in school."[28] However, as those critics who emphasize the apocalyptic element in the poem recognize, its mood is more one of urgent anxiety than of confident, schoolteacherly censure.[29] What we should also recognize is that the source for the mood lies in the embedded, sometimes conscious, sometimes at most half-conscious, generational conflict as well as in the conscious allusions to Antichrist and the Last Days. It is the old man's frightened, sorrowful response to the rising young and to a society dominated by childishness that gives to the poem much of its energy, force, and complexity. The same can also be said of *The Dunciad* and *The Waste Land.* Each of these poems develops a highly complex response to its subject, a response that can be traced back in large part to the underlying, implicit opposition between old speaker and young world.

The source for both the conflict and the anxiety that each poet shows lies ultimately in the cultural conditions he was living through. Theirs were ages of transition, and the immature, threatening figures of the three poems belong firmly to the emerging new. Wolsey, Skelton's "calf," was the embodiment of the upstart new man, not only because he rose from a buther's shop to possess "Law in his Voice, and Fortune in his Hand" but also by virtue of his interest in Greek, his self-confidence, and his taste in pictures. Although his Catholicism allied him to some extent with the old ways (and this probably accounts for Skelton's shift from enmity to support for Wolsey), his annexation of Church authority paved the way for the creation of the Church of England.[30] The, for Pope, senescently juvenile Cibber was a new man in a slightly different way. Without Wolsey's power or energy, he was more the representative of a class than a danger in himself. The action of *The Dunciad* over which he dozes rather than presides is "the Removal of the Imperial seat of Dulness from the City to the polite world" (*Poems* 5:51). It is the triumph of the urban middle class, of their tastes and values, over the old aristocratic order. The clerk and the typist are also representative types. He belongs to the people Orwell identifies as "of indeterminate social class," those who are most comfortably at home in the modern world, "the technicians and the higher-paid skilled workers, the airmen and their mechanics, the radio experts, popular journalists and industrial chemists."[31] Orwell was writing two decades later than Eliot, and he does not mention estate agents, but the unplaceable office worker, moving from flat to flat as he does in the original version, is as much a member of this indeterminate modern group as anyone (*Facsimile*, 45). As for the typist, she is rather strikingly, though this is generally ignored, a version of "the new woman." Although she lacks emancipatory zeal, she has the independence that Wells's Ann Veronica aspires to, living in her own room, earning her own money and conducting herself by her own code of sexual morality.

The conflict in *Speke Parott, The Dunciad,* and *The Waste Land* is essentially the conflict between the old order and these new men and women. By presenting the new men as youths and themselves as aged protesters, Skelton, Pope and Eliot are figuring forth the conflict as a conflict of generations. The figure is a peculiarly appropriate one for, as Curtius says, "the opposition of generations is one of the conflicts of all tempestuous periods whether they are under the sign of a new spring flowering or an autumnal decay."[32] The remarkable thing, though, is not so much the degree of historical or sociological acuteness on the parts of the poets, but the fact that some kind of intuition (and that seems to be the best word for it) of historical conditions determines a whole way of looking at things and a whole frame of mind. As I have emphasized, the poems are characterized by a complexity of response, a complexity that, while it must have resided in each poet's mind, also (with its mixture of self-defensive aggression and more disinterested fear for the future) reflects something of the complexity of contemporary conditions. To say that is not completely to endorse Leavis's view that the poet is "the most conscious point of the race in time."[33] Very often the poet is only half-conscious even of his imaginative insight into history, and very often his insight recognizes only half "the race in time." Thus, the adoption of an aged perspective by Skelton, Pope, or Eliot offers no hint of the hopeful developments in the poet's "tempestuous period" but only a strong impression of the fear and insecurity of the threatened generation. Nevertheless, Leavis has a point. *Speke Parott, The Dunciad,* and *The Waste Land* each rests upon a conflict of generations that is the conflict of its times, and each expresses an anxiety that is both the anxiety of a recognizable personal predicament and the more general anxiety of a disappearing order.

Part Three
The Few and the Many

4
Massed Ranks

Profusion

The kind of conflict I have been describing is essentially one in which the poet or his speaker (an old man) is threatened by other people (the young), tries to respond to the threat (with an assertion of aged authority), but fails to neutralize it. The frame of mind that belongs with this conflict is characterized chiefly by anxiety in the face of a threat which cannot be contained. A similar conflict and a similar anxiety are also present in another common concern of the three poems, the concern with profusion. In each poem, the ideas of large numbers of objects, of large quantities of knowledge and experience, of crowds of people, of contending voices, and of a possible consequent madness form a cluster of images that reinforces and helps determine the meaning of the more prominent images. So, the presumption, impiety, and madness of *Speke Parott,* the dark and the dullness of *The Dunciad,* and the aridity and sexual failure of *The Waste Land* all acquire part of their significance from this cluster. The idea of profusion adds to the poems' apocalyptic tenor, but it also, like the idea of youth, serves as much to suggest the fear of the speakers and of the poets themselves as it does to delineate a degenerate society. Profusion is peculiarly frightening as its swarming, undefined vastness denies the individual firm points of reference and threatens to swallow him up. The threat, again like the threat of youth, has its roots in the periods in which the poems were written. Transitional periods like theirs are periods of expansion and proliferation, with the arrival of new men, new ways of behaving, new ideas and attitudes, new books, and new forms of literature. But they are also periods that have not yet developed the kind of outlook which tends to exist in a "renaissance" period, the outlook which has assimilated and can, to some extent, accommodate this newness. Each of my three poets is in the awkward position of being faced with a bewildering profusion while lacking the means to comprehend it. Instead of comprehending, each responds with attempts at rejection and reduction that are ultimately vain. I discuss these in the subsequent chapters, while concentrating here on profusion itself.

The general problem of coming to terms with profusion was one that engaged all three poets during the periods in which they were writing the poems I am dealing with. In *Magnyfycence,* Skelton is concerned with the proper regulation of wealth but also with the danger of moving expansively outward from a fittingly circumscribed and limited sphere. The vices draw Magnificence away from temperance and toward the excess of unfettered liberty (2088–2100) and the crowded confusion of folly (1803–40). On the other hand, the virtues insist on limits, that "In ponder, by nomber, by measure all thynge is wrought" (118), where "nomber" means specifically limited numbers. Magnificence's rejection of measure and his surrender to the (admitted) delights of excess lead to hardship, despair, and almost to suicide. If *Magnyfycence* dramatizes an individual's mistaken choice of excess, the late satires also involve the idea of dangerous multiplicity, but in a different way: they present a whole world that is already given over to it. The Skeltonic, though probably originating as a medium for meditations upon death, is a perfect vehicle for this, as its speed and energy, captured in Hall's phrase "angry *Skeltons* breathlesse rimes," allow the author to match profusion with profusion.[1] The description of beer-swilling women in *Elynour Rummynge* is fairly typical:

> Some be flybytten,
> Some skewed as a kytten;
> Some with a sho clout
> Bynde theyr heddes about;
> Some have no herelace,
> Theyr lockes aboute theyr face,
> Theyr tresses untrust,
> All full of unlust;
> Some loke strawry,
> Some cawry-mawry,
> Full untydy tegges,
> Lyke rotten egges.
>
> (141–52)

Such snowballing lists suggest exhaustion as well as exhilaration. The poet's weariness is conveyed partly by the almost desperate energy of the verse and partly by the division of the poem into sections, with each break between the sections existing as kind of resting spot for him.[2] There is a similar structure in *Collyn Clout* and *Why Come Ye*

Nat to Court? Both are poems of bursts and pauses, their pauses sometimes announced by the poet and sometimes marked by an interlocutor's questions or (in *Collyn Clout*) by references to the people and defenses of the verse. This structure and the frantic energy imply a poet beginning to be worn down in his attempt to grapple chaos.

Pope's late satires also sometimes present the bewildering variety of the world through (albeit statelier) lists, but a more explicit treatment of the subject occurs in the account of the relation of people to profusion in *An Essay on Man*. The first epistle expresses at once a fear of and attraction toward the multitudinous creation.[3] Pope's advice throughout, delivered at times with imperative urgency, is that we should not "act or think beyond mankind" (1:190), for to do so would be to enter an unmanageable vastness. This danger can be seen in the picture of the destructive effects of man's leaving his sphere, in which the general disorder has alongside it the shade of a more personal fear of uncontrolled and uncontrollable numbers.

> Let ruling Angels from their spheres be hurl'd,
> Being on being wreck'd, and world on world,
>
> (1:253–54)

Yet the same numbers can be exciting. When Pope asserts toward the beginning that only he who can see "worlds on worlds" can understand creation (1:24–28), he is enjoying his own presumptuous poetic flight as well as warning against presumption. The simultaneous knowledge of and inability to grasp the "worlds unnumber'd" of the universe are central to the dilemma of man's middle state. The section on the blessings of ignorance includes the example of the lamb who can "skip and play" under the butcher's knife (1:81–84). Human beings are like the lamb in not knowing the future but quite different from it in knowing that there is a future. So

> Hope springs eternal in the human breast:
> Man never Is, but always To be blest:
>
> (1:95–96)

The couplet's reassuring solidity is somewhat undermined by its implication of a deep uncertainty in the human condition. While people know enough to be drawn toward the vast, and, in the immediately preceding paragraph, catastrophic,[4] future, they cannot ultimately know it, or cope with it.

An interesting early example of Pope's ambiguous attitude toward profusion is found in the opening paragraphs of his 1715 preface to *The Iliad*.[5] Although, on the surface, these simply offer praise of the "wild Paradise" of Homer's work, there is an underlying note of unease. It appears first in the explanation of critics' preference for a judicial rather than a fruitful genius,

> because they find it easier for themselves to pursue their Observations through an uniform and bounded Walk of Art, than to comprehend the vast and various Extent of Nature. (*Poems* 7:3)

If the clause aims to expose the limitations of critics, it may simultaneously evince a certain sympathy for their "easy" preferences. Later, the problem that Homer's copious imagination poses for readers becomes more apparent. Pope shifts from the image of nature to those of fire and movement, summing up the effect of Homer's fiery rapture at two key points. Firstly, he explains how "the Reader is hurry'd out of himself by the Force of the Poet's Imagination," and secondly, finding an analogy between the movement of Homer's verses and Homer's own description of a moving army, he claims that *"They pour along like a Fire that sweeps the whole Earth before it"* (*Poems* 7:4). In both cases, Pope's admiration is uppermost, but the images also imply a threatening quality in the strength, which is related to the size, of Homer's imagination. By the time Pope came to write *An Essay on Man* and *The Dunciad*, the balance had shifted, and while he could still find pleasure in abundance, he was more inclined to be afraid of it.

The attitude toward large numbers that emerges from Eliot's writings of about the time of *The Waste Land* is principally one of dislike and fear. In the 1916 prospectus for a course of lectures, he defines the romanticism he opposes as *"excess* in any direction,"[6] and in his 1922 essay on Dryden, he selects the phrase "all the sad variety of Hell" for special commendation (*SE*, 312). The fear implicit in these examples is more obvious in a passage about the contemporary "vast accumulations of knowledge" in the 1920 essay, "The Perfect Critic."

> When there is so much to be known, when there are so many fields of knowledge in which the same words are used with different meanings, when everyone knows a little about a great many things, it becomes difficult for anyone to know whether he knows what he is talking about or not. (*SW*, pp. 9–10)

The main clause emphasizes the danger to individuals in the increase of knowledge, since that increase makes inevitable not only ignorance about the current state of learning but the more radical ignorance about the extent of one's ignorance. Addressing in 1923 the different question of the postwar proliferation of manufactured objects and entertainments, Eliot again brings out the threat to people of a too-numerous world. "When every musical instrument has been replaced by 100 gramophones, when every horse has been replaced by 100 cheap motor-cars," civilized people might, he argues, like the Melanesians, die "from pure boredom"—they might, that is, be smothered by those escalating numbers of new things (*SE*, 459). Finally, there is a similar anxiety evident in the early poetry. After being bombarded with all the varied experiences of his life, Prufrock exclaims desperately, "It is impossible to say just what I mean," and Gerontion's confusion toward the end of his poem is a result of the legion of thoughts and the "thousand small deliberations" that "multiply variety / In a wilderness of mirrors." Both personae are faced with, and threatened by, an experience too many-sided and diverse to be easily or safely managed.

The sense of the danger of profusion is central to *Speke Parott, The Dunciad,* and *The Waste Land.* In *Speke Parott,* it is most clear in the final invective, where the "so manys" and "so muches" suggest (at least in part) a country in which evil is superabundant and superabundance is evil. The section is related to the burgeoning lists of the Skeltonic satires, although there is in its rhythm and organization a somewhat greater sense of control. Earlier in the poem, profusion is less explicit an idea and more personally threatening to Parrot and to Skelton behind him. The virtuoso account, toward the beginning, of the copious variety of chatter and languages that Parrot both meets and employs in England leads to his recommendation of moderation, followed by the qualification:

> But reason and wytte wantythe theyr provynciall,
> When wylfulnes ys vicar generall.
>
> (53–54)

The couplet has both an external and an internal reference. In politics, the rule of will, which Skelton associates with Wolsey and with excess, takes away from the qualities of reason and wit their prestige and power, while in the personality, an excessive will can destroy reason. However, if the couplet has two levels of meaning, these are not completely separate from each other. In fact, a good deal of its suggestiveness lies in the interplay between them, in the way that the social meaning affects and involves the moral meaning. By implication, the outward, political excess of Wolsey makes it hard for anyone, even those as gifted as Parrot or Skelton, to maintain the inward integrity of reason. A few lines earlier, Parrot asserts "Phronessys for frenessys may not hold her way" (47), that all understanding is defeated by the contemporary madness of excess, and his own apparently less-than-sane babblings lend weight to the assertion.

In *The Dunciad,* the idea of profusion appears in the crowds of dunces and their works, in a number of mock-heroic similes, and in the description of mysteries at the end. The epoch of Dullness is to be one of disorderly abundance, and Pope demonstrates the psychological effects of such abundance early on in two complementary passages in book 1. Dullness looks into her chaos:

> There motley Images her fancy strike,
> Figures ill pair'd, and Similies unlike.
> She sees a Mob of Metaphors advance,
> Pleas'd with the madness of the mazy dance:
> (B1:65–69)

Dullness's pleasure, which is essentially the pleasure of meeting large numbers and variety and of losing one's grip on ordinary reality, bears some resemblance to Pope's imaginative pleasure at soaring into the cosmos in *An Essay on Man.* However, the passage is different from *An Essay on Man* in that the loss of grip is to the fore, and Dullness, with all her excitement, is being drawn into the madness of swarming creation. Colley's glimpse into chaos, that is, into his own "monster-breeding breast," is a more somber experience:

> Then gnaw'd his pen, then dash'd it on the ground,
> Sinking from thought to thought, a vast profound!
> Plung'd for his sense, but found no bottom there,
> Yet wrote and flounder'd on, in mere despair.
> (B1:117–20)

The lines, which recall both Dullness viewing chaos and Satan journeying through it,[7] demonstrate how an individual can lose himself in his own overcrowded mind. Pope, of course, presents this as a condition of dullness from which he and others like him are safely immune. Yet the poem is, in one respect, a record of his entry into the dull world of myriad books, myriad ideas, and myriad dunces and of his struggle to give that world form and the limits implied by form. While the finished piece bears witness to some success, there remains an uneasy tension between the reductive (in a neutral sense) order of his imagery and verse and the teeming disorder of his subject. The tension serves as a reminder of the effort needed to avoid being engulfed, like Colley, in profusion.

Finally, there are in *The Waste Land* several points at which the copiousness of experience is threatening. The stifling atmosphere of the lady's room in "A Game of Chess" is a result of the "rich profusion" of the scene, the speaker at the beginning of "The Fire Sermon" imagines the cluttered waste the summer lovers left behind (177–79), and the fragments of the last paragraph are too many and varied to be happily ordered. In earlier drafts, these examples are reinforced by the images of "the swarming life" of London and the "chaotic mischmasch potpurri" of Fresca's learning (*Facsimile* 31, 27). However, it is not so much through individual phrases and passages that Eliot conveys the danger of profusion as through the whole structure of his poem, through its confusing range of speakers, situations, allusions, and meters. In my first chapter, I argue that there is a dominant speaker behind *The Waste Land,* a speaker who is a version of Eliot. The reason every reader of the poem must clarify for him- or herself the nature of its speaker or speakers or "unifying consciousness" is that the existence of the kind of coherent authorial voice we expect is neither obvious nor certain. David Spurr suggests that *"The Waste Land* shows us a fragmented persona whose different voices express opposing factions of the poet's consciousness."[8] Although this view is not (I think) completely correct, Spurr has quite a strong case. The many intruding voices and experiences undermine, if not actually destroy, the substantial identity of the main speaker, and they simultaneously undermine the reader's expectations. A dominant consciousness, expressed through a dominant voice, remains, but it is one that struggles before the diversity of experience and that the reader sometimes must struggle to locate. The sense that emerges of someone almost annihilated by profusion reflects the anxieties of *Speke Parott* and the more implicit tensions of *The Dunciad*.

The distaste for profusion that I have briefly outlined is not peculiar to Skelton, Pope, and Eliot. Arnold, for example, writes in "Stanzas in Memory of the Author of 'Obermann'" of "The hopeless tangle of our age" and of its "change, alarm, surprise," and he complains in letters to Clough of the "multitude of new thoughts and feelings" that a modern has to deal with and of the "world's multitudinousness."[9] Yet *Speke Parott, The Dunciad,* and *The Waste Land* possess features that distinguish them from the writings of Arnold and others—in particular, the tendency to see profusion always as a threat and never as a source of delight; the markedly dangerous quality of the crowds in the poems, which I discuss below; and the way, also discussed below, that profusion becomes central to their structure through the different voices incorporated into them. By contrast, Arnold is able to view the dangers of profusion with a "philosophical" detachment and, also, to feel drawn toward what he calls "the world without."[10] The difference between Arnold and the three poets I am discussing is essentially one of period. Louis Menand describes the early twentieth century as "not a period *without* values so much as a period with *too many* values."[11] Each of the three poets was living through a period of "too many values," a period in which the values, literary and other, that had been in place for over a century were still just about in place, but under threat from new influences. It was in large part the result of this kind of cultural situation that Skelton, Pope, and Eliot should feel experience to be terrifyingly too much.

Crowds

One form of profusion that has an important place in all three poems is the profusion of people. The image of crowds shares some of the general significance of large numbers, the crowds in the poems becoming the human embodiment of the burgeoning new that the poets have so much difficulty with, but it also has three more specific associations of its own. Firstly, for people of aristocratic (or elitist) temper, crowds can represent democratic anarchy, the rule by the "many-headed beast" in place of that by the intelligent, self-controlled few. In *Upon the Dolorus Dethe,* Skelton attacks the "commons most unkynd" who killed the earl of Northumberland (56); Pope pictures the apotheosis of vice in the first epilogue to the satires, imagining how "thronging Millions to the Pagod run" (157); and one of Eliot's early essays asserts that "the forces of deterioration are a large crawling mass, and the forces of development half a dozen men."[12] Secondly, although this does not apply to Skelton, crowds can connote the invasion of barbarians that results in the sack of the city and the fall of civilization. Pope makes this meaning explicit in Cibber's vision in the third book of *The Dunciad* (B3:85–100), and *The Waste Land*'s "hooded hordes," associated as they are with falling cities, imply a similar invasion (368). Finally, crowds can present a more immediate and physical threat to individuals than the rather abstract threat of profusion in general.

Skelton's work contains a number of very muscular, bustling crowds, and he is often caught up in the throng. This happens to Dread, for example, in the prologue to *The Bowge of Courte*.

> Thus, in a rowe, of martchauntes a grete route
> Suwed to Fortune that she wold be theyre frynde.

They thronge in fast and flocked her aboute,
And I with them prayed her to have in mynde.

(20–23)

It is the rough physical presence of all these people, together with the
way that Dread is "with them," that makes the image striking. Its
vividness, and possibly its appropriateness to its time, can be emphasized by comparison with another allegorical dream of a crowd,
Langland's "feld ful of folk," which is just as packed and noisy as
Skelton's wharf.

> Bothe bakeres and breweres, bochers and other,
> Webbesteres and walkeres and wynners with handes,
> As taylers and tanners and tulyers of þe erthe.[13]

However, there is the important difference that Langland only observes the horde, while Skelton, through Dread, is there in the thick of
it, shoving and being shoved. The crowds in *Garlande or Chapelet of
Laurell* have a similar immediacy. Skelton's first experience of them is
when Dame Pallas challenges him to "put hymselfe in prease /
Amonge the thickeste of all the hole rowte" and to compete in
noisemaking with the rest (239–41); later, he walks to and fro among
the multitudes pressing around Fame in her palace (491–516); and
finally, he watches from above the "Innumerable people" who mill
round the English gate of fame until they are blasted away by cannon
(602–43). The obvious comparison to make here (and again, the
difference in period is important) is with Chaucer's *House of Fame,* to
which Skelton's poem owes a clear, if undefined, debt. The comparison serves to bring out the physicality, closeness, and threat of
Skelton's crowds. Although Chaucer moves among the supplicants to
Fame and seems to enjoy making the goddess deny large numbers
their wish, he neither competes with them (claiming to have no
interest in fame for himself) nor does he resort to desperate gestures
like Skelton's cannon.[14] Indeed, Chaucer in the 1370s or 1380s could
relish the busy variety of his crowds:

> Ther saugh I pleye jugelours,
> Magiciens, and tregetours,
> And Phitonesses, charmeresses,
> Old wicches, sorceresses,[15]

The people outside Skelton's English gate are a much more unsavory
bunch of "medelynge spyes," "dysdanous dawcokkis," "Fals flaterers,"
and "kurris of kynde" (617–19), and all he relishes is firing the
cannon in imagination to make "sum lympe-legged" and others

"pevysshe, porisshly pynk iyde" (625–26). The nature of the crowd and the fancying of its destruction are the fruits of a sensibility that can no longer take delight in masses of people.

In *Speke Parott,* large groups of people are also threatening, although not in exactly the same way as the crowds in *The Bowge of Courte* and *Garlande or Chapelet of Laurell.* The most dramatically direct way in which Skelton presents the conditions in England is through the conversation of Parrot with his ladies. While the fairly frequent, anonymous interjections imply there are quite a number of these women, they are not, on the surface, a danger to Parrot, since they busy themselves feeding him and making sweet his bower. Yet the relationship is less simple than that. The bower the ladies dress is also a cage, and Parrot is expected to perform for his food. More importantly, having urged him to speak very early on (13), the ladies (with the exception of Galathea) devote most of their energy to trying to shut him up, and Parrot must plead repeatedly, "I pray yow, let Parot have lyberte to speke" (98, 141, 210). The dramatic conflict between the silencings of the women and Parrot's pleas for speech suggests someone struggling against being hemmed in and stifled by other people. What is more, a further effort to silence Parrot is being made by the detractors beyond the ladies, out in the world, who decry his words. These "nodypollys" do not speak in the poem but are presented only through the four attacks on them in the envoys and the lines that follow. Nevertheless, the recurrence of the attacks implies that the "some" who disdain Parrot are pretty numerous, and Skelton's violence in attack implies that they threaten. Again, the impression given is of Parrot (and Skelton) being terribly alone among dangerous people.

In addition to the groups who appear in the poem specifically in their relation to Parrot, there are other groups in his analysis of the evils facing England. His account often suggests multitudes.

> *Ulula,* Esebon, for Jeromy doth wepe!
> Sion is in sadness, Rachell ruly doth loke;
> Madionita Jetro, our Moyses kepyth his shepe;
> Gedeon is gon, that Zalmane undertoke,
> Oreb *et* Zeb, of *Judicum* rede the boke.
> Now Geball, Amon and Amaloch—"Harke, harke,
> Parrot pretendith to be a bybyll clarke!"—
>
> (113–19)

By following the references to Psalm 83 and, more particularly, to the commentaries on the psalm, F. W. Brownlow has identified the threat-

ening names toward the end of the stanza as belonging in an eschato-
logical context and as connoting different aspects of Antichrist, and of
Wolsey.[16] The stanza, though, works by multiplication as much as by
allusion, and the packed lists of names are threatening, like Milton's
lists of devils or Pope's of dunces, even without the reader knowing
the exact significance of each one. The overall effect, as Brownlow
points out, is to imply at once a single source of evil and a "teeming
army" of it.[17] Furthermore, the disguised warning in the interruption
at the end emphasizes the special danger of this teeming, unified evil
for Parrot. When, a little later in the poem, he turns his attention to
the abuses of learning, crowds are prominent once again.

> Set *Sophia* asyde, for every Jack Raker
> And every mad medler must now be a maker.
>
> (160–61)

The "everys" convey the idea of large numbers of these meddlers, and
they add an extra element to the lines' expression of Skelton's usual,
and lifelong, irritation at upstarts.[18] Here, the upstarts are taking
over, and worse still, they are taking over his own privileged position
as a maker. It is hardly surprising, in the face of such usurpation, that
Parrot should end the section by asking for nutmeg to steady his mind
(183–84).

Like Skelton throughout his career, Pope in his late poetry often
presents crowds as palpable and threatening. This is perhaps most
marked in the opening of *An Epistle to Dr. Arbuthnot.*

> What Walls can guard me, or what Shades can hide?
> They pierce my Thickets, thro' my Grot they glide,
> By land, by water, they renew the charge,
> They stop the Chariot, and they board the Barge.
>
> (7–10)

Pope is working here in the tradition of satire in which the poet enters
the poem in the character of the wit, buttonholed and bothered by a
dunce or a number of dunces. Donne is in a similar position when he
is trapped, in his fourth satire, into conversation with "A thing more
strange, then on Niles slime, the Sunne / E'r bred," and so, too, is
Marvell when forced to listen to Flecknoe's poetry.[19] Another example, and one slightly closer to the figure of Pope in *Arbuthnot,* is the
Rochester who is bullied into dining with five "brave *Fellows*" or who
hurtles back and forth at Tunbridge Wells in order to get out of the
way of the various groups there.[20] However, the scene in *Arbuthnot* is

different from those in the other poems, and the difference owes
something both to Pope himself and to the pressures of his era.
Firstly, it is more crowded, as the people making demands on Pope's
attention are everywhere. Secondly, it is much closer to home. Pope
does not encounter his dunces out in society, but they come to him,
and their arrival is significantly described in the language of siege. For
all the self-consciously humorous exasperation and comedy of these
lines, the picture in them is of someone who is dangerously sur-
rounded by other people and can only narrowly, possibly only provi-
sionally, escape into the safety of his home.[21] The personal element is
also present in poems that depict crowds in a less dramatic way.

> Sons, Sires, and Grandsires, all will wear the Bays,
> Our Wives read Milton, and our Daughters Plays,
> To Theatres, and to Rehearsals throng,
> And all our Grace at Table is a Song.
>
> (*Epistle* 2.1.171–74)

Pope has not only multiplied Horace's examples of those seized by the
poetic itch but has also moved them to a more distinctly domestic
setting.[22] In doing so, he implies again the dangerous invasion of
private space by throngs of others.

Although the crowds in *The Dunciad* do not appear at Twickenham,
they possess a robust physicality that is both immediate and threatening, and they are constantly moving, pushing, and making noise. At
the beginning of book 2, the dunces arrive for their queen's games.

> A motley mixture! in long wigs, in bags,
> In silks, in crapes, in Garters, and in rags,
> From drawing rooms, from colleges, from garrets,
> On horse, on foot, in hacks and gilded chariots:
>
> (B2:21–24)

The idea of the mob here owes something to Dryden's frequent
strictures on "th'ignoble crowd" and to the tradition in which those
belong, but Pope's description differs from Dryden's usual approach.[23] Dryden tends to concentrate on the abstract idea of the
multitude, as when he apostrophizes and defines it in *The Medall:*
"Pow'r is thy Essence; Wit thy Attribute!"[24] Even in as dramatic a
poem as *Absalom and Achitophel,* where the mob figures among the
forces of rebellion, the description remains on the level of ideas:

> But far more numerous was the herd of such,
> Who think too little, and who talk too much.[25]

Occasionally Dryden claims to see the crowds he represents and occasionally his representations have some of the vividness of sight, but the general impulse in them is toward abstraction.[26] Pope's general impulse is the opposite. The duncaes flocking to the games are distinct physical presences, and his most symbolic crowds retain the same quality. The progeny of Dullness, seen in book 3 in a vision in a dream and associated with the idea of invading barbarians, are as physically present as the duncaes of book 2.

> Each Songster, Riddler, ev'ry nameless name,
> All crowd, who foremost shall be damn'd to Fame.
> Some strain in rhyme; the Muses, on their racks,
> Scream like the winding of ten thousand jacks.
>
> (B3 : 157–60)

The activity and noise in this passage image the characteristics of a real crowd, and with its violence and its torture of the muses, it has a more palpably threatening quality than Dryden's mob.

The bustle of the crowds in *The Dunciad* can be further emphasized by comparison with three sources. The procession of supplicant duncaes before Dullness in book 4 derives most immediately from the procession in *The Temple of Fame* and from *The House of Fame* behind that. Although the crowds in *The Temple of Fame,* a poem written in a more secure period of Pope's life and of English cultural history, are as large as those in the fourth book, they are much less muscular. This can best be seen in the verbs used for the arrival of the succeeding groups before Fame's throne: the first group "appears," its displacement by the second is signaled by no verb but simply by "next these," two more groups "come," and we are told to "behold" another.[27] Similarly, the various companies in *The House of Fame* all blandly "come" before the goddess, with the slight exception of the "shrewes," who "come ther lepynge in a route, / And gonne choppen al aboute."[28] The fourth book's crowds, on the other hand, have a vigor of their own.

> Now crowds on crowds around the Goddess press,
> Each eager to present the first Address.
> Dunce scorning Dunce beholds the next advance,
> But Fop shows Fop superior complaisance.
>
> (B4 : 135–38)

The sense here of a heaving crowd is reinforced later when Bentley and his cohorts arrive demanding space, when the pedants are pushed aside by the "gay embroider'd race," when Annius and Mummius quarrel, and when the virtuosi turn up. Finally, the general idea of crowds of writers that is present throughout *The Dunciad* owes something to the "Sessions of the Poets" poems of the seventeenth century. The one sometimes attributed to Rochester begins

> Since the Sons of the Muses, grow num'rous and lowd
> For th'appeasing soe Clam'rous and Factious a Crowd;
> Apollo, thought fit, in soe weighty a Cause,
> T'Establish a Government, Leader and Laws:[29]

Although the poet refers to the factiousness and noise of the mob of courtly poets, his cheerful dog-trot rhythm betrays the gentleman's complacent good humor before them rather than any anxiety. It was for a poet of a later generation to perceive the real danger of numerous writers and to convert that perception into images of crowds which capture their threat.

Although Eliot's crowds are never quite as robust as Pope's, he sometimes catches their physical presence. The idea of the unruly populace that lurks behind his 1923 essay "The Function of Criticism" derives largely from Arnold. The title is from Arnold, he is mentioned twice (though to qualify his judgments), and another passage alludes to him.

> The inner voice, in fact, sounds remarkably like an old principle which has been formulated by an elder critic in the now familiar phrase "doing as one likes". The possessors of the inner voice ride ten in a compartment to a football match at Swansea, listening to the inner voice, which breathes the eternal message of vanity, fear, and lust. (*SE*, 27)

"Doing as one likes" refers the reader to *Culture and Anarchy,* and the football fans are a modern equivalent of Arnold's "rough," "asserting his personal liberty a little, going where he likes, assembling where he likes, bawling as he likes, hustling as he likes."[30] Yet Eliot's description is both more specific in its details than Arnold's and rhetorically much shriller. Instead of ironic urbanity, the passage exhibits a certain emotional excess, and it raises such unintended awkward questions as how those hapless passengers are going to satisfy their lust at a football match. Even less like Arnold is Eliot's earlier comparison of criticism to a "Sunday park of contending and contentious orators" (*SE*, 25). Arnold sees criticism in terms of "very subtle and indirect action" and himself as outside the "rush and roar of practical life,"[31] and Eliot, too, consciously deplores noise and contention. But by going on to contend with Middleton Murry and to use the kind of contentious rhetoric mentioned above, he places himself, in imagination, within the fractious throng. As with the differences I outline above, the one between Arnold and Eliot is a difference of generations. Arnold can retain his urbanity because his cultural tradition is safe from the philistines of his age in a way that Eliot's tradition is not.

The most obviously threatening crowd in *The Waste Land,* and the one that has the most direct relation to the speaker, can be found in "What the Thunder said." Although the "sweaty faces" and the "shouting and the crying" of the first paragraph have biblical sources in Jesus' encounters with "great multitudes," the details give to the description a feeling of direct experience. A little later, the speaker bemoans the lack of solitude in the mountains:

> But red sullen faces sneer and snarl
> From doors of mudcracked houses
>
> (344–45)

Here, the sense of the speaker's experience and of the antagonism he detects in others is very apparent. It is, at least partly, in an attempt to escape that antagonism that he (as well as the poem) moves toward the introspection and the implied isolation of the responses to the thunder and of the final lines.

Earlier in *The Waste Land,* the crowds are less aggressive, and they threaten the speaker in a different way, though their threatening quality is just as pronounced. The association of crowds with danger is established early on when Madame Sosostris's warning "Fear death by water" is followed by "I see crowds of people, walking round in a ring" (55–56). A few lines later, the speaker meets a city crowd.

> Unreal City,
> Under the brown fog of a winter dawn,
> A crowd flowed over London Bridge, so many,
> I had not thought death had undone so many.
>
> (60–63)

There is a note of pity here that is absent from *Speke Parott* and *The Dunciad,* but there is also fear. An early draft has "terrible" in the place of "unreal" (*Facsimile,* 9), and its substitution by the later word indicates the nature of the city's terror, a terror that resurfaces later in *Coriolan:* "And such a press of people. / We hardly knew ourselves that day, or knew the City." The idea of the "press" undermining knowledge of the external world and of oneself is reinforced in the passage from *The Waste Land* by the phrase "under the brown fog." As well as implying the dimming of perceptions, the image of fog, with the preposition "under," recalls Madame Sosostris's warning of death by water and looks forward to the disintegration of body and self that Phlebas undergoes. Under the fog, the members of the crowd are without personality, and even the personality of the speaker, for all the air of detachment and perceptiveness that the echoes of Dante afford, appears to be no very coherent one—when he greets Stetson, he sounds insane. The same threat to the self posed by large numbers of others appears elsewhere in the poem in a different way. Just as *Speke Parott*'s allusions give the picture of a "teeming army" of evil, *The Waste Land* with its various speakers, allusions, names, and situations creates "a small army of characters."[32] As I argue above, this profusion (and it is primarily a profusion of people) threatens to overwhelm the dominant speaker, to push him out of the poem, and that threat, however differently it might be expressed, is closely related to the threat of crowds in *Speke Parott* and *The Dunciad*.

Other Voices and Madness

Perhaps the most important and distinctive way in which the threat of profusion is registered in *Speke Parott, The Dunciad,* and *The Waste Land* is through the presence in the poem of many competing voices. In the discussion of the opening paragraph of *The Waste Land,* which introduces the main themes of his book, Calvin Bedient argues that "first the poem registers a crisis of heteroglossia, and, beyond that, a crisis of meaningless identity."[33] The word "imperilled" would, I think, be preferable to "meaningless," as it is hard to see how identity, given such a thing exists, can be meaningless, and some sense of identity remains in the poem; but Bedient's focus is still a happy one. *The Waste Land*'s first paragraph of eighteen lines contains the disillusioned voice who complains about April; the flatter, more social voice of the visitor to the Starnbergersee; a line of German that alludes to Russia; Marie recollecting her childhood and rediscovering her childhood's idiom; her cousin's instructions concerning sledging; Marie speaking with the regret of an adult; and finally, a disillusioned voice again. As I suggest in my first chapter, the voice that opens the paragraph and the voice that closes it may belong to the same speaker, the dominant speaker of the whole poem,[34] but what is not made explicit is this person's relation to the other voices. Nevertheless, it is this relation and the implied relation of the poet that are most important. Those relations can be inferred by the reader only from two principal sources. Firstly, there is the mood of retreat in the first seven lines, with their complementary dislike of the breeding, stirring, and desire of April, and preference for the forgetfulness and oscitation of winter. The speaker wants to escape experience, and although the cause of this wish is not given, the placing of the lines before the multiplicity of voices that follows suggests the two might be connected. The weariness of the speaker is, by implication, a result of the effort needed to live with, and manage, all those different dialects. Secondly, there is the reader's impression of the poet's labor behind the paragraph. Even those readers who recognize no dominant speaker know that the hegerogeneous voices have been assembled, shaped, arranged, and ordered by one person, and are, in a sense, being repeated by him. What is more, every reader has experienced the bewilderment that the variety can provoke, and the struggle involved in trying to accommodate all its elements in one, unifying interpretation. The reader's struggle in interpretation, I assume, reflects to some extent the poet's struggle in composition, the struggle to discover, or create, some kind of coherence amid a babel of different tongues. The fact that a coherence does emerge is chiefly a testimony to the writer's considerable discipline and skill in the face of great obstacles.

Bedient's analysis of the opening of *The Waste Land* includes the attempt to fix the poem's peculiar quality by contrasting its multivocal style with "the unitary style of almost every other poem."[35] This use of "poem" is rather a limited one, as it takes the word to mean only those poems where the writer's experience, or his poetic struggle with experience, is in the foreground. Poems in which experience itself takes center stage, poems such as *The Canterbury Tales* or *Macbeth,* are often just as multivocal, or as "heteroglossic," as *The Waste Land.* However, the kind of poetry that puts the poet to the fore, whose main forms are the lyric and satire, is generally more unitary in style, although the allusiveness of modernism and the mock-heroic of the Augustans tend to impair that unitary quality. Two poems that are quite as "heteroglossic" as *The Waste Land,* though, are *The Dunciad,* which I will come onto in a moment, and *Speke Parott.* In his first one hundred lines, Parrot uses English, Latin, French, Greek, Dutch, Scots, Punic, Welsh, a lingua franca, the "language of the Beme," and he claims to know Hebrew, Chaldee, and Spanish; he varies his style from the stately dignity of the introduction, to the waggish banter with the ladies, to the dark hints by which he exposes Wolsey; he quotes proverbs and ballads, as well as Horace and Persius, and he probably alludes to a great many more writers; he hears, and records in his poem, the chatter of the ladies and one snatch of Irish. There is in all this the difference from *The Waste Land* that Parrot uses his various languages, whereas Eliot seems more to mimic his various voices, but the difference is more apparent than real. Parrot is in a country where the learning of previously unknown languages is rife, and he imitates, and denounces, the variety of the English babel.[36] His imitation is not very far removed from Eliot's mimicry of the voices of postwar Europe.

Like that of *The Waste Land,* the "multivocality" of *Speke Parott* poses problems for the reader which reflect the problems of the writer and his protagonist. The effect on some readers is evident in the charge against Parrot, recorded in the first envoy, of those fools who "say ye arre furnysshyd with knakkes, / That hang togedyr as fethyrs in the wynde" (292–93). The phrase "feathers in the wind" is also applied, though with amused indulgence, by Magnificence at the very height of his extravagance to the words of Folly. Folly has claimed,

> I saw a foxe sucke on a kowes ydder;
> And with a lyme rodde I toke them bothe togyder.
> I trowe it be a frost, for the way is slydder;
> Se, for God avowe, for colde as I chydder.
>
> (1814–17)

The readers who object to Parrot are largely in the position of those who listen to Folly, of being confused by the way that disparate ideas (in Parrot's case, disparate languages) are brought, apparently without sense, together. The lack of sense is only apparent in Parrot, since the envoys insist that his enemies denigrate him out of ignorance,[37] and that under his "Langagys divers," there lie

> Maters more precious than the ryche jacounce,
> Diamounde, or rubye, or balas of the beste,
> Or eyndye sapher with oryente perlys dreste:
>
> (365–68)

However, the existence of this precious matter does not cancel the difficulty of getting at it, the difficulty of those "Langagys divers," and even Parrot (and, it must again be added, Skelton), for all his boasts of learning, does not find the modern array of tongues altogether easy to master. He complains about the spread of language learning, partly because he considers the newly learned to be ignorant (145–49) and partly because the spread is an important element in the frenzied excess that is ruining the country (45–50). His own difficulty in the face of this linguistic excess is betrayed by his handling of the languages then current in England. It is a dazzling virtuoso performance, and as with any virtuoso performance, the audience admires the skill and poise of the performer, always with full knowledge of the severity of the task. This brings us back again to the comparison with *The*

Waste Land. Parrot arranging his impossibly diverse range of languages so that they contain, and cover, his precious matter is a very similar figure to Eliot arranging his equally diverse voices into the peculiar coherence of his poem.

Another similarity is that both poems further multiply their voices in a set of notes. Whatever else they do, Eliot's notes make a display of the poem's learning and range, of the way that it has managed to comprehend a whole series of ancient voices as well as those of early twentieth-century Europe. The virtuosity of this act of comprehension is underlined in those notes where Eliot himself appears, for he assumes, in his familiar reference to Sappho (221n) or in his initiate's recommendation of Henry Clarke Warren's pioneering work in Buddhist studies (308n), the nonchalant manner of the expert, a manner that is always ultimately intended to direct attention toward the expert's expertise. As pointed out above, the spectator's recognition of such expertise, or virtuosity, depends upon a knowledge of the difficulty of the task, in this case the difficulty of putting some order into all those sources, languages, and voices. To turn to Skelton's notes, only a handful of what was, presumably, a fuller original set survives.[38] The surviving notes give either references to authority, or the laconic comments on Parrot's performance of someone else, or Parrot's own equally laconic comments, and while they are too slight and too few to be of much significance, they both add voices to the poem and draw lighthearted attention to Parrot's skill.[39]

More important than the notes of either *Speke Parott* or *The Waste Land,* however, are those of *The Dunciad.* Although some of Pope's notes, like Eliot's, identify allusions (thus testifying to the poet's skill) or offer information, others provide space for the dunces themselves to speak or for the imitations of them by Pope and his collaborators. Perhaps the best example of this is the first note to the 1743 edition.[40] The single word "Dunciad" is glossed in four fairly hefty paragraphs that are ascribed to Theobald, Bentley, Anon, and Scriblerus, and in which the contending scholars dispute, with ponderous scholarly politeness, about the spelling of the word. Later, different idioms appear in the quotations of the notes (for example, the violence of Dennis [A1 : 104n] and the eccentricity of Henley [A3 : 195n]), and to these idioms may be added the many opinions about Pope, expressed in many styles, that are preserved in the prefatory "Testimonies of Authors" and the appendical "A Parallel of the Characters of Mr. Pope and Mr. Dryden." The overall effect of prefatory materials, notes, and appendixes is to surround the poem with a multitude of muttering voices—it is almost comparable to a play being performed with the audience allowed, even encouraged, to discuss the performance as it takes place.

In the poem itself, different voices are held together in the strenuous fusions of the mock-heroic. Although mock-heroic is often seen as being chiefly "the systematic application of heroic conventions and language to unheroic subjects,"[41] it consists as much in the combination of disparate kinds of language as in the combination of disparate language and subject matter. When Pope uses epic sentence structures or images in ironic praise of dullness, or when he puts otherwise positive words, such as "peace," into the mouths of dunces, he is at once creating a kind of special dunce-heroic idiom, and he is referring the reader to those idioms in which the structures, images, and words are used properly. Moreover, the dunce-heroic idiom also includes, of necessity, reference to the idioms of those Pope regarded as real dunces—the unheroic subject can enter the poem only through unheroic words that belong in an unheroic dialect. So, while a phrase like "Smithfield Muses" in the second line applies an incongruously exalted word to a fairground and places the fairground in an incongruously exalted couplet, it also draws upon, must draw upon, the language of Smithfield in order to make its point; here, the word "Smithfield" itself belongs to a linguistic context as well as denoting a social and geographical one. This creation of a special idiom that exploits and combines at least two other idioms, a high and a low, is common to all mock-heroic poetry. What distinguishes *The Dunciad* from earlier and less anxious mock-heroic poems such as *The Rape of the Lock* or *Mac Flecknoe* is its scope, a scope reflected in its length, in the amount of heterogeneous material it incorporates, and in the consequent density of the verse.

Pope's characteristic "packing" in his combinations of idioms is particularly clear when the dunces speak. Toward the beginning of his first speech, Colley says,

> Dulness! whose good old cause I yet defend,
> With whom my Muse began, with whom shall end;
> E'er since Sir Fopling's Periwig was Praise,
> To the last honours of the Butt and Bays:

> (B1 : 165–68)

While the second line alludes to Horace and Vergil (A1 : 146n), "good old cause" in the first is a phrase associated with Puritanism and Whiggism (A1 : 145n). The religious and political loyalties implied in the phrase are inappropriate to the poem's original hero (less so to

Cibber), and Pope's chief reason for using it is to give his hero's defense of Dullness its place in typical duncely controversy and to mimic the typical duncely language of any dunce's defense. In the second couplet, the word "Periwig" is annotated by a long quotation from Cibber, the effect of which is to identify its origins in Cibber's idiom and to demonstrate the way it fits in that (B1:167n). "Butt" and "Bays" are also from Cibber, this time in his official role as poet laureate, with his butt of sack and his laurel crown, but both are puns, "Bays" meaning the hero of an antiscribbler satire and "butt" meaning an object of ridicule. Cibber's last honors, in fact, have been to become the butt and the Bays of Pope's poem. What Pope does in these lines, then, is to create a kind of "Colley-speak" out of the varied ingredients of the real Cibber's language, the classical heritage, and a satiric tradition.

The passages of narrative in *The Dunciad* work is a similar way. To take another early example, Colley in the first book looks at his library, remembering his many thefts.

> How here he sipp'd, how there he plunder'd snug
> And suck'd all o'er, like an industrious Bug.
> Here lay poor Fletcher's half-eat scenes, and here
> The Frippery of crucify'd Moliere;
> There hapless Shakespear, yet of Tibbald sore,
> Wish'd he had blotted for himself before.
>
> (B1:129–34)

Two words in the passage are given glosses that indicate their origin in a less gentlemanly kind of language than Pope's. Never having "blotted" is identified as "a ridiculous praise which the Players gave to Shakespear" (B1:134n), and Pope's contempt for players is amply set out in his preface to Shakespeare,[42] while "Frippery" derives from a remark of Cibber's about himself (B1:132n), and it is associated in a note to *The Dunciad Variorum* with Rag Fair (A1:27n).[43] Another odd word is "crucify'd." The sense in which Pope uses it does not appear in Johnson's dictionary, and the omission suggests that the usage is very colloquial, possibly one principally connected with the theater. At the same time, the fact that Moliere is robbed of his clothes as well as crucified recalls the word's literal and biblical meanings, thus highlighting its devaluation in the modern vernacular. Finally, the first couplet contains two opposing kinds of experience and language. The "industrious Bug" is a version of Swift's image from *The Battle of the Books* of the genuine poet as a bee who ranges through nature collecting honey from every flower, an image that goes back, via Sir William Temple and others, to Plato;[44] but the words "suck'd" and "Bug" place the image in quite a different social and linguistic context.[45] Even "snug," which the *Oxford English Dictionary* records as a cant word used by villains to signify that the coast is clear, seems, in its place next to "plunder'd," to be drawn from a very "low" idiom. So, in this passage, as in the one where Colley speaks, Pope has integrated several voices into one style, voices from Grub Street, the theater, and the underworld, as well as those from revered tradition.

The procedure is typical of *The Dunciad;* Pope's apparently unified style is put together throughout the poem from many styles. Although these usually exist in the poem only as individual words and phrases, the words and phrases are expanded by the notes, or by the reader's knowledge, into complete and independent idioms. This returns us to *Speke Parott* and *The Waste Land. The Dunciad* appears different from either poem in its integrated style, but like that between *Speke Parott* and *The Waste Land,* this is not a real difference. Behind, and within, Pope's single style, there are quite as many voices as those of the other two poems. Furthermore, the prodigious skill with which Pope integrates diverse materials into one style has its equivalent in the virtuosity with which Parrot masters diverse languages or with which Eliot arranges different speakers and quotations. Like that virtuosity, Pope's skill always draws attention to itself and to the difficulty of its task, the difficulty, that is, of fashioning something unified and coherent from all those contending voices.

The fracturing of language into many, often mutually incomprehensible, dialects is connected with the collective madness that grips the world of each poem. In *Speke Parott,* an important part of the frenzy Parrot deplores is the attempt by all manner of, predominantly young, people to master languages and to develop eloquence. Since these aspirant polyglots are unequipped for the role, they fail to make much progress in the new languages, with the result that (since they have also abandoned their proper study of Latin) "the rest of good lernyng is roufled up and trold" (168). As Parrot presents it, England is a country where everyone talks and no one understands. Pope's dullness, a kind of madness just as active as Skelton's frenzy, is intimately associated with the way the dull use language and the effect they have on it.[46] Queen Dullness's own concern for unintelligibility is reflected early on in her birth, "e'er mortals writ or read," to Chaos and Night (B1:9–12), and in her project to bring the "Smithfield Muses to the ear of Kings" (B1:2). Later, the dunces demonstrate the complete opacity of these muses and their language in, for example, the cacaphony, the braying, and the droning of book 2 (B2:235–68, 2:379), or in Bentley's giving up "Cicero to C or K" in book 4 (B4:222). Unlike *Speke Parott* or *The Dunciad, The Waste Land* does not explicitly identify madness as the prevailing condition of its world. Instead, the people of the poem are characterized by the kind of isolation described by F. H. Bradley in the passage Eliot quotes from him: "In brief, regarded as an existence which appears in a soul, the whole world for each is peculiar and private to that soul" (411n). However, such isolation, implying as it does the inability to grasp the external reality either of other people or of the world of objects, is itself allied to madness. Its neurotic, if not quite psychotic character is evident in the scene in "A Game of Chess," where the typically isolated lady badgers the poem's speaker for some contact (111–34). The scene also shows the place of language in the neurosis, as the two people are unable to communicate only because they have no common idiom. Throughout *The Waste Land,* it is the failure of language, the tendency of each person to create his own idiom and the resulting variety of idioms, that conditions the isolated, neurotic lives Eliot exposes.

In each of the three poems, the main speaker—and each speaker has a close connection with the poet—is infected by the madness of his world. Parrot rattles on like a madman, is accused of talking as if he were *"ebrius"* (68), and needs to take nutmeg to steady his mind (183). Pope, ironically identifying himself with the dull, witnesses the world's collapse into lunacy and foresees his own disappearance in darkness (B4:1–16). And when Eliot's speaker enters into the dramatic action of the poem to converse with others, he sounds insane or on the verge of insanity. However much solemn annotation is piled upon the greeting of Stetson, the principal effect of the lines is to suggest a character who, like Ferdinand in the last act of *The Duchess of Malfi,* is of less-than-sound mind (69–76). Similarly, some of his dark thoughts in silent reply to the neurotic lady in "A Game of Chess" border upon paranoia (115–18). Of course, these speakers, although they may be a mask for the poet or a vehicle for his ironic utterance or a version of part of him, are not quite the same as the poet himself, the person who orders the poetic material and puts the poem together. But even that figure is threatened by something like madness. In discussing the way the three poets face and arrange a multitude of different voices, I have several times used the word *virtuosity,* and it seems to me an appropriate one. The deliberate display of prowess in taking on and controlling a number of languages and idioms much greater than any ordinary person would attempt is a virtuoso display, and like every virtuoso display, it is carried out on the edge of disaster. The poets are like the tightrope walker dancing, of course without a net, over the abyss; or they are like the pianist playing a piece so complicated and fast that at every moment the harmony threatens to disintegrate into discord. In their case, the abyss or the discord is the madness of Babel.

5
The Citadel

The Poet's Authority

Skelton, Pope, and Eliot all resort, in the face of the profusion they perceive, to assertions of poetic authority, or rather to assertions of their own peculiar poetic authority. One aspect of this is the aged poetic voice I discuss in chapter 2, since the assumed age and venerability of the poet allow him to oppose and, he hopes, to silence the young. More generally, the poets tend, in their writing about poetry and about themselves as poets, to establish the value of their work by reference to an external institution, group, or tradition, which is the privileged keeper and defender of the truth—it is the poet's allegiance to this institution that accredits his work. Such attitudes, set out most explicitly in critical passages (and it is to these we must turn first), appear in *Speke Parott, The Dunciad,* and *The Waste Land* through some of their distinctive rhetorical approaches, particularly through the use of allusion and through the ambiguous projections of the poet in the poems. Furthermore, just as the aged voice is a response to the youthful world and, ultimately, to the contemporary situation, the more general poetic authority responds to contemporary profusion, for its most essential feature is reduction. The exclusive nature of the authoritative institution sets limits on the number of members and of legitimate voices, while the poet's obedience to it and its ideology provides him with a reduced version of experience and a circumscribed knowledge by which to define himself. However, the assertions of authority are undermined by the fragility of the institutions and by the irascible crankiness of the individuals who represent them, with the result that the poems do not, ultimately, express authority and confidence. Their insecurity is the subject of my next chapter, but here I look at some aspects of authority itself: the appeal to it in critical writings, its function for the poet, its place in the three poems, and its implications for the reader.

Commentators on Skelton's aesthetics usually concentrate on the later parts of *A Replycacion* in order to identify his argument for divine inspiration and to distinguish his attitudes from those of earlier medieval poets.[1] Just as striking in the passages, though, is the way that Skelton deals with opinions contrary to his own by insisting on his authority as the appointee of higher institutions. It is true that all poets who wish to establish a point must in doing so establish their own right to speak, just as writers generally at some point and in some way usually seek to impress upon readers their special qualifications. The typical medieval pose of modesty is, as Curtius points out, a rhetorically roundabout way of doing this,[2] and the modern critic's apparatus of notes and bibliography serves to identify his labors as much as to place his arguments in a context. Skelton's self-proclamations, however, differ from these in the openness and loudness of his assertions of authority and in their reliance on external institutions. The important section of *A Replycacion* begins

> A confutacion responsyve, or an inevytably prepensed answere to all waywarde or frowarde altercacyons that can or may be made or objected agaynst Skelton laureate, devyser of this Replycacion, etc.

> Why fall ye at debate
> With Skelton laureate,
> Reputyng hym unable
> To gainsay replycable
> Opinyons detestable
> Of heresy execrable?

> (300–305)

Skelton's defense, characteristically mounted in answer to a number of imagined "waywarde or frowarde altercacyons," that is, in answer to dissenting readers, relies at this point less on the authority of poetry than on that of Skelton, graduate of three universities. The essence of the defense is indignation at the sheer impertinence of opponents, and it implies the attitude "how dare you disagree with me, with my position and qualifications!"

Barclay recognizes this reflex appeal of Skelton's to institutions in an allusion to him in one of the eclogues.

> To be with princes of power excellent,
> Some fooles counteth a thing preeminent.
> Or that men should him a kinges tutour call,[3]

Here, Skelton is shown resting (so to speak) on the laurels of a former position at court, and Barclay's rancor implies that the appeal to courtly status played some part in the disagreement between the poets.

But Barclay identifies only what is evident throughout Skelton's poetry. He constantly enters his poems in the character of a weighty
speaker with an even weightier institution behind him: as a priest, or
as *orator regius,* or as a graduate, or, most often, as "Skelton laureate."
Even in *Garland or Chapelet of Laurell,* a poem specifically celebrating
his achievements as a poet and the works he has produced, the greatest
dignity is conferred by the garland that the countess of Surrey and her
ladies sew for him and that he wears as a badge of office (1105–6). It
is the possession of this garland that distinguishes him from Chaucer,
Gower, and Lydgate (397).

Skelton's emphasis on his serious function, high office, and divine
appointment as a poet has often been regarded as anticipating the
arguments of the English Renaissance, particularly those of Sidney in
the *Defence of Poesie.*[4] However, the differences between the positions
of Skelton and Sidney are, significantly, far more marked than the
similarities. Right at the start of his essay, Sidney announces his
motives and his authority for writing about his "unelected vocation"
with the self-deprecating remark that "selfelove is better then any
guilding, to make that seem gorgios wherin our selves be parties."[5]
Later, he ironically exemplifies his own tendentiousness by including
in his examples of the divinity of poetry not only the psalms but also
the Delphic oracles and the ancient practice of prophesying by ran-
domly opening Vergil.[6] Since this use of Vergil is an example of
ancient enthusiasm and since the Delphic oracles were sometimes
associated with the devil,[7] Sidney is evidently pursuing his argument
only half-seriously, and he arrives from it only at the qualified conclusion that poetry "deserveth not to be scourged out of the Church of
God."[8] The qualified, ironic, urbane style at this, and other, points of
the *Defence* is connected with Sidney's conception of the poet's relation to his audience, and of the true nature of poetic teaching. Assuming that everyone possesses the "erected wit" or the "inward light" to
know perfection, if not to practise it, he regards the poet's task as a
kind of sweet, delightful enticing of the reader toward virtue.[9]
Nothing could be further from Skelton's attitude and approach in *A
Replycacion.* He flatly asserts his special right to lay down the law, and
he attempts to admonish heretics and potential detractors into silence
rather than to ravish them into goodness.

Sidney's attitude toward the authority of the poet and his difference
in this respect from Skelton are shared by other Renaissance poets,
including those of a more despotic temper than he. Jonson, who is
sometimes thought of as a kind of literary dictator lording it over his
subjects at "The Devil," often cites precedent, argues that poetry
"utters somewhat above a mortall mouth," and has the elitist's vig-

orous contempt for "the beast, the multitude."[10] He also left an impression of arrogance on such contemporaries as William Drummond of Hawthornden, who reports "he was wont to name himself the Poet" and who calls him "a great lover and praiser of himself, a contemner and Scorner of others." However, with regard to Drummond, Jonson seems, in remarks like "Owen is a pure Pedantyque Schoolmaster sweeping his living from the Posteriors of little Children," to have been playing the role of Peregrine from *Volpone* and having fun at the expense of his sensitive Scottish host.[11] More seriously, he emphasizes in *Discoveries* that persuasion can be effected only through the good opinion of a persuader's wisdom and honesty, and he holds nothing "more ridiculous, then to make an Author a *Dictator*."[12] Moreover, the same rule applies to himself, for he declares, "I am neither *Author,* or *Fautor* of any sect. I will have no man addict himself to mee."[13] Something of this is evident in one of his most defensive poems, "Ode to himselfe." Although he compares his detractors to usurpers and to swine, the poem does not really attempt to assert authority in the face of them. Rather, addressed to Jonson himself, it seeks to console and encourage him, and it ends by suggesting that his critics will confess his eminence "when they heare thee sing / The glories of thy *King*."[14] They will, that is, be drawn to admiration by his poetry rather than awed to silence by the power of the institutions behind him.

Later in the century, Milton's grand style and his claims to divine inspiration represent an appeal to a kind of authority, but it is not one that seeks the unquestioning acquiescence of the reader. Marvell's commendatory verses for *Paradise Lost,* which appeared in the second edition, reproduce the responses of a qualified reader, and Marvell as reader is respectful, not submissive. He begins by "misdoubting" Milton's intent in undertaking so enormous a project, and is won over to it only as he reads.[15] Marvell's comments are in keeping with the attitudes of Sidney, Jonson, and Milton himself. They reflect the Renaissance regard for a kind of urbanity whereby the writer tries to persuade, not to direct, his reader, and for a kind of limited skepticism whereby he honors but does not slavishly follow his predecessors. All this is quite different from Skelton's representation of himself as the spokesman of authoritative institutions and his demand that readers accept his word because it his word and not presume to question it.

Belonging to a later phase of the Renaissance tradition, Pope often expresses the values of his forebears in his critical writing. In the preface to the *Works* of 1717, he takes it for axiomatic that "no single man is born with a right of controuling the opinions of all the rest" (*Poems* 1:3), and in *An Essay on Criticism,* he urges critics to avoid being too blunt, because "Men must be *taught* as if you taught them *not*" (573–74). Such attitudes also underpin the arguments in reply to Madame Dacier in the final part of the postscript to his Homer. After ironically insisting on his own orthodoxy in defending Homer against "all the Hereticks of the age" (*Poems* 10:392), Pope moves on to define more seriously the differences between him and his opponent.

> that I offer *opinions*, and she delivers *doctrines;* that my imagination represents *Homer* as the greatest of human Poets, whereas in hers he was exalted above humanity; infallibility and impeccability were two of his attributes. (10:394)

The argument relies in part upon the negative weighting in this context of the words "doctrines" and "infallibility," a weighting that derives from the critical tradition as well from Protestantism. A further extension of this modesty about the poet's authority is Pope's rather affected and unconvincing habit of referring to poetry as a trivial amusement. According to the preface of 1717, it is "only the affair of idle men who write in their closets" (*Poems* 1:3), and according to one of his letters, he is become "almost the only trifler in the nation" (*Corr.* 1:324).

However, despite his disclaimers and his general air of moderation, Pope sometimes exposes a desire for, or makes an appeal to external authority in his writings about poetry and about himself as a poet. His conventionally measured attitude toward the rules and their limits in *An Essay on Criticism* gives way to inflexibility when he considers them in relation to modern writers.

> But tho' the *Ancients* thus their *Rules* invade,
> (As *Kings* dispense with *Laws* Themselves have made)
> *Moderns,* beware! Or if you must offend
> Against the *Precept,* ne'er transgress its *End,*
> Let it be *seldom,* and *compell'd by Need,*
> And have, at least, *Their Precedent* to plead.
>
> (161–66)[16]

In the first couplet, the ancients, regarded only as the discoverers of nature's laws and as potential guides earlier on, have been transformed into a version of Jonson's scorned writer-dictator, kings who make their own laws. The rest of the passage embodies a curious conflict, as Pope moves between his express belief that the rules may be broken and his evident desire to prevent any moderns from doing so. By the end, he has qualified the possibility of praiseworthy transgression so much that ancient rule and precedent stand absolute. A similar conflict is present in some of Pope's early attempts at self-defense. He draws toward a conclusion in the preface to Homer by submitting his translation, with conventional modesty, "to the Publick, from whose Opinions I am prepared to learn" (*Poems* 7:23). But immediately after this he states exactly which members of the public he will listen to and which not, and he goes on to list all the wits who encouraged him in his undertaking, to refer to some of the nobles who patronized him, and to thank Oxford University for favoring him (*Poems* 7:23–25). In effect, Pope is asserting his authority by gesturing toward the groups and institutions behind him, and though the assertion is slightly qualified by the submission to public opinion, it is not so very different from the assertions of Skelton.

The later poetry continues to place expressions of tentative modesty alongside those of assured rank, but the assertions of authority in it are more frequent and more definite than earlier. Increasingly in his later years, Pope relied, like Swift and Johnson at times, on his position and eminence to give his words weight. The first imitation of Horace is not altogether ironic in its appeal to law, and Pope supports his own behavior, in typical fashion, by calling on the exalted precedents of Montaigne and Eramsus (*Satire* 1.1.141–43, 52, 66). Although *An Epistle to Dr. Arbuthnot* represents Pope treating poetasters with urbane politeness and includes the claim that he writes only to make life bearable, it also seeks to certify his poetry.

> But why then publish? *Granville* the polite,
> And knowing *Walsh,* would tell me I could write;
> Well-natur'd *Garth* inflam'd with early praise,
> And *Congreve* lov'd, and *Swift* endur'd my Lays;
> The Courtly *Talbot, Somers, Sheffield* read,
> Ev'n mitred *Rochester* would nod the head,
> And *St. John*'s self (great *Dryden*'s friends before)
> With open arms received one Poet more
>
> . . . .
>
> From these the world will judge of Men and Books,
> Not from the *Burnets, Oldmixons,* and *Cooks.*

(135–46)

The last lines indicate a context of critical controversy, which (together with the controversial nature of the whole poem) suggests that the earlier section is largely a piece of self-defense in reply to disparagement. What Pope does in his own defense is to refer to, and help create, a high tradition of writers and prominent men, albeit partly men of the opposition, whose approval testifies to his quality as a poet and licenses him to write. Instead of surrending his work to the judgment of the reader in the manner of Jonson, he proclaims his authority by parading extrinsic qualifications in the manner of Skelton. Finally, in the second *Epilogue to the Satires,* Pope speaks of ridicule in similar terms to those used by Skelton for poetry.

> O sacred Weapon! left for Truth's defence,
> Sole Dread of Folly, Vice, and Insolence!
> To all but Heav'n-directed hands deny'd,
> The Muse may give thee, but the Gods must guide.
>
> (212 –15)

The lines emphasize not so much the divinity of ridicule as the special possession of this divine gift by Pope, and they treat the heavenly faculty not as a means of creating delightful or instructive fictions but as a power for silencing the wicked and, significantly, the impertinent.

The authoritarian strain in Pope becomes particularly evident when he is compared with Dryden, with whom he has in some other respects so much in common. Occasionally, Dryden makes high claims for poetry, such as when he talks of Anne Killigrew's "Heav'nly Gift of Poesy" in his elegy for her, and occasionally, he deliberately adopts the style of the "Law-giver," as he explains in his preface to *Religio Laici.*[17] Yet far more characteristic of him is a hesitancy that reflects a genuinely skeptical temper.[18] The preface to *Religio Laici* ends with the standard argument that a man is "to be reason'd into Truth," and it begins with Dryden expressing, it seems genuinely, "the due sense of my own weakness and want of Learning."[19] There is the same due sense in works such as *An Essay of Dramatic Poesy* that enter into literary controversy. Although Dryden wrote the dialogue in response to Sir Robert Howard and although he addresses such important issues as the debate between ancients and moderns, he does not attempt to enforce his own views in it by dint of some external authority. Instead, he keeps his promise not "to reconcile, but to relate" different opinions, and he goes so far as to poke mild fun at himself, under the guise of Neander, for being so carried away by his own arguments as to fail to hear his friends or to notice their journey's end.[20] Even at the end of his life, long after his conversion to Catholicism, Dryden still retained that diffidence. Having submitted his work to the judgment of the reader in the preface to the *Fables,* and having foreseen the possibility of condemnation, he writes,

> I have the Excuse of an old Gentleman, who mounting on Horseback before some Ladies, when I was present, got up somewhat heavily, but desir'd of the Fair Spectators, that they count Fourscore and eight before

they judg'd him. By the Mercy of God, I am already come within Twenty Years of his Number, a Cripple in my Limbs, but what Decays are in my Mind, the Reader must determine.[21]

It is interesting that Dryden should refer so explicitly to his age and that the reference should have so different an application from those of Skelton and Pope in their declining years, but the real point is Dryden's modest tone. Unlike Pope, at least in the later part of his career, he feels no need to draw support for himself and his poetry from outside witnesses and outside institutions.

The later tradition, from which Eliot emerges, is considerably more suspicious of assertions of authority by a writer, whether the writer be poet, critic, or poet-critic, than is the tradition of the Renaissance. If the romantics lay stress on the poet's high calling, they do not attempt to validate this with an external institution. When Wordsworth compares himself to a priest, it is a priest listening to an inner voice,[22] and Keats writes that

> The Genius of Poetry must work out its own salvation in a man: It cannot be matured by law & precept, but by sensation & watchfulness in itself— That which is creative must create itself—[23]

Although Arnold, in some ways a more direct influence on Eliot, nurtured his doubts about romanticism, there is a similar reluctance to seek outside help in his critical writing. He sees criticism in terms of *"disinterestedness"* and of "a free play of the mind on all subjects which it touches," defines the "language of genuine poetry" with Wordsworth's phrase as "the language of one composing with his eye on the object," and refuses to exploit his professorial position in argument, choosing instead to stand "as a plain citizen of the republic of letters, and not as an office-bearer in a hierarchy."[24] Eliot's attitude toward Arnold is, in proper skeptic's fashion, one of only qualified admiration, but his criticism still flaunts some of these values. In "The Perfect Critic" alone, an essay that begins with a piece of slightly qualified praise for Arnold, he calls criticism "the disinterested exercise of intelligence," honors Aristotle for looking "solely and steadfastly at the object," urges (rather coercively) that "in matters of great importance the critic must not coerce," and ticks Dryden off for his "tendency to legislate rather than to inquire" (*SW*, 11–12). Elsewhere, Eliot puts himself in the role of the disinterested critic by adopting the vocabulary and some of the rhetorical gestures appropriate to it. He sets out to "test" a book, admits to earlier failures of perception, and describes himself as merely "struggling to attack" a point (*SW*, 3, xi,

56). It was presumably this kind of language along with Eliot's more open claims that led one commentator to write of the "diffused scepticism that had made the earlier criticism possible."[25]

Eliot's approach, however, is far less genuinely skeptical than all that suggests, and he shares the tendency toward authoritarian and total-itarian solutions so common among the modernists. His critical style, for example, tends to veer between the rationally cautious and the unbendingly dogmatic.[26] In later retrospective comments, he con-cedes something of this by writing mockingly of his former "assump-tion of pontifical solemnity" (*SW*, vii)—and we must assume that the Anglo-Catholic of 1928 was using "pontifical" carefully—or of the way that he obtained "partly by subtlety, partly by effrontery, partly by accident, a reputation amongst the credulous for learning and scholarship" (*CC*, 145). The second comment nearly, but not quite, identifies the ingenious assertions of the writer's authority that play so important a part in *The Sacred Wood*. One such device is the appropria-tion of the language of science. Having at one point castigated "that familiar vague suggestion of the scientific vocabulary which is charac-teristic of modern writing," Eliot goes on to state, apparently without irony, that the "verbal disease above noticed may be reserved for diagnosis by and by" (*SW*, 2). His objections to the "verbal disease" are not scientific, but they are given weight by the implication of a scientific authority possessed by the writer.[27] Another, and more ubiquitous, device is the casual display of breathtaking erudition, as when, for instance, he takes Charles Whibley to task.

> On Surrey's blank verse he is feeble; he does not even give Surrey the credit of having anticipated some of Tennyson's best effects. He has no praise for Golding, quite one of the best of the verse translators; he apologizes for him by saying that Ovid demands no strength or energy! There is strength and energy, at least, in Marlowe's *Amores*. And he omits mention of Gawain Douglas, who, though he wrote in Scots, was surely a "Tudor" translator. (*SW*, 36)

The focus of this passage is less on its ostensible subject, which is treated quite cursorily, than on Eliot and on his special credentials for pronouncing about literary matters. What is more, although the allu-sions to "Tennyson's best effects" and to Golding seem to ground his authority in knowledge, their rapidity and their arch knowingness place Eliot less in the light of a scholar than that of an insider. The passage identifies him as an initiate in the arcane mysteries of literature in the same way as does his superior reference to the "quite uninitiated reader" of Dante (*SW*, 14), or his curious estimate that Jonson might appeal to "about three thousand people in London and elsewhere" (*SW*, 121). The impulse behind these identifications is not to develop a "free play of the mind" but to establish authority, an impulse that becomes still more apparent in the language of "orthodoxy" and "heresy" of *After Strange Gods* (*ASG*, 21).

Eliot associates "orthodoxy" with "tradition" in that essay, and it is the idea of tradition that provides the most explicitly and consciously authoritarian element in the early criticism[28] and in Eliot's conception of the poet. The idea, originally set out in "Tradition and the Individual Talent," is recapitulated in "The Function of Criticism."

> I thought of literature then, as I think of it now, of the literature of the world, of the literature of Europe, of the literature of a single country, not as a collection of the writings of individuals, but as 'organic wholes', as systems in relation to which, and only in relation to which, individual works of literary art, and the works of individual artists, have their significance. There is accordingly something outside of the artist to which he owes allegiance, a devotion to which he must surrender and sacrifice himself in order to earn and to obtain his unique position. (*SE*, 23–24)

It is important to remember that in the early criticism in general and in this essay in particular, Eliot was engaging in controversy. Like Skelton and Pope, he meets real and potential opposition by appealing to a privileged, higher group, to what he calls "literature." It is the poet's membership of this group, his place in the institution of literature, that, like Skelton's laureate or the testimonies quoted by Pope, gives him his significance and authority, and the passage hints fairly strongly at Eliot's own membership. I chose to quote from "The Function of Criticism" rather than from "Tradition and the Individual Talent" because it was written after the publication of *The Waste Land,* when Eliot had some claim to be one of the true artists he was discussing. But what is striking is that any implicit claim to a unique position here is made not on the strength of the reader's judgment of his poem but on the strength of the poet's "allegiance," his "devotion," and, it might be added, his belonging to "something outside of the artist."

Authority, the Poet, and Others

Two further points can be drawn out of the passage from "The Function of Criticism." Firstly, there is the emphasis not only on the artist's accreditation by the external institution but on his necessary submission to it. It is a curious coincidence in this respect that Eliot and Pope should both choose to parody the same passage of Scripture in order to illustrate the poet's duty. While Eliot argues that the "Arts insist that a man shall dispose of all that he has, even of his family tree, and follow art alone" (*SW*, 32), Pope writes that to "follow Poetry as one ought, one must forget father and mother, and cleave to it alone" (*Corr.* 1:243). The scriptural associations impart to the statements as strong a sense of the poet's need to surrender to the institution of literature as of his need to labor over composition. Although Skelton does not use the same parody, he, too, can see the poet's task in terms of service, as when he represents himself in the livery and the household of Calliope (*Calliope*, 9–14). The second point to be drawn out of the "Function of Criticism" passage is that the poet's devotion to literature is in part, or is part of, a process of self-definition and self-formation—through devotion he becomes a devotee. This tendency is perhaps most obvious in Skelton's renaming himself "Skelton laureate," but it is also present in Pope's comparisons of himself with his ancient forebears and in Eliot's ruminations on "the mind of Europe." Of course, any discussion of a poet's attempt to define himself must be qualified by the consideration that it is impossible to know exactly how far the private man, in his most private moments, regarded himself as a poet and as a servant of Poetry. Nevertheless, we can say that when these three men write of poetry, particularly of their own poetry, they seem to be trying to define themselves as poets belonging in a larger tradition. Moreover, the tradition, however large, is limited, and it excludes far more writers and ways of writing than it admits. It is the exclusiveness of a tradition that makes it such a good means of self-definition, for the exclusiveness promises to reduce the unsettling profusion of experience and the bewildering variety of voices.

When Skelton appears in his poems it is almost always as a poet standing in a tradition of poetry. He bustles into Jane's meditations in *Phyllyp Sparowe* not as a lover but as the "laureate poet of Britain," announcing himself loudly, tossing off classical allusions, calling upon his muses, and boasting of how her fame will spread through his praise (834–88). The kind of self-image implied here is present in more definite form in *Garlande or Chapelet of Laurell* when Skelton meets Occupation, who as "Fames Regestary" will eventually ensure his place among the great poets (522).[29] She recollects their earliest acquaintance.

> whan broken was your mast
> Of worldly trust, then did I you rescu;

Your storme dryven shyppe I repared new,
So well entakeled, what wynde that ever blowe,
No stormy tempeste your barge shall overthrow.

(542–46)

The lines are personal and they represent Skelton, with the well-worn sea/ship imagery, as having been saved from the dangers of the world by his dedication to poetry and his hope of future fame. The exact nature of the salvation is embodied in the movement of the whole allegory. Skelton progresses from his place among the noisy suitors to Fame into her palace, where "If xii were let in, xii hundreth stode without" (490). Later, he is accorded a privileged view of the crowds outside the gates to Fame, he visits a garden of the Muses and the peaceful chamber of the countess of Surrey, and he returns to the court of Fame to hear a catalog of his own works. By the end of the dream, the "thowsande thowsande" suitors contending noisily and variously for admittance to Fame have been transformed into the "thowsande, thowsande" poets and orators who repeat the single word "triumpha" in honor of Skelton (250–58, 1505–6). What has happened is that Skelton has escaped, by industrious application to his art, from a world of variety and contention into a simpler realm, just as More does, in a different way, by his imagination of Utopia. In this context, the final addendum after the dream, the conventional complaint against the abuses of the world offered in three languages, is not as incongruous as it first seems, for it serves as a reminder of the "stormy tempeste" that Skelton has left behind. To return to *Phyllyp Sparowe*, there is a hint of something similar in that poem. Having made his grand entrance in the role of poet, Skelton proceeds not to praise his mistress but to anticipate the objections of envy against his writing and to answer the objections by reference to his poetic authority and conventionality, that is, he tries to use these to silence (970–83). One great irony of the poem, though, is that neither the objections of the envious nor the worries of Jane were neutralized by his comments, and Skelton had to compose the later addition as a further piece of self-justification.

Pope's Horatian poems project, or perhaps enact, the process of deliberately creating a self,[30] and the most marked feature of Pope's self in the poems is that he is a poet belonging in a distinctive literary tradition. This is not to say that Pope was unaware of the dangers (the temptation to vanity, for example) involved in comparing oneself to literary predecessors. His interlocutor in the first *Epilogue to the Satires* complains that "'Tis all from *Horace*" (7), while he himself mocks the uncritical reverence frequently accorded dead authors (*Epistle* 2.1.83–

84), at the tendency of writers to ascribe to themselves the gifts of Milton or Shakespeare (*Epistle* 2.2.135–37), and at the absurd flatteries of those who compare him in physique to Ovid, Vergil, or Homer (*Arbuthnot,* 115–24). What is more, the relationship that Pope develops with his forebears, especially with Horace, is, as commentators have often remarked, usually a more complex affair than his simply ransacking them for characteristics he would like to have.[31] Nevertheless, what chiefly emerges from the poems is the portrait of a man as an extremely literary (in the sense of belonging in a tradition) poet. Poetry is so fundamental a part of Pope's character that it engrosses his consciousness (*Satire* 2.1.12–14), that it was present in his earliest speech (*Arbuthnot,* 127–28), and that the greatest misery of age would be to lose the faculty (*Epistle* 2.2.76–77). More importantly, he is a poet among other poets and their friends. Even when he decides to give up writing it is with the blessing of literary precedent, for if Pope resolves to put verse aside now, Horace has done the same before him, and the reader probably responds to both resolutions with about as much conviction (*Epistle* 1.1.17). To take a wider perspective, the whole personality that is so strong a presence in the imitations and the other poems of the 1730s is, as Maynard Mack has shown, a version of the "beatus vir" of literary tradition.[32] By drawing upon literary tradition in this way, or more accurately, by drawing upon one literary tradition in this way, Pope simultaneously creates himself out of it and places himself firmly inside it.

The tradition from which Pope fashions himself is, like every tradition, a very exclusive affair. By putting himself in a line of poets, Pope emphasizes not only his resemblance to them but also his difference from the writers who are not, must not be allowed to be, in the same line. The "beatus vir" embodies this wish to shut out in a peculiarly appropriate way, for, in addition to possessing a select set of antecedents, he is physically removed from pretenders and contenders by his retirement away from the city and in the country. Like Skelton behind the walls of the Palace of Fame, Pope at Twickenham is cut off from those other people and other voices which are potentially so threatening, and he often chooses to stress this seclusion.

> I sought no homage from the Race that write;
> I kept, like *Asian* Monarchs, from their sight:
> (*Arbuthnot,* 219–20)

His invisibility from the "Race that write," which is desirable because it prevents their trying to define him, implies at the same time their invisibility from him, which is desirable because it acquits him from having to take account of them. The attitude is essentially snobbish, and some of the snobbishness may have been learned from Bolingbroke.

> I have sometimes represented to myself the *vulgar,* who are accidentally distinguished by the titles of king and subject, of lord and vassal, of nobleman and peasant; and the *few* who are distinguished by nature so essentially from the herd of mankind, that (figure apart) they seem to be of another species, in this manner.

Bolingbroke goes on to compare the behavior of the "herd" in the world with that of "Dutch travellers" in foreign countries, and the behavior of the few with "men who are sent on more important errands."[33] It is hard to avoid the conclusion in reading a passage like this that the writer includes himself and his friends among the few, while the herd comprehends just about everybody else, and one must be struck by the arrogance of this division of humanity into two species, with only the grudging, parenthetical admission that members of each look alike. Pope's attempt to make himself in the image of the retired poet-sage and to shut himself in a select tradition has something of this about it, but to his credit he is never quite successful in banishing the dunces from Twickenham, and he seems perhaps not entirely to want to.

Eliot's early criticism is couched in the language of objective inquiry, and there is consequently little overt self-presentation in it. However, the essays in *The Sacred Wood* can legitimately be read as personal statements, expressing Eliot's preoccupation with his own nature as a poet as well as his theories about poetry in general.[34] The first point which emerges from them is that the poet finds himself, or makes himself, in tradition. The assertion of the necessity of following the arts alone, which I quote above, is followed by:

> For they require that a man be not a member of a family or of a caste or of a party or of a coterie, but simply and solely himself. A man like Wyndham brings several virtues into literature. But there is one man better and more uncommon than the patrician, and that is the Individual. (*SW,* p. 32)

It is a curious paradox that devotion and obedience (the arts "require") should be associated with individuality, and the paradox indicates the way that, for Eliot, submission leads to self-formation. The idea is central to "Tradition and the Individual Talent," in which he argues that "not only the best, but the most individual parts of his [a poet's] work may be those in which the dead poets, his ancestors, assert their immortality most vigorously" (*SW,* 48). The focus on the poet's work rather than on the poet himself in that quotation is part of the whole attempt in the essay to distinguish not only between the poet and other men but also between the poet as poet and poet as man. Eliot insists that "the more perfect the artist, the more completely separate in him will be the man who suffers and the mind which creates" (*SW,* 54), and he argues further that it is not in his "personal emotions . . . . that the poet is in any way remarkable or interesting" (*SW,* 57). But the poet is remarkable and interesting—and Eliot is talking about the poet rather than poetry—in the poetic part of himself, and that, as the essay stresses, must be created through tradition. By implication, then, there are two Eliots: the man who lives his messy, emotional life, and the poet who stands in a tradition and writes.

Poetry (along with the poetic Eliot) provides a kind of haven into which he (the most essential Eliot) can escape from the emotional Eliot, the man of the world. It is a little citadel into which he can retreat from his evil age. Perhaps the most famous part of "Tradition and the Individual Talent" comes in the sentences that close the second section.

> Poetry is not a turning loose of emotion, but an escape from emotion; it is not the expression of personality, but an escape from personality. But, of course, only those who have personality and emotions know what it means to want to escape from these things. (*SW,* 58)

Although the imprecision of words like "emotion" and "personality" makes it hard to extract from this a coherent theory, the "human" meaning is plain enough. Personality and emotion belong in the realm of the world, of "the man who suffers," and poetry, both when it is written and presumably when it is read, offers an escape from that realm. In this respect, Eliot's impersonal theory of poetry is similar to Skelton's imagination of himself in the Palace of Fame and to Pope's re-creation of the traditional figure of retirement literature, for all three represent a psychological sanctuary. It is also similarly exclusive. The above quotation excludes those who have not even sense enough to want to enter Poetry, and throughout the essay Eliot is concerned to set limits. He contrasts the "confused cries" of the newspaper critics giving "the names of poets in great numbers" with the rarity of the real poem (*SW,* 53), and focusing his attention in the final paragraph more singly on readers, he emphasizes that only "very few know when there is expression of *significant* emotion, emotion which has its life in the poem and not in the history of the poet" (*SW,* 59). This limitation is essential to Eliot's theory. The tradition through which a poet achieves impersonality and by which a reader knows it may be vast and difficult to master, but it is also orderly and strictly limited. Indeed, the vastness and difficulty of mastery work toward the limitation, for they help to keep out the noisy, contentious, emotional people (both writers and readers and even Eliots in some aspects of their personality) whose entry into literature would transform it from a peaceful retreat into another version of the world.

Allusion in the Three Poems

One striking way in which the desire both for self-definition and for the exclusion of others is present in *Speke Parott, The Dunciad,* and *The Waste Land* is through the images of the Flood that I discuss in my first chapter. As I say there, by predicting a second deluge, the poets take on for themselves the character of the prophet, a character endowed with enormous external authority. Furthermore, the flood they prophesy is essentially an agent of reduction, the myth of the Flood being, so to speak, a reduction myth. The first chapter concerning Noah begins:

> And it came to pass, when men began to multiply on the face of the earth, and daughters were born unto them, That the sons of God saw the daughters of men that they were fair; and they took them wives of all which they chose. (Gen. 6:1–2)

According to later verses, the Flood is sent by God when he sees that "the wickedness of men was great in the earth" (Gen. 6:5), but the emphasis at the start suggests it is some kind of answer to multiplication itself. The solution is a beautifully simple one. The Flood puts an end to proliferation and replaces the teeming life of the earth with smaller, more manageable numbers. At the same time, the variety and complexity of the landscape is reduced to one undifferentiated mass of water. Such a quiet, empty world is a kind of imaginative, more radical version of "tradition," with all those troublesome, rowdy others finally shut out and silenced.

More important than the images of flood, however, and probably the most important device by which the set of attitudes I have been discussing appears in the three poems is allusion. If each of the three poets tends to rely on extrinsic authority when answering opposition, to define himself by his membership in a tradition, and to emphasize that the tradition is an exclusive one, these gestures are present in the poems largely through the references to the tradition. It hardly needs adding that each of the poems is highly allusive, even in an age of allusive writing. Different critics have awarded the prize for the most allusive poet in English to both Pope and Eliot,[35] and while no one has made the same claim for Skelton, he (through Parrot) points to his own dense use of allusion:

> Suche shredis of sentence, strowed in the shop
> Of auncyent Aristippus and such other mo,
> I gader togyther and close in my crop,
>
> (92–94)

However, it is not so much the extent of allusion that is important as the fact that the three poems employ it in similar ways, and in ways that accord with the set of attitudes outlined above. The allusions of *Speke Parott, The Dunciad,* and *The Waste Land* are usually deployed to assert the poet's insider authority in the face of opposition, they help to constitute his personality in the poem out of tradition, and they imply the exclusion of others from that tradition. These uses of allusion are not common to every allusive poet. When Milton alludes to classical epic precedents in *Paradise Lost,* he both draws authority from his relation to Homer and Vergil and he carefully distinguishes himself, as a Christian poet, from them.[36] Even his place in the Christian tradition fails to confer on him a final authority, for the poet of the Fall is himself a fallen poet. Furthermore, Milton's allusions do not exist in implied situations of satiric conflict, functioning as markers of the poet's superiority, but rather they reach toward comprehensiveness. A very different use of allusion, the use of it to set limits, and the relation of this kind of allusion to the images of chaos, provide the focus of the following pages.

Most of Skelton's allusions in *Speke Parott* are put into the beak of his "wonderowus" bird, and something of their purpose and effect can be seen in the exchanges between Parrot and his ladies.

> Aram was fyred with Caldies fyer called Ur;
> Jobab was brought up in the lande of Hus;
> The lynage of Lot toke supporte of Assur;
> Jereboseth is Ebruc, who lyst the cause dyscus.
> "Peace, Parrot, ye prate as ye were *ebrius!*"
>
> (64–68)

The allusions here, as with the other Old Testament allusions in the poem, suggest a similarity between the ancient enemies of Israel and

the modern degenerates Skelton is attacking, especially Wolsey, and
the lines seem further to point to a figure of the "one upright man"
(Haran, Job, and Gideon/Jerubbesheth) who withstands the degeneracy of the times. The two sets of references (to evil and to the one
good man) represent, beneath their difficult surface, an interpretation
of Skelton's England that reduces its complexities to the long-standing
and fairly straightforward struggle between good and evil. The rhetoric of the passage rests less on an attempt to make this interpretation
persuasive than on the authority of the speaker, since the rapid string
of references to the Bible and, just as important, to a way of reading
the Bible serves chiefly to identify the speaker's learning and authority. Wolsey is like a Chaldean not because he is made to look like
one but because an accredited Parrot says so.

The implication in this that the lines focus as much on the mes-
senger as on his message is also contained in the lady's comment on
the way he speaks. The word "ebrius," which she applies to him, has,
in addition to its hint of his less-than-stable mental condition, at least
two further functions. Firstly, it is a pun that means "Hebrew" as well
as "drunk" and that takes us back to the statement in the previous line,
"Jereboseth is Ebrue." The lady has, however unwittingly and
obliquely, identified Parrot as Jerubbesheth, a type of the one upright
man, and as always, behind Parrot is Skelton. It is significant that he
should define his role as Wolsey's, and evil's, opponent by reference to
Haran, Job, and Gideon, that is, by placing himself in a tradition. The
second, and equally important, extra function of the word "ebrius" is
that, used by another to express irritation and incomprehension, it
effectively differentiates Parrot from his interlocutor. He speaks a
language that she cannot penetrate, and thoughout the poem, Parrot
protects himself in this way not only from political oppression but also
from intrusion by others. The final envoy boasts:

> Wherfor your remorders ar madde or else starke blynde,
> Yow to remorde erste or they know your mynde.
>
> (369–70)

Parrot has, the lines imply, preempted his detractors by making his
mind and himself unknowable to them.

There are two impulses at work in all this, impulses that appear to
be somewhat at odds with each other but that combine quite happily
in Skelton's characteristic self-projection. On the one hand, he needs
to create a strong presence for Parrot and for himself in order to exert
authority; on the other, he craves the kind of anonymity and retreat
that will enable him to keep his little world inviolate. What Skelton

does to combine these impulses is to create a fabulous Parrot who inhabits a remote but authoritative realm and whose words should be attended to, whether the listeners fully understand them or not. Parrot's riddling references prevent the lady from knowing exactly what he thinks and from becoming intimate while also letting her see his general cast of mind and his generally anti-Wolsey opinions. Her interruption, which like the earlier "*Tycez-vous,* Parrott" (56), and the later "ware the cat" (99) is partly a warning, shows that she has grasped the essence of his argument, but no more than the essence. It is only in the single figure of Galathea that Parrot finds a fully sympathetic listener, and it is only in the final invective that, at her prompting, he speaks out plainly enough to be understood by all. But even then he retains a certain aloofness, as the invective is largely conventional, and coming after nearly 450 lines of allusive obscurity, it carries an air of remote condescension. As for Skelton's own presence, this is projected for most of the poem through Parrot (thus being a further degree removed), and the bird's distant authority is mirrored in those parts where Skelton himself appears. The second epigraph's reference to his golden reputation *("Skeltonidis aurea fama")* is repeated in the final epigraph, while another burst of Latin in the middle numbers him in the catalog of the muses (*"In Piereorum cathalogo numeratum"* [232]). References such as these direct the reader not toward a man but toward a figure, the figure of the inspired poet, and similarly, the difficult style of the envoys implies this figure and that his message is only for the few. Skelton makes the latter point explicitly—lords, ladies, and "notable clerkes" may, he says, behold his poem (358–59), but the other kind of people are too stupid to understand and should keep off (319).

Although Pope does not comment on the exclusive function of *The Dunciad*'s allusive style quite as directly as Skelton does on *Speke Parott*'s, he makes it plain that the allusions shut the dunces out. In his prefatory essay, Martin Scriblerus comments on the "allusions infinite."

> yea divers by his exceeding diligence are so alter'd and interwoven with the rest, that several have already been, and more will be, by the ignorant abused, as altogether and originally his own. (*Poems* 5:52–53)

The point is borne out by the notes. The majority of the notes that give the sources for allusions do so anonymously and simply, and the contrast between these brief, unidentified notes and the lengthy annotations of the identified contributors suggests that they are the work of one properly learned reader. Against this reader are set the

others, whose ignorance makes them miss the allusions and whose
false learning, equally a handicap, makes them misread. Scriblerus, for
example, is sometimes reliable, especially in his prefatory essay, but
just as often he misses the point, as when he agrees with Thomas
Hearne that obsolete words should be preserved.

> Little is it of avail to object that such words are become *unintelligible*. Since
> they are *Truly English*, Men *ought* to understand them; and such as are for
> *Uniformity* should think all alterations in a Language, *strange, abominable,*
> and *unwarrantable*. Rightly therefore, I say again, hath our Poet used
> ancient words, and poured them forth, as a precious ointment, upon good
> old *Wormius* in this place. (A3 : 183n)

Scriblerus's learning has allowed him to understand the word "arede,"
which is the supposed subject of the whole rambling note (only part of
which is given here), but he fails to see what he elsewhere recognizes,
that Pope is writing ironically. What is more, the note shows him
moving away from any attempt to understand the poem as he becomes
more and more entangled in the self-preening pleasures of learned
argument. A worse offender than Scriblerus is Bentley (or the character "Bentley" Pope creates by ascribing notes to him), who offers
seminonsensical new readings (B1 : 218n) or who exploits the notes to
advertise his own work (B4 : 544n). Both Bentley and Scriblerus
betray the same thing, that Pope's meaning is largely inaccessible to
the dunces, just as Skelton's is to the newly ignorant.

In the poem proper, Pope constantly projects himself, albeit
through a filter of irony, as belonging to a limited and defined tradition that is set apart from the noisy, troublesome world of the duncas.
The early allusions to Vergil, Ovid, and Dryden identify the classicality of his muse, while the inscription to Swift places him as a
member of a modern literary elite.[37] The difference between Pope and
the duncas in this respect becomes particularly clear when he describes
his hero's library.

> But, high above, more solid Learning shone
> The Classics of an Age that heard of none;
> There Caxton slept, with Wynkyn at his side,
> One clasp'd in wood, and one in strong cow-hide;
>
> (B1 : 147–50)

Although these lines are far more appropriate to Theobald than to
Cibber, Pope seems to have retained them in the final version in order
to emphasize that the duncas belong to a whole culture, like that of the
Middle Ages, which is distinct from his. They do not read classical

literature, or if they do, they fail to understand it. To underline the point, Pope included in the editions after 1735 a long footnote that begins by mocking Caxton's treatment of the *Aeneid* "as a History" and his speaking of it "as of a book hardly known," and that goes on to quote some of the printer's barbarous comments on the "*Eneydos* (made in latyn by that noble poete & grete clerke *Vyrgyle*)" (A1:129n). The implicit contrast to Caxton and his modern counterparts is Pope, who has not only heard of and read the classics but is so immersed in them that his poetic style and personality, as the allusions elsewhere in the poem demonstrate, have been crystallized by the immersion. It is this generalized, classical Pope who is set against the dunces, and the contrast is typical of *The Dunciad*. Pope and the dunces are presented as belonging to different worlds, and his habitation of a superior, simpler world both allows him to comment authoritatively on their chaotic minds and activities and (it is hoped) protects him, by virtue of the elevation and relative unpopulousness of his Parnassus, from the dangers of that chaos.

In *The Waste Land*, the function of allusion is sometimes exposed through dramatic situations which are closer to that of Parrot among his ladies than to the implied conflict of *The Dunciad*. The best example of this occurs in "A Game of Chess."

> 'What is that noise now? What is the wind doing?'
>> Nothing again nothing.
>>> 'Do
> You know nothing? Do you see nothing? Do you remember
> 'Nothing?'
>
>> I remember
> Those are pearls that were his eyes.
> 'Are you alive, or not? Is there nothing in your head?'
>>> But
> O O O O that Shakespeherian Rag—
>
> (119–28)

The speaker (or really, he should be called the thinker) here is even more withdrawn than Parrot, for while Parrot hides behind his riddling, allusive chatter, this speaker is silent toward his companion. Nevertheless, his unspoken thoughts work in a similar way to Parrot's words. Firstly, they distinguish and separate him from the woman he is with—even if she could read his mind, she would be incapable, like Skelton's ladies and Pope's dunces, of piercing the meaning of the allusions to *The White Devil, The Tempest,* and *Hamlet*. Secondly, by distinguishing him in this way, the allusive thoughts confer on the speaker a superiority over the woman and a right to judge her. So, his silence implies that she is not worth talking to, his deep thoughts turn her accusations back on her, and his reference to that "Shakespeherian Rag" mocks her cultureless existence. Much of the allusion in *The Waste Land* turns on this kind of condemnatory contrast. If it does not contrast a glorious past with the degraded present in the manner of some of Eliot's earlier poetry, it does at least contrast the poet's cultured mind, which has access to the past, with the empty minds of other moderns. A further important element in the scene from "A Game of Chess," and one that underlines the speaker's distinction and superiority, is the way his thoughts are available to the reader. While Eliot confronts the woman with silence, he carefully exposes to us the way the speaker's, probably a version of his own, mind works and draws our attention to the difference between his unhappy but highly literary meditations and her neurotic and empty interrogations.

There is the same quality to the allusions in those parts of *The Waste Land* which represent no dramatic conflict. The statement of the first Thames-daughter, for example, that "Highbury bore me. Richmond and Kew / Undid me" (293–94), echoes, as Eliot's note indicates, the words of La Pia in *Purgatorio*. As in the scene discussed above, one major effect of the allusion is to distinguish the woman from the poet (and, in that case, from the speaker). While she repeats La Pia's melancholy admission and her pathetic sentence structure without knowing she is doing so, he is consciously reworking the poetry of a predecessor. His knowledge of *The Divine Comedy* implies he has access to a sphere the Thames-daughter cannot enter, and the nature of this sphere is clarified in the 1929 essay on Dante. There, Eliot emphasizes the simplicity and intelligibility of Dante's allegorical method (*SE,* 242), and he gives particular attention to the "universality" of his language (*SE,* 238–40). By this, he means that Dante wrote from a unified culture held together by an orderly system of thought rather than from a fragmentary culture of many voices. The idea is related to his famous earlier proposal that English history be seen as suffering from a "dissociation of sensibility" somewhere about the middle of the seventeenth century (*SE,* 288). The poets who came before that dire event, he argues, "possessed a mechanism of sensibility which could devour any kind of experience" (*SE,* 287). This peculiar mixed metaphor reiterates a central idea of Eliot's criticism, that a work of literature, and indeed a Literature, should join different experiences in a unified whole, and the conception of Dante's universal language seems to be a slightly different version of the same idea. To return to the allusion to La Pia: by making it, Eliot implicitly positions his poetic consciousness in the simplified, orderly sphere of universal languages and associated sensibilities. There is, of course, another part of his consciousness, that of "the man who suffers," which must bear all the fragmentariness and dissociation of modern life. Nevertheless, in the context of the poem, the allusion suggests a creative mind that is quite distinct and aloof from those of the Thames-daughter and others like her, somewhat contemptuous of them, and largely in retreat from their world.

The poetic presences of Skelton, Pope, and Eliot differ greatly in their degree of aggression or wit or depression. Yet there is also the underlying similarity that each is both authoritative and elusive.[38] Much of the poet's implied personality derives from his place in a tradition, and it is this that allows him, sometimes explicitly, sometimes only by implication, to condemn his untraditional contemporaries. At the same time, it protects him from them. The traditional nature of his character confers on him a kind of impersonal generality that makes it hard to pin the particular man down. So, Skelton is a Job or a Gideon, Pope a member of a classical family, and Eliot a submitter to his ancestors. What is more, the different traditions of the three poets are all distinct from the worlds depicted in the poems, and they represent a kind of citadel into which the frightened poet can retreat. The problem for the poet (and one important reason why the allusive appeals to authority do not, ultimately, work) is that in order to write about the world he must leave his citadel and go out to meet it.

The Reader

If the allusions are meant, in the context of the conflict between the satirist and his butts, to keep those butts away, they have a similar function in relation to readers. Their learning requires a certain kind of reader, and effectively "screens" readers, allowing only those with the proper credentials of reading, knowledge, and ideology to enter the inner sanctum of the poem's meaning, while barring all others. A consequence of this is that all readers, even those who pass the test, must experience some degree of discomfort, since all readers are being tested. The relationship between author and reader that is implied here—the author as an austere examiner and the reader as his nervous examinee—is rather an unusual one. Although Milton demands that his heavenly muse should "fit audience find, though few," he is not really concerned with shutting potential readers out.[39] On the contrary, *Paradise Lost,* for all its difficulty, has an immediate accessibility that serves to draw the reader into further reading and deeper understanding, and, as B. Rajan argues, "learning is what the poem recommends rather than what it stipulates."[40] A kind of writing that is at first sight closer to the rhetoric of *Speke Parott, The Dunciad,* and *The Waste Land* is that involving the essentially snobbish trope of irony.[41] But most irony works by appealing to the desire of all readers to feel superior, and it only pretends to be directed at a specially select group. The appeal of irony emerges very clearly in one of the pamphlets that was written in response to Swift's Bickerstaff hoax. The writer contrasts the way that the hoaxer and his friends will "laugh often and plentifully in a corner" (thus including himself, in imagination, in that group), with the "many hundred thousand fools" taken in by the joke, whom he considers to be "Mr. Bickerstaff's choicest cullies."[42] However, Swift's hoax was such a success not because it duped large numbers of credulous fools but because it gave the impression of doing so and afforded readers the luxurious feeling of being in on a secret.[43] Swift's later irony refuses readers this kind of comfortable complicity, and the allusiveness of *Speke Parott, The Dunciad,* and *The Waste Land* has more in common with that kind of rhetorical gesture. It sets up real obstacles for the reader, and makes penetration of the poem a genuinely difficult and strenuous task. Behind such obstacles, one can sense a similar prickly defensiveness to that of Lawrence when he says of his book that "the generality of readers had better just leave it alone," or when he declares that *"the great mass of humanity should never learn to read."*[44]

Critics have disagreed about the nature of Skelton's relations with his readers in *Speke Parott.* It has been argued that contemporary readers would have been equipped for the poem, that the allusions are intended to entice the reader into conspiratorial complicity with the poem's subversive meaning, that Skelton used obscurity for self-protection, that "bewilderment is exactly the effect Parrot desires," and that the poem "is of approximately the same degree of difficulty as *The Waste Land."*[45] The range of opinions reflects the impossibility of reconstructing an early sixteenth-century reader on whom to test *Speke Parott,* and because of that impossibility, it is best to rely on the considerable internal evidence about how the poem will be, and is being, read, some of which I have dealt with already. The confusion of Parrot's ladies must be an image of the confusion of at least some of Skelton's readers, while the envoys mention explicitly and repeatedly the detraction and incomprehension that the poem has met with. The point is further reinforced by the Latin interjection to the effect that "they shall scarcely understand your poem, who read you and your poem" (372),[46] and by the comparison with Persius, the most obscure of Roman satirists, which follows it. It is, moreover, implicit in the poem's representation of a world losing its traditional knowledge, a world in which Parrot and Skelton are so out of place that even "In *Achademia* Parrot dare no probleme kepe" (162). Of course, some elements in the portrayal of the world can be put down to satiric exaggeration, but when this is allowed for, there still remains the question of where, in Wolsey's England, Skelton will fit audience find. The most probable answer is that the fit contemporary audience was small. Most readers would have struggled and many would have failed to understand the poem fully, and both the struggle and failure are the results of Skelton's deliberately exclusive rhetoric.

Angus Calder argues, in developing a contrast between *The Waste Land* and *Epistle to Dr. Arbuthnot,* that Pope's relation with his audience was more harmonious than this.

> Pope's satire, and notes, are based on a confident belief that his audience is at home with three types of reading matter; the Latin classics; the Bible and John Milton's *Paradise Lost* as a kind of annexe or extension to it; and a tradition of verse and drama in English going back to Chaucer.[47]

Calder, however, does not advance any convincing evidence,[48] and Pope and many of his contemporaries were actually less sanguine about the reading public's level of erudition than he suggests. The usually optimistic Steele quips in the *Spectator* that "MANY of my fair Readers, as well as very gay and well-received Persons of the other Sex, are extremely perplexed at the *Latin* Sentences at the Head of my Speculations," while Gay writes in a letter that "People have now forgot Homer, and Virgil & Caesar, or at least they have lost their ranks," and the *Craftsman* inveighs against the decline of learning as part of the general depravity of the age.[49] It is toward a readership of this kind that the last sentence of the prefatory "Letter to the Publisher," quite probably written by Pope, gestures.

> To his Poem those alone are capable to do Justice, who to use the words of a great Writer, know how hard it is (with regard both to his Subject and his manner) VESTUSTIS DARE NOVITATEM, OBSOLETIS NITOREM, OBSCURIS LUCEM, FASTIDITIS GRATIAM. (*Poems* 5:19)

The first part of the sentence limits Pope's fit readers to "those alone" who know the difficulty of his task, and the later quotation from Pliny is taken from his preface, addressed to Vespasian, in which he singles out the emperor as his proper reader.[50] In this context, the promise to bring light to the obscure is in one sense ironic.

The real difficulty Pope's later poetry presented to contemporary readers can be seen in their responses to it. Isaac Watts commented privately on his obscurity and incomprehensibility when compared with Horace; Swift recommended that notes should be added to *The Dunciad* identifying "the parodies (as they are call'd)" as well as the dunces; and Johnson remarked retrospectively about the poem that "the plan, if not wholly new, was little understood by common readers."[51] Even some of the contemporary publications explaining, and attacking, *The Dunciad* testify to this lack of understanding, since their authors' self-conscious displays of erudition seem intended to establish expertise, and assume that expertise is needed to read the poem.[52] As with *Speke Parott,* the difficulties for *The Dunciad*'s reader arise from its deliberately difficult allusiveness, from the rhetorical, to borrow Aubrey Williams's apt phrase, "hide-and-seek" that Pope constantly plays with us.[53]

Eliot plays the same game in *The Waste Land.* His promise in the introductory paragraph to the notes that "Miss Weston's book will elucidate the difficulties of the poem much better than my notes can do" directs the reader toward the hard path to elucidation, and a generation of critics dutifully set out to solve the poem's grail mystery. More recently, commentators have sought elucidation in Eliot's character, and have tried to read the allusions in relation to that.[54] Although both approaches can be illuminating, neither has really "solved" the puzzle of the poem or produced its meaning. A third approach, and one that is also illuminating and partial, is not to look primarily for the poem's meaning but to look at what might be called its dynamics, the relations between the speaker and the other characters and the relations between the poet and the reader. Indeed, this kind of approach is even more appropriate for *The Waste Land* than it is for *Speke Parott* and *The Dunciad,* since there is the strong possibility that the poem has no distinct, defined meaning and that it is predominantly a matter of dynamics or, to use the earlier image, a kind of serious game. Eliot's part in the game is to drop hints and leave clues for the reader to follow. The implication is that when we have finally solved that next puzzle, or discovered that next fact, or read that next book, we will be ready to be initiated into the poem's secret. But, at least in my experience, the secret is never revealed, and as one barrier is removed another springs up, as one test is passed another presents itself. Thus, reading *The Waste Land* involves taking an unending series of tests, and Eliot's rhetoric, rather than weeding out unfit readers in the manner of that of *Speke Parott* and *The Dunciad,* seems designed to exclude everybody.

Despite this difference, the reader-testing that goes on in each of the poems has the same function of protecting the poet and asserting his authority. By hiding himself and his meaning in allusion, the poet attempts to force the reader to submit to his testing and to acquire his kind of learning. If we want to understand these poems, we must achieve the standards the poets set. But a poet can only try to assert his authority over readers in this way. In her stimulating essay on *Phyllyp Sparowe,* Susan Schibanoff argues that Skelton's earlier attempts to control his readers give way in *Garlande or Chapelet of Laurell,* in its invitation to readers to amend *Phyllyp Sparowe* (*Garlande,* 1257–60), to "a belated laureation of the reader, a recognition that the reader will always have the last word."[55] Although Skelton does not recognize the reader's power quite as unequivocally as this suggests, Schibanoff's point is a good one. Readers do have the last word, we all know this, and the knowledge plays a part in the relationship between writer and reader. However much he may try to assert his authority, to make us jump through his hoops, to browbeat us into reading according to his instructions, he knows, as we know, that we need not listen and we can always put the book down.

6

Breaches in the Wall

Poetic Heightening

The claims to authority in *Speke Parott, The Dunciad,* and *The Waste Land* are undermined by other elements in the poems besides our shared knowledge of the reader's independence. Something of the resultant insecurity is evident in the notes, for while the notes to each poem support the poet's authority, they also subvert it. Graham Hough writes of Eliot's:

> The notes to *The Waste Land* are a joke, but they suggest that he would be quite willing to be edited like an ancient classic. Here we see him cutting a solemn caper between excessive deference and excessive disrespect for traditional authority.[1]

Eliot not only displays respect for traditional authority but also, with his initiate's knowing air, tries to claim a share in it, yet at the same time the notes very often seem somewhat mocking. The overplayed casualness of the observation, "This may not appear as exact as Sappho's lines" (221n), for example, both exhibits Eliot's familiarity with Greek poetry and laughs at the exhibition. Some of the notes to *Speke Parott* have a similar effect. One allusion to Horace is glossed with "hear Horace and observe what a diabolic tangle,"[2] which directs the reader toward Skelton's learning and his learned obscurity while also hinting that the poem may be simply irritatingly incomprehensible. Lastly, if Pope's notes on the one hand work toward emphasizing his classical authority, they encourage on the other an ironic attitude toward him. When one footnote commends the poet for his *"Candour and Humanity"* (A1:39n), the reader is invited to laugh at Pope's malice and at his denials of it, and when "Bentley" comments on the hidden mysteries (B4:4n), the note alerts us to the difficulty of some passages in a way at once serious and ridiculous. More generally, the absurd solemnity with which Scriblerus treats the poem suggests the desirability of other, less earnest attitudes, and the tendency of these is to undercut authority.

The ironies of the notes reflect, albeit lightheartedly, an anxiety about the position of the poet that is also present in the tensions of the poems. Each of the poets tries to secure himself in the citadel of tradition, but each poem exposes considerable uncertainty about the strength of the citadel and about the poet's position in it. The claims to authority are countered in the first place by the attempts to "heighten" the poems. Each poet emphasizes the evil condition of the world by showing its rejection and ignorance of his tradition, but since the power of a tradition depends upon centrality, a marginal position deprives it and its would-be representatives of power. A similar effect comes about through the evident wish of the poets to engage with the world. Alongside the insistence of each that he inhabits a different sphere is his obvious involvement with the world, and alongside the "traditional" character belonging with that higher sphere is an individual who is distinctly cranky and flawed. At the same time as the poet engages with the world, the world seems also to enter his poem, destroying its order. Finally, and this is related to all the tensions I have mentioned, the authority is subverted by the poets' dramatizations of their situations. Each dramatizes his own struggle by representing it as one man against the world, but since this dramatizes the struggle in the sense of making it a drama as well as in the sense of elevating it, the reader is afforded a spectator's perspective and a spectator's freedom to judge actions and motives.

The effect of the poetic heightening, dramatization, and so on is to work against the claims to authority as they are made, and thereby to create tensions that imply a failing authority, or (to use the metaphor of my title) that expose breaches in the walls of the poets' psychological citadels. The word *effect* in that sentence suggests that it is principally the reader who detects the failure and who uses the reader's prerogative to reject the poet's claims, which takes us back to the question of intention. The tensions in the poems are sometimes so acute and so apparent as to imply uncertainty and anxiety, unacknowledged, perhaps, on the part of the poet himself. The anxiety is rarely on the surface and, at times, it is almost hidden. Nevertheless, we are justified, I think, in assuming that the uneasy tensions in a poem are the products of an uneasy imagination. The poet may have been unaware of his anxiety in much of his conscious life, as any human being is, and he may have spent many hours as a contented snob, as every human being does. But if his poem will not let such self-satisfied contentment be, the credit for the imaginative honesty is not finally the reader's but the poet's.

In *Speke Parott,* Skelton tries at once to establish his authority by displaying credentials and to intensify his satirical portrait by showing the disappearance of authority from the world. His inspired poet, "Skelton Lawryat" (520a), is accredited by three institutions, and each of the three is presented as corrupt, perhaps to an irreparable degree. Firstly, the use of his title of laureate identifies him as a graduate and seeks to draw strength from the universities, but a good portion of the poem is devoted to exposing their lamentable condition (141–82). Secondly, his other title of "Orator Regius" (520b) places him as a faithful and trusted servant of the monarchy, and this aspect of character is underlined by the professions of loyalty scattered throughout the poem. However, Skelton is also concerned to show that the monarchy has betrayed itself to Wolsey, so that "Bo-ho doth bark wel, Hough-ho he rulyth the ring" (130). Henry, who conferred on Skelton his impressive title, is reduced in this line to Wolsey's performing dog. Finally, and perhaps most importantly, Skelton is a good son of the Church, and in particular, he is a priest, with the priest's special authority. Even though there is no direct reference to his vocation, contemporary readers would have known of it, and it is implied in the dazzling sets of biblical allusions I discuss in the previous chapter. F. W. Brownlow's invaluable account of these argues convincingly that Skelton refers not "to primary sources so much as to later interpretations of them,"[3] that is, his approach to the Bible is traditional. It was also becoming old-fashioned in the wake of the kind of new learning referred to in the poem. The notes to Erasmus's Greek New Testament (and the Testament is the target of a couplet of *Speke Parott* [153–54]) prefer a literal interpretation whenever possible,[4] and Erasmus, for all the controversy surrounding his edition, was respected by Henry and Wolsey. In addition to Skelton's kind of religion becoming "dated," the central institution of the Church itself was endangered by Wolsey's preeminence in England and his moves to be made pope, and again these have their place in the poem (411–14). Whatever Skelton may have thought about the supremacy of the papacy, he implies in the poem that a Pope Thomas would be extremely damaging for the authority of the Church. So, *Speke Parott* embodies a curious conflict, with Skelton relying for his own authority on the very institutions he exposes as degenerate.

The case of *The Dunciad* is somewhat different from this, since Pope's authority does not derive from distinctive institutions but from tradition. There is, however, the similarity that Pope's tradition, like Skelton's institutions, is authoritative because it is, or has been, central, established, and powerful. When Pope signals his position in a line of English poets going back to the Renaissance and, with a jump, to Chaucer, he is placing himself in the mainstream, and when he numbers Bolingbroke, Swift, and Peterborough among his friends, he is aligning himself with the powerful figures of Queen Anne's time. The significance of such gestures lies in their insistence that Pope belongs to what has been the central tradition, and that his friends have been high in the establishment. But Pope—and this is close to Skelton—also represents new forms of literature as marginalizing his tradition, and a new kind of leader as firmly settled in the establishment. In effect, he attempts at once to gain authority from his own centrality, and to create a striking satiric picture by emphasizing the removal of himself, and all he values, from the center. Something of this conflict can be seen at those points of *The Dunciad* where Pope reworks passages from his earlier poetry.[5] For example, Smedley bursting from the mud of Fleet Ditch to describe the "wonders of the deep" (B2:325–46) recalls and contrasts with the appearance of Father Thames in *Windsor Forest* (329). Father Thames, decked out in the appropriate trappings of classicality and literary precedent, celebrates the growth of London under Anne and the spread of English peace, while Smedley celebrates dirt and the contagion of forgetfulness and insensibility. As well as indicating a decline since the days of Anne, the allusion reveals the difficulty of Pope's position. It directs us toward a poet who is both essentially conservative, drawing strength from the established and the establishment, and who is a bitter opposition outcast. The two opposing aspects of character are present throughout the poem, and of course, the fact that Pope is an outcast tends to throw doubt on his implicit assertions of an authority based on centrality.

The kind of authority Eliot claims is also based on centrality, although it has nothing to do with distinctive institutions or (even lost) political power. The important paragraph of "Tradition and the Individual Talent" dealing with the poet's relation to the past argues that he must be conscious of "the main current" and of "the mind of Europe" (*SW*, 51). Both images emphasize centrality, and in *The Waste Land,* Eliot demonstrates his place in the central tradition, and claims the authority conferred by that place, through his constant allusion. But if the allusions beckon toward the "mind of Europe," it is a mind that is inaccessible, even unrecognizable, to most Europeans. Although we are not given the reactions of any other characters of *The Waste Land* to the speaker's literary meditations, they are easy enough to guess. If the neurotic lady of "A Game of Chess" could read her companion's thoughts, she would presumably be unimpressed as well as incomprehending. And if any stray nymphs and heirs were to happen upon the solitary walker from the beginning of "The Fire Sermon" and to hear his monologue, they would be struck less by his superiority and erudition than by his eccentricity. This is really the hub of the matter: authority rests on a special status, which even when not generally understood is generally recognized. Consequently, a figure of authority cannot be marginal or eccentric. But while one part of Eliot wishes to establish centrality and to assert authority, another wishes to show in as vivid as possible a way a world that has cast the kind of tradition from which these derive out to the margin. The result is that Eliot's authority in *The Waste Land,* like Skelton's in *Speke Parott* and Pope's in *The Dunciad,* is of a very uncertain and unconvincing kind.

Engaging with the World

If the poetic heightening of Skelton, Pope, and Eliot works against their claims to authority, so, too, does their engagement with the world. The assertions of authority represent an attempt on the part of the poets to define themselves by tradition and to shut others out, but by engaging with the world, they allow their worldy character to emerge and they place themselves among other people. The tension here is related to, though not identical with, the tension in all satire between the two roles of the satirist, between his role as custodian of public morality and his role as character assassin or, more generally, as malicious attacker. The differences of *Speke Parott, The Dunciad,* and *The Waste Land* from much other satire are partly that their claims to authority are not quite the same as the standard pose of public moralist, although they have something of that in them, and partly that the tension is particularly acute in these poems. Most satirists deemphasize the tension by emphasizing one satiric role at the cost of the other. The personal satirist, for example, often discards any claim to moral purpose and simply sets about destroying his victim, with the implicit acknowledgment that his satiric character is aggressive, violent, and, to use Wyndham Lewis's word, "non-moral." In a slightly different development, Elizabethan writers of satire became so taken up with expressing this kind of satiric character that, as Alvin Kernan writes, "it often appears that they were more interested in creating a sensational satirist than in writing satire."[6] At the other pole of satire are those writers who hide their violence and aggression behind a cloak of morality. Dryden's famed "air of fairness" in *Absalom and Achitophel* is, according to Bernard Schilling, "much more apparent than real,"[7] and its rhetorical function is precisely to cover the poet's partiality, aggression, and unfairness. Even the Juvenalian strand of satire tries in a sense to obscure the poet's aggression by reclassifying it as moral indignation. Comparing Juvenal and Horace, Dennis writes:

Juvenal attacks the pernicious outrageous Passions and the abominable monstrous Crimes of several of his Contemporaries, or of those who liv'd in the Age before him, which is the Business of Tragedy, at least of imperfect Tragedy. . . . There is almost every where in *Juvenal,* Anger, Indignation, Rage, Disdain, and the violent Emotions and vehement Style of Tragedy.[8]

The description both justifies Juvenal's anger by identifying its cause as "abominable monstrous Crimes" and ennobles it with the reference to tragedy. It is, of course, just such a noble, implicitly unmalicious anger that Johnson tries to imitate in his two Juvenalian poems. But if most satirists work to suppress or to camouflage the tensions in their satire, those in *Speke Parott, The Dunciad,* and *The Waste Land,* somewhat different, as I have said, from the tensions in other satire, are very pronounced.

Perhaps the most pervasive, and yet also the least tangible, way that the tension is present in the three poems is in a conflict of methods for dealing with other people. In my fourth chapter I refer repeatedly to the virtuoso handling of different voices, and in my fifth to assertions of authority in response to other people, without indicating in either chapter that these are very different kinds of actions usually performed by very different kinds of people. While an assertion of authority rests on extrinsic institutions, a virtuoso performance rests on intrinsic skill, and while one tries to reduce, the other tries to face difficulty, to cope with as great a problem, in this case as great a diversity, as possible. Skelton, Pope, and Eliot try to be at once both authority figure and virtuoso, and there is an implicit tension between their attempt to identify themselves with a reductive tradition in a reductive way and the dazzling skill with which they incorporate different voices into their poems. To return to one of my earlier examples, Colley remembers his thefts.

> How here he sipp'd, how there he plunder'd snug
> And suck'd all o'er, like an industrious Bug.
>
> (B1 : 129–30)

The rather obscure allusion to the bee image from *The Battle of the Books* contains the appeal to authority. It implies both Pope's position in a tradition of poets from the Greeks to the English Augustans, and the difference between him in that tradition and Cibber in the Grub Street "tradition." The very obscurity of the allusion emphasizes the inaccessibility of the classical tradition to mere grubs like Cibber and, perhaps, to the reader. Moreover, the word "Bug" harks back (the couplet is a late addition) to the portrait of Sporus in *Arbuthnot* and to Pope as Sporus's adversary. This is the Pope who appears as friend of the great, or at least of the sometime great, and as someone removed from the sordid court life by his superior character and his residence at Twickenham. Yet if all this reflects the impulse to appeal to authority, there are also other impulses at work in the couplet. Alongside the impulse to retreat from Cibber and his ilk into tradition there is the impulse to engage with them and to try out their kind of language, and alongside the impulse to protect meaning by obscurity there is the impulse to show off skill and mastery. Indeed, even the allusion to Swift's bee imagery appears not just as evidence of classicality but as a feat of poetic comprehension—the idea of the poet as a bee is another of the colored skittles that Pope keeps aloft. So, the couplet tries to deal with experience, particularly the experience of other people, in two opposing ways. While it implies that the poet is safely removed from all that and all those in his classical garden, it also shows him getting to grips with them. This conflict implies a poet torn between the wishes to retreat from the world and to be involved with it.

The same kind of tension is also present in the three poems in other ways, and differently in each poem. In *Speke Parott*, Skelton dramatizes Parrot's dilemma as a bird who belongs in Paradise and in Wolsey's England, and who consequently both recoils from and engages with the present.[9] The opening lines define very emphatically the paradisaical side of Parrot's character.

> My name ys Parott, a byrde of Paradyse,
> By Nature devysed of wonderowus kynde,
> Deyntely dyetyd with dyvers delycate spyce,
>
>   (1–3)

As the poem develops, Parrot continues to insist on this side of his character, the side that separates him from the world, by reminiscing on the good old days in Eden, by demanding the kind of food he was used to there, and by exercising his distinctive gift of being able to speak every language "aptlye." Yet Parrot in England is not, cannot be, simply a bird of paradise, and just as frequently as he retreats into his Edenic character through reminiscence or food, he advances into the world with chatter to amuse his ladies, with hints of Wolsey's corruption, and eventually, with ever clearer, ever-more-animated denunciations. In these opposing movements, we witness a desire for retirement that is at odds with a desire for involvement, a conflict that reflects Skelton's own. His appeals to authority imply the wish to withdraw into a traditional character that his character as satirist will not allow, and the movement of the poem shows the satirist gradually becoming dominant. Whatever aloofness Skelton retains in the final invective, the poem does move away from obscurity and separation and toward plain speaking, openness, and involvement. A further element in the appeals to authority is that they signal an attempted intellectual retreat, in that authority offers a reductive version of experience, and a weighty dismissal of awkward parts of it. But Skelton's experience of English profusion will not be reduced or denied. This appears most clearly in the structure of the poem, for like other of Skelton's poems, *Speke Parott* gives the impression of growing with a life of its own. In the first part, Skelton seems to reach his conclusion twice, only to start again (140, 225–29), and in the second he introduces a new character (Galathea), new materials (the song "My propir Besse"), then goes on with more pieces of Latin, no fewer than four envoys, more complaint, and, finally, the invective. Such growth suggests that far from having reduced the problems of England to his own satisfaction, Skelton is continually drawn back to reconsider and rework them. This is not to argue that his analysis undergoes any dramatic change but simply that he cannot leave the subject alone.

The conflicting impulses to retire and engage are matched by inconsistencies in the characters of Parrot and Skelton, for both possess personalities in which traditional authority sits uncomfortably beside worldly eccentricity. However much Parrot may claim that he deserves to be set alone above all other birds because of his special qualities conferred by God, he behaves in a way that is exhibistionistic, sexually suggestive, boastful, changeable, and, as his detractors point out, railing. Perhaps more importantly, Skelton's poetic character is also very mixed, and the inconsistencies that are present in his poetry in general can be seen in his contemporary reputation. While Caxton supposed "he hath dronken of Elycons well" and Erasmus hailed him as "that incomparable light and ornament of English letters,"[10] he was also known as the jestbook character who, in the first of the *Merie Tales,* aggressively demands a drink of an innkeeper, and who, in the ninth, defecates on a friar who is trying to share his bed. Later, it was the unconventional side of Skelton, as poet and man, that was most well known. Even in this century, and after the "Skelton revival," G. R. Owst associates him with an age that (and Owst is presumably not thinking of the ninth *Merie Tale*) "begins to delight in fouling the nest which reared it" and in which the realist poet is "without any spark of Idealism transcending what he sees."[11] A more balanced view is taken by William Nelson, who finishes his book on Skelton by arguing that "precisely this violence, this lack of restraint is his chief poetic virtue," then contrasting his violent expression with his "cool, moderate, considered" philosophy.[12] The contrast between violent expression and cool philosophy is an important one, though it may be more accurate to see it as a division in Skelton himself, a division between two of the most prominent aspects of his character, the academic priest and the aggressive, rather cranky scoffer. In *Speke Parott,* the latter side of Skelton is projected through his choice of a lascivious bird as persona, through the playfulness, however under-lyingly serious, with which he treats his subject, through the calcu-lated impudence he directs at Wolsey and even at Henry, and through the violence of some of his expressions, particularly in the envoys and the final invective. All these elements direct the reader toward a Skelton who is rather different from the figure of the inspired poet or of the Old Testament one good man, and by doing so, subvert that figure.

The Dunciad differs from *Speke Parott* in its lack of a protagonist related to the poet, and consequently, Pope does not present his conflict quite as directly, and perhaps not as consciously, as Skelton sometimes does. Nevertheless, the poem does expose an imagination at odds with itself, an imagination of which one side is drawn toward classical dignity while another is drawn toward the chaotic world of Grub Street in all its most unpleasant detail.[13] The conflict is already evident in the involved explanations of the prefatory "A Letter to the Publisher" (purportedly from William Cleland) as to why Pope wrote *The Dunciad.* Cleland (or more probably Pope himself) leans over backward to make it clear that it was only after a long period of silence, and after the dunces had resorted to personal abuse of himself and, more especially, his friends, that Pope retaliated, and the letter writer also explains that he himself would have remained silent had the dunces not attacked his friend's moral character (*Poems* 5:12–13). The letter must go to these lengths to establish that Pope wrote despite himself because his engagement with the dunces is out of keeping with his projected public character. If Pope is really the independent, virtuous, contented friend of the great, the character who appears in the letter (*Poems* 5:18) and who is later developed in the imitations, he should not be bothering with dunces.

There are two principal explanations of how this Pope got mixed up with Grub Street. Firstly, there is the argument that is hinted at by Cleland and that appears more explicitly in Scriblerus's essay and in the notes, the argument moreover that most modern critics adopt in one way or another, that the dunces represent a danger "common to all" and that Pope is performing a public service in opposing them (*Poems* 5:13). No doubt Pope did regard his poem in part as defending certain cultural values and no doubt these were threatened, but even given that, a tension remains between Pope the devotee of friendship and Pope the heroic adversary of evil. Furthermore, *The Dunciad* is, as Pope's contemporaries all knew and as the prefatory letter acknowledges, as much concerned with particular enemies and with paying off old scores as with cultural decline.[14] The second explanation of motive, that he was only retaliating for personal injury, responds to this element in the poem. Again, there is some truth in the picture of Pope as the victim of scurrility, but that does not quite explain why he, to whom the dunces are supposedly mere gnats, their libels mere gnat bites, should expend such a vast amount of energy in swatting them and imagining them. The only explanation for that can be that the virtuous friend of the great is only one side of Pope, and that as well as the ancient cultivating his flowers and his friendships at Twickenham, there is another Pope who must travel in imagination to Grub Street and must experience in imagination the Grubean way of life.

The presence of the other Pope in both his poetry in general and in *The Dunciad* in particular has long been recognized. Dennis's first attack on Pope, his *Reflections* on *An Essay on Criticism,* begins, interestingly, by seeing the *Essay* as part of a general decline in taste brought on by the popularity of opera, and goes on to accuse Pope of hypocrisy.

> I not only found myself attack'd without any manner of Provocation on my side and attack'd in my Person, instead of my Writings . . . I not only saw that this was attempted in a clandestine manner with the utmost Falshood and Calumny, but found that all this was done by a little affected Hypocrite, who had nothing in his mouth at the same time but *Truth, Candor, Friendship, good Nature, Humanity* and *Magnanimity.*[15]

The smarting of an injured vanity is obvious here, the language is intemperate, and the argument suffers from the intemperance. Still, Dennis has a valid point,[16] that the ideals which Pope professes and by which he defines himself do not always square with his real character or with the character which emerges, through subject and style, in his poetry. The disruptive, unconventional side of Pope appears in *The Dunciad* in several connected ways. Firstly, there is the aggression toward the dunces, which, though somewhat hidden behind the impersonal tone of mock-heroic, is unmistakable in the way that Pope makes them dance humiliatingly to his tune. Secondly, there is the disguised iconoclasm in, for example, some of the biblical parodies, as when the dove descending on Jesus is reenacted in Dullness's bird descending on her son (B1:287–92). Thirdly, there is a kind of compulsive indecorousness or offensiveness, which possibly covers a certain aggression toward the reader. The poet who dedicates *The Rape of the Lock* to the gentlewoman whose pubic hair he refers to in the poem also enjoys presenting the reader of *The Dunciad* with images of urinating competitions and aristocratic dinners where the learned watch Annius being delivered of the contents of his stomach (B4:391–94). Fourthly, there is the pleasure that Pope himself finds in "dirty" images, what Johnson calls his (and Swift's) "unnatural delight in ideas physically impure."[17] Lastly, there is the way in which, as Emrys Jones and others since him have pointed out, Pope's imaginative involvement with the dunces releases a secret sympathy with their world of play, irresponsibility, and sleep.[18] The poet emerging from all this is a far cry from the honest professor of virtue and friendship, and if it is not quite fair to dismiss Pope as a hypocrite, it is true to say that his poetic personality is a divided one.

   The Waste Land, too, possesses a number of "unofficial" features that imply a consciousness in conflict with itself,[19] as well as apparently more deliberate indicators. (I write "apparently" because the extent to which the conflict is consciously portrayed or is imaginatively felt and portrayed out of that feeling is largely a matter of guesswork.) Perhaps the most important of the, so to say, unacknowledged elements is the characteristic attitude of Eliot's imagination toward its subject, an attitude that is mirrored in Tiresias. While the ancient prophet seems to want to distance himself from the "event" by his clipped account, his grandiose memories, and his reminders of his bisexuality, he is also interested enough to watch and to report. Similarly, there is in Eliot's typically oblique approach to experience, particularly sexual experience, the suggestion of a mind at once fascinated and disgusted, attracted and repelled. It is almost as if the poet is turning his head away from all that squalor while straining desperately and obsessively to focus on it from the corners of his eyes. Also—and this is a connected point—the would-be loftily prophetic style of parts of the poem is undercut by a more personal animus.[20] There is in the warning to "Consider Phlebas" not merely the prophet's urgent address to his people but also, implicitly, a vindictive delight that the "handsome and tall" will eventually suffer Phlebas's fate. Lastly, the poet's traditional character, which is implied in the allusions and which is related to the ideas about poets put forward in *The Sacred Wood*, is awkwardly opposed by more personal energies. The extent to which a poet appears as traditional and orthodox or as aberrant and heretical, depends to a very great extent on his acquired reputation. Eliot's later career as the grand old man of English letters and his still-central place in university English courses make it easy to regard him as mainstream, just as Skelton's three centuries of dubious fame as a madcap poet must have made it hard for Owst to see him in any other way than that. But, as Bernard Bergonzi argues, *The Waste Land* was initially thought to have "subversive as well as solemn aspects,"[21] and we must not forget the effort it once took to "place" it as traditional. The poem's discontinuities, obscurities, and sterile atmosphere make it an unexpected setting for all those literary jewels, and Eliot's ransacking of the tradition to adorn his strange object could place him as much in the role of the barbarian looting the citadel as in that of the loyal soldier defending it.

In addition to all this, there are aspects of *The Waste Land* that suggest a slightly more self-conscious presentation of an erratic, wayward poetic personality. The line "These fragments I have shored against my ruins" (430), for example. seems meant to sum up the purpose and function of the poem, and it implies chiefly three things: that the allusions are fragments rather than manifestations of a coherent tradition and of the poet's place in it; that they have been used by him as pyschological props; and that his personality is in ruins. There are similar implications elsewhere in *The Waste Land*. In the previous chapter, I discuss the exchange between the speaker and the lady of "A Game of Chess," suggesting that the allusions to Shakespeare are intended to confirm his, and Eliot's, superiority over the woman and others like her. But the drama of the scene, with the gloomy intellectual harried by the nervously energetic woman, presents the allusions not just as confirmations of superiority but as attempts to confirm, that is, as defensive reactions to the worrying of the woman. Moreover, if the allusions and the air of superiority are a defensive reaction, then the whole sense of a special sphere of tradition to which the speaker has access is likely to be his invention, with the function of supporting his rickety personality. So, Eliot here seems at once to be claiming authority and superiority, and to be deliberately contextualizing the claims in a way that undermines them. In other parts of the poem, the instability of the speaker is even more apparent. The greeter of Stetson is decidedly unbalanced; the figure at the beginning of "The Fire Sermon," walking by the river, mangling lines of poetry and thinking of other people's sexual activities, is eccentric at least; and the answerer to the thunder is taken up with his former sexual experiences and sexual failures. All in all, the character that Eliot presents, of his speaker and himself, has as much in it of the private and odd as of the impersonal and traditional.

In each of the three poems, then, the poet, while on the one hand suggesting his authority and his habitation of an authoritative realm, reveals on the other his involvement with the world and the character that goes with that involvement. One result of this conflict in the poems is that the traditions for which the poets are supposed to stand are partly exalted and enshrined and partly demeaned and bespattered. As I argue in the previous chapter, each of the poets defines himself by identifying himself with his tradition, but this also has the effect of identifying the tradition with the poet. Consequently, the personal defects of the poet become associated also with the tradition, and he becomes an image of its decay. A corollary of this is that the poets fail to fashion for themselves in their poems a convincingly coherent, traditional personality. They seem, that is, not to reach the secure psychological haven toward which their claims to authority point. As the reader notices the different sides of each poet's character, he becomes more and more aware of their incompatibility with each other, of the traditional character as a mechanism for dealing with difficulties, and of its fragility. And importantly, the reader's awareness is a reflection of the poet's anxiety. Every contradiction and tension in the poems implies the poet's anxiety, implies that his traditional character is not all it might at first seem and that the citadel is far from secure.

Failures of Order

Another way in which the failing authority of the three poets is revealed is in their failure to create a fully satisfactory poetic structure or order. Of the critical comments of the three, those from Skelton emphasize order least. His acceptance by the Queen of Fame in *Garlande or Chapelet of Laurell* depends chiefly on the volume of his writings, for, as she says, "his name can not ryse / But if he wryte oftenner than ones or twyse" (1154–55), and his defense of poetry in *A Replycacion* rests on its "spyrituall," "mysteriall," "mysticall / Effecte energiall" (365–68). Even so, the importance placed on measure in *Speke Parott* implies the necessity of order in poetry, and more explicitly, Parrot, refers to his art as *"Confuse distrybutyve,"* or "ordered confusion" (198). Both Pope and Eliot give a more prominent place to order in their critical writings. Pope calls beauty the "joint Force and full *Result* of *all*" in *An Essay on Criticism* and talks of it in terms of a "well proportion'd Dome," a whole at once *"Bold, and Regular"* (245–52), while Eliot's central idea of the creative process is that of making new wholes from disparate materials (*SW,* 55). However, as I have said, none of the three is successful in molding his poem into a strong, regular whole. C. S. Lewis writes of Skelton's poetry in general that there "is no building in his work, no planning," and William Nelson suggests, with somewhat more truth, that the second part of *Speke Parott* is "simply a series of more or less discrete envoys or afterthoughts appended to the poem."[22] Even this view is slightly overstated, but if the poem has a discernible direction, shape, and conclusion, it is still something of a loose and baggy monster. Similarly, the four books of *The Dunciad* follow a clear enough outline in their representation of "the restoration of the reign of Chaos and Night, by the ministry of Dulness their daughter, in the removal of her imperial seat from the City to the polite World" (*Poems* 5:50, l.23n). On the other hand, the discontinuities between the fourth book and the other three, between the visions of the third and the games of the second, and between individual passages throughout the poem, give it a very disproportioned, irregular shape. Finally, Eliot is, as Stephen Spender has put it, "a poet of fragments,"[23] and if *The Waste Land* follows a general drift and has a vague kind of form, it lacks a striking and unified architecture.

The failures of order in *Speke Parott, The Dunciad,* and *The Waste Land* have a similar source and are of a similar kind, that is, the poems seem to grow in response to the experiences they deal with and they disturb settled structures with their growth. The poet's need of a discipline that will severely control and limit the growth of his poem is emphasized in some of the critical remarks of Pope and Eliot, although the same cannot be said of Skelton. Pope laments that "copious Dryden, wanted, or forgot, / The last and greatest Art, the Art to blot" (*Epistle* 2.1.280–81), while Eliot urges his reader to compare *Education Sentimentale* with *Vanity Fair* "and you will see that the labour of the intellect consisted largely in purification, in keeping out a great deal that Thackeray allowed to remain in" (*SW,* 65). The three poems are also marked by a failure to keep out or even to have done. In *Speke Parott,* Skelton gives in to his habit of "forever adding to a poem"[24] as events develop or as thoughts occur, and the finished piece carries marked traces of this addition and growth. Similarly, *The Dunciad's* development from the poem of 1728 to *The Dunciad Variorum,* through a few minor changes in the 1730s, to *The New Dunciad,* and finally *The Dunciad* of 1743, is evident in the final poem, and Pope reminds the reader, if any reminder is needed, that this is a new version of an old poem in the jocular "notice" which begins the 1743 volume (*Poems* 5:252). The case of *The Waste Land* is not quite the same, as it has not grown since publication, except by the addition of the notes and, unintentionally on Eliot's part and coincidentally for my argument, the publication in 1971 of the early drafts. These drafts are important in confirming what must be inferred from the published poem about its final composition. The "poem" was originally an unwieldy collection of fragments, passages, and discrete poems, to which Eliot kept adding but which he could not reduce to a manageable size without the help of Pound. Such addition and failure to stop are evident in the published poem, though less obviously than in the drafts, in its disorderly mélange of scenes, fragments, characters, and allusions.

The growth of the poems implies the disturbing presence of chaos within them, the chaos of profusion, crowds, and other people. I speak in my previous section of the way that the poets fail to preserve an authoritative character because of their opposite impulse to engage with the world. As well as subverting the poet's authority, this impulse has the effect of letting "the world"—and the world is characterized by profusion—into the poem in a curiously palpable way. So, Skelton tries to finish his poem and to write off the state of England with a neat allegory, an allusion, or an insult, but he must repeatedly pick up his pen again and write on. The tension between the poet's desire to finish and the world's thrusting itself upon upon his notice exposes both the real presence of the world (in that it alters the poem) and its threat to the poet, a threat he must keep trying to contain anew. In the same way, Pope seems to bite the matter off with every decisively closed couplet, but the matter will not be bitten off like this, and more couplets must be added, and more names named, and more notes attached, and finally, a whole extra book must be written. The sense is very much that the dunces are (as they were) real people who impinge upon the poem, upon the poet, and upon his sense of himself, and whose continuing threat must be countered again and again. Finally, *The Waste Land* is (again) rather different from the other two poems in that it is not tied so firmly to historical personalities and events , although Countess Marie Larisch has her place in "The Burial of the Dead" and parts of "A Game of Chess" recall Eliot's first wife and his maid. Despite the difference, though, the poem's repeated assaults on the same, or the same kind of, experience indicate the poet's struggle with his subject, a struggle that remains unfinished. This is the key point. The three poets all seem to struggle inconclusively with their world, and both the energy of the struggle and its inconclusiveness betray the presence and the power of the chaos they are grappling.

Speke Parott, The Dunciad, and *The Waste Land* are not, of course, chaotic poems. Each of them displays considerable organization, a recognizable structure, and some clarity and point. However, if they are not chaotic poems, they are equally not poems in which the multiplicity of life is either successfully ordered or viewed with detachment from a position of authority. Rather, profusion enters the poems and forces the poets to respond to it in a makeshift, contingent, minute-by-minute way. Earlier, I drew the distinction between virtuosity and authority. The three poems are more virtuoso than authoritative, and even the appeals to authority have a kind of virtuoso effect in that they keep the world temporarily at bay. The virtuosity of the poems, with the constant effort and alertness it requires, emphasizes the immediacy of the world and its potential threat: if profusion has not engulfed the poet yet, *Speke Parott, The Dunciad,* and *The Waste Land* each implies the possibility that it soon might.

The Dramatic Context

The poet's authority is further weakened by his isolation in the world that has rejected his values and, paradoxically, by the heroism that is associated with his lonely struggle. By identifying themselves in their different ways as the only just or classical or knowing men in a rotten world, the poets take on the heroic role of Abdiel, the one angel among Satan's host to resist the invitation to rebellion. In *Collyn Clout* and *Why Come Ye Nat to Courte?* Skelton draws on popular discontent for support, so that, as C. S. Lewis says, "in them Skelton has ceased to be a man and become a mob."[25] This is the rhetorical approach that underpins the modern political petition and that lies behind the closing, and scarcely veiled, threat in Defoe's pamphlet in defense of the Kentish petitioners, *"Our Name is Legion, and we are Many."*[26] *Speke Parott,* on the other hand, rests on the opposite assumption, "my name is single, and I am one." Parrot is without supporters except for Galathea, and he complains bitterly of the cowardly unwillingness of other people to oppose Wolsey, "For drede ye darre not medyll with suche gere" (394). His own readiness (and Skelton's) to involve himself, however cryptically at times, with such gear marks him out as different from others, and alone in his fight. Pope is also alone in *The Dunciad.* Although the "Testimonies of Authors" includes passages written in his support, and although the preface to the Dublin edition, reprinted as an appendix in later editions, reckons his admirers to number a hundred thousand (*Poems* 5:202–3), the poet behind the poem, especially in the fourth book, is essentially the poet of the second *Epilogue to the Satires.* He is the final member of the old band, drawing the "last Pen for Freedom" against the forces of a degenerate age (248–53). The aura with which Eliot surrounds himself is considerably less swashbuckling than this, but he, too, suggests his isolation

in the modern world. What is more, the speaker's cultivated difference
from nymphs, heirs, and other inhabitants of the waste land, the
struggle (both speaker's and poet's) in the final part toward meaning,
and the poet's attempt to keep in touch with "the mind of Europe" all
imply a quiet kind of heroism. While all around are unresistingly
losing their memories, their wills, their most genuine and most valuable emotions, Eliot sets himself against the trend and tries to preserve
something.

If the isolation of the poet/hero underlines his heroism, it also, by
bringing the dramatic conflict between poet and world into the foreground, undermines his authority. This takes us back to Irvin
Ehrenpreis's description of satire as a situation where one person
abuses a second person while watched by a third. In fact, the satirist's
audience is not usually one other person but, implicitly, everybody
else, and the audience's involvement in the conflict is greater than
Ehrenpreis suggests. It is, after all, their wish to be one of the
dominant majority spurning a pariah, their malicious support and
laughter, and their pleasure at the victim's humiliation that give the
satirist his power. Because the audience is involved in this way, the
context of an observed conflict is not acknowledged, or at least not
stressed, in the working of most satire. *Speke Parott*, *The Dunciad*, and
The Waste Land are different—they turn upon a satiric situation in
which one person presents himself as resisting a whole population
before the eyes of another person. In one sense, the audience is more
numerous than just "another person," since every reader knows that
the poem has many other readers, but the emphasis on the universality
of evil has the effect of implying a single, privileged (if not fully
trusted) reader. More important, though, is the way that the heroism
of the poet's resistance draws attention to itself and to the conflict.
The reader, never invited to feel comfortably at one with the poet, is
aware that a clash of mighty opposites is taking place, and that he is a
spectator to the clash. But the more the reader's position as spectator
is confirmed, the more he is enabled to judge the behavior of the poet
by its dramatic context, and this applies to the poet's assertions in
respect to us as well as those in respect to his objects. So, from his
spectator's vantage point, the reader can interpret the poet's assertions
of authority more as responses to a desperate situation than as testimony of real authority, more as moves and psychological gambits
than as rubber stamps and certificates.

The effect is pervasive throughout the poems, but it can also be
illustrated with brief, if rather arbitrarily chosen, examples. Among
Skelton's attacks on the condition of England is the comparison with
Heshbon.

O Esebon, Esebon, to the is cum agayne
Seon, the regent *Amorreorum,*

(120–21)

Skelton here is declaiming against both Wolsey and a general state of
corruption similar to that in the Old Testament city. His authority to
declaim rests on the possession of a special knowledge demonstrated
by the allusions, and on the implied relationship to Jeremiah, the
denouncer of the real Heshbon. The access to knowledge, the prophetic air, and the heroic role of one man against general corruption
all help to keep the reader at a distance, but from that distance the
reader can easily conclude that the composite pose of initiate/prophet/
hero could be put on for the occasion and that Skelton might be
affecting authority to justify a personal grouse against Wolsey and the
times. The effect is even more marked in *The Dunciad,* largely as a
result of Pope's insistence in the apparatus and notes on his struggle
with Grub Street and his poem's place in the struggle. The note to the
first couplet, for example, has Scriblerus rebuking an early commentator for misreading it, quoting Vergil to put him in his place, and in
his usual fashion, seizing the opportunity of a few lines of Latin to
offer his own *"Conjectural Emendation"* (A1 : 1n). In addition to the
joke at Scriblerus's and scholarship's expense, the note serves to cite
classical precedent, to refer to a pamphlet written against Pope and,
thereby, to his war with the dunces, and to hint at his role as the real
hero of the poem and the era. Once alerted to the war and the role, or
rather, when reminded of them, the reader is in a position to see the
classical precedents less as evidence of Pope's real classicality than as
weapons for silencing dunces.

Although Eliot does not represent himself specifically in the role of
the lone warrior, the projected difference, both from world and from
reader, of his poetic presence is so distinct as to allow for doubts about
the truth and the motive behind the projection. His exhibitionistic
cleverness may not, for some readers, serve to locate him in a central
tradition but rather to identify him as someone trying to be special
and superior. When Tiresias mentions Thebes, the reference seems
meant to suggest that he has experienced everything and that the poet
has been, in reading and in imagination, to places where the clerk, the
typist, and others like them will never journey. But the rather incongruous interjection of "And I Tiresias etc." into the sordid love
scene can also sound like someone (Tiresias and the poet) almost
comically bent on establishing his distinction, at least in some respects,
from the less-than-passionate couple. As with *Speke Parott* and *The
Dunciad,* the result of such an interpretation—and it is Eliot's empha-

sis on his difference that invites it—is to undermine authority, for it regards the gestures of authority as actions the poet performs in a context rather than as trustworthy indicators of what he is.

The creation of a context is at the heart of all those points in the poems at which the reader can recognize the poet's weakness. The possibilities of seeing that his authority is based on questionable assumptions, of judging and condemning his satiric character, and of recognizing the effect upon the poem of those people the poet is trying to control all arise out of the dramatic context of the poet or his speaker or the poet and his speaker versus the profuse world. It is in this context that a note of desperate bravado can be heard in the claims to a special authority or a splendid isolation, and that these claims can begin to be questioned. Recognizing the context and beginning this kind of questioning, the reader soon arrives at the conclusion that none of the poets is very secure in his psychological citadel and that all are threatened and anxious. Moreover, the close identification that exists in each poem between the poet and his tradition leads to doubts about the security of the tradition itself. These conclusions are only those to which the imagination of each poem leads. In imagining the crisis of his times, and his own role in that crisis of resisting the new and defending both the established and himself, each of the poets recognizes, though probably not consciously, the weakness of his position and, implicitly, the vulnerability of his cause.

Epilogue

This book has attempted to establish, or at least strongly to suggest, two principal ideas. Firstly, it should by this point be fairly certain that the three poems I have concentrated on are alike in some very essential respects, that the three poets perceive their worlds, and respond to them, in strikingly similar ways. Secondly, the most likely explanation for the affinities between the poems seems to lie in affinities between the cultural conditions of the periods in which the poets wrote. Not simply observers of, but also participants in, the cultural crises of their times, the poets were shaped and influenced by the worrying transitions they were living through. Given that, however, a number of questions still remain, questions which, with one partial exception, can only be raised, and must remain unanswered, here. There is, for example, the important question of why cultural traditions should grow old and decay. Although we tend nowadays to reach for social or economic explanations of such phenomena, it is rather hard in looking closely at the periods of the three poets to find firm points of comparison of this kind, beyond the fact that each is transitional in some way. Graham Hough's argument about the relations of literature and society may be relevant here.

> Literature, by a fortunate dispensation, does not reflect very accurately the convulsions of the social order. Its revolutions sometimes precede the social ones, sometimes follow them, sometimes, it would seem, overlap them quite pointlessly.[1]

But if Hough is right, what are the causes of literary revolutions or literary declines? Further, there is the question of how it is that cultural conditions come to affect an author as deeply and as inwardly as I have suggested they do. How is the state of a culture translated into feelings so personal and so important? And lastly, in a more limited sphere, there is the question of what characterizes the imagination from phases of literary traditions other than the end. If we can detect a Trojan sensibility at the end, what can we detect at the beginning or in the middle?

It is this final question for which I can offer the partial, crude and

tentative beginnings of an answer by returning to the subject of my
third section. While the imagination of each of the three poets from
the end betrays a fear of large numbers and a defensive constriction in
the face of them, the imagination from the beginning is generally
expansive itself and excited by experience. In his second anniversary,
Donne writes of his own coming death.

> Thirst for that time, O my insatiate soule,
> And serve thy thirst, with Gods safe-sealing Bowle.
> Be thirstie still, and drinke still till thou goe
> To th'only Health, to be Hydroptique so.[2]

Although the soul's insatiability here has a specially religious sense, the
words "insatiate" and "hydroptique" could be applied to Donne's
imagination generally. There is in his characteristic searching for
ideas, experiences, images, novelties, and definitions a kind of greediness for more, which stands in sharp contrast to the desire in Skelton,
Pope, and Eliot for less. A similar frame of mind can be detected in
Donne's contemporaries, and even in the representation of a tragic
figure like Faustus. When Mephostophilis has presented him with
books containing all necromantic, astronomical, and botanical knowledge, Faustus protests, "O thou art deceived," with the disillusion that
is at the heart of his tragedy.[3] His disillusion arises from the fact that,
wanting a profusion of knowledge and experience, he is profoundly,
shatteringly disappointed when he discovers that the world can offer
so little.

   The Renaissance greediness, if it might be called that, of Donne
and, by inference, of Marlowe is also characteristic of the early romantics. "Our destiny," writes Wordsworth (with words that capture a
good deal of the spirit of the age), "our being's heart and home, / Is
with infinitude, and only there."[4] By contrast, the poets in the three
poems I have dealt with locate their being very firmly with finitude,
and for them the more defined and limited the finitude, the better. In
similar fashion to Wordsworth, Shelley in a famous passage of *Epipsychidion* scorns the narrowness of "the heart that loves . . . One
object," and exalts instead the imagination

> which from earth and sky,
> And from the depths of human fantasy,
> As from a thousand prisms and mirrors, fills
> The universe with glorious beams, and kills
> Error, the worm,[5]

The word, "thousand" in an early romantic poem like this carries quite
different associations from the "thousand small deliberations" that

plague Gerontion, a difference that can be traced back to the different positions of Shelley and Eliot in their tradition. Shelley at the confident beginning is able, if not quite to comprehend, at least to welcome newness and variety, while Eliot at the threatened terminus can only shrink before them. The same shift in sensibility that can be seen in the contrast between Shelley and Eliot is marked in the difference between Keats's excited "MUCH have I travell'd in the realms of gold" and Prufrock's gloomy "For I have known them all already." The vastness of experience that was a stimulation for Keats has become a burden for Eliot.

These remarks, as I have said, represent only the crudest beginnings of any attempt to delineate the characteristic sensibility of the early phase of a tradition. They suggest nothing of the complexity of the sensibility, of its internal tensions, of its energy, of how most typically it manifests itself in imaginative literature, or of awkward exceptions. Even so, they draw in a rough way the contrast between the sensibility of the beginning of a tradition and that of the end, and they sketch, just as roughly, one of the features of the former. More generally, they indicate something of the direction in which future study could go and, thus, bring us to the larger implications of this book. Although its scope is deliberately circumscribed and limited, the book might represent the beginnings of a fuller commentary on the ways in which writers are shaped by the age of their tradition and, more broadly still, on the pattern of English literary history. Needless to say, a close reading of three poems, however important each of them may be, is too flimsy a foundation on which to construct a secure account, or a solid theory, of literary history. But it is toward the building of such an account and such a theory that this study ultimately tends. If the Trojan imagination exists, and if it is shaped by the decline of the poet's tradition, it seems likely that a characteristic sensibility might attach to other stages of a tradition's development. And once that is granted, it is probable that some recurring pattern of changes in sensibility will be discernible generally in the rise and fall of English cultural traditions.

Notes

Chapter 1. Introduction

1. Samuel Johnson, *Johnson on Shakespeare,* ed. Arthur Sherbo, vols. 8–9 of *The Yale Edition of the Works of Samuel Johnson* (New Haven: Yale University Press, 1968), 8:82.

2. Ibid. 8:3.

3. Anne Wright, *Literature of Crisis, 1910–1922: "Howards End," "Heartbreak House," "Women in Love" and "The Waste Land"* (London: Macmillan, 1984), p. 1. Wright's project is, in some respects, similar to mine in that she seeks to read in conjunction authors who are usually regarded as different from each other. The obvious difference, of course, is that her authors are from the same period while mine are from different periods. Surprisingly enough, given the readiness of contemporary criticism to challenge existing groupings and preconceptions, no one has attempted, as far as I know, to draw the parallels in imagination, as opposed to the parallels in theme or genre, between authors from different periods.

4. Joseph Spence, *Anecdotes, Observations and Characters of Books and Men Collected from the Conversation of Mr. Pope and Other Eminent Persons of his Time,* ed. Samuel Weller Singer (London: Centaur, 1964), p. 117. In his note to the line from the first epistle of the second book that contains the phrase "beastly Skelton," Pope describes his poetry as "consisting almost wholly of Ribaldry, Obscenity and Scurrilous Language."

5. *Selected Poems by Ezra Pound,* ed. T. S. Eliot (1928; reprint, London: Faber and Faber, 1948), p. 18.

6. David B. Morris, *Alexander Pope: The Genius of Sense* (Cambridge: Harvard University Press, 1984), p. 1.

7. David Ward, *T. S. Eliot, Between Two Worlds: A Reading of T. S. Eliot's Poetry and Plays* (London: Routledge and Kegan Paul, 1973), p. 141. There has been something of a *Waste Land* "revival" since Ward wrote, but the poem does not enjoy the reputation it once did.

8. The earliest critic I know who compares *Speke Parott* and *The Waste Land* is Ian Gordon (*John Skelton: Poet Laureate* [Melbourne: Melbourne University Press, 1943], p. 158), while more recently, A. C. Spearing has also made the connection (*Medieval to Renaissance in English Poetry* [Cambridge: Cambridge University Press, 1985], p. 265). Among those who compare *The Dunciad* and *The Waste Land* are Patricia Meyer Spacks (*An Argument of Images* [Cambridge: Harvard University Press, 1971], pp. 84–132); J. S. Cunningham ("Pope, Eliot and 'The Mind of Europe,'" in *"The Waste Land" in Different Voices,* ed. A. D. Moody [London: Edward Arnold, 1974], pp. 67–86); and Maynard Mack (*Alexander Pope: A Life* [New Haven: Yale University Press, 1985], p. 782).

9. Grover Smith, *"The Waste Land"* (London: Allen and Unwin, 1983), p. 47.

10. The quotation (from T. S. Eliot, *The Use of Poetry and the Use of Criticism* [1933; reprint, London: Faber and Faber, 1964], p. 62) is:

The age of Dryden was still a great age, though beginning to suffer a death of the spirit, as the coarsening of its verse-rhythms shows; by the time of Addison theology, devotion and poetry fell fast into a formalistic slumber.

Although Eliot refers to "the time of Addison" rather than "the age of Pope," the major poet of the period must by implication be included in his strictures.

11. A. R. Heiserman, *Skelton and Satire* (Chicago: University of Chicago Press, 1961), pp. 178–80.

12. Robert Griffin comments on both ("Pope and the Prophets," in *Modern Critical Views: Alexander Pope,* ed. Harold Bloom [New York: Chelsea House, 1986], pp. 136–37, 141–42).

13. Jeremiah refers apparently to a real drought, but he regards it always as a drought caused by the wickedness of Jerusalem.

thou hast polluted the lands with thy whoredoms and with thy wickedness. Therefore the showers have been withholden, and there hath been no latter rain; (Jer. 3:2–4)

Other relevant passages are Jer. 2:15, 12:4, 14:1–6, 23:10; and from the other prophets, Isa 19:5–8; Ezek. 30:12.

14. Douglas Brooks-Davies discusses Pope's use of the image (*Pope's "Dunciad" and the Queen of Night: A Study in Emotional Jacobitism* [Manchester: Manchester University Press, 1985], p. 78), examples of which occur in B1:8, 119, 329; B2:271–322, 405–10; B3:44, 89; B4:84, 202, 275, 596, 625.

15. Francis Noel Lees ("Noah and *The Waste Land,*" *Critical Quarterly* 23 [Spring 1980]: 80) is the exception among critics in offering this kind of interpretation.

It would seem certain that Eliot's readers should understand that what is portended is not a restorative downpour but an annihilating deluge, a Noah's flood; not a blessing but a distinct and definite doom. We might, so to say, for 'Himavant' read 'Ararat.'

16. This fits with the apocalyptic readings of the poem: F. W. Brownlow, "*Speke, Parrot:* Skelton's Allegorical Denunciation of Cardinal Wolsey," *Studies in Philology* 65 (1968): 124–39; Arthur F. Kinney, *John Skelton; Priest as Poet* (Chapel Hill: University of North Carolina Press, 1987), pp. 15–30.

17. Pope's apocalyptic imagery owes a good deal to Dryden, but Dryden tends to suggest that the purging fire has passed and the great days have arrived. Examples can be found in lines 1169–72 of *Annus Mirabilis;* lines 1026–31 of *Absalom and Achitophel;* and lines 70–85 of "To the Duchess of Ormond."

18. David Lawton, "Skelton's Use of *Persona,*" *Essays in Criticism* 30 (1980): 11, 19–20.

19. S. E. Fish, *John Skelton's Poetry* (New Haven: Yale University Press, 1965), p. 140.

20. Dustin H. Griffin, *Alexander Pope: The Poet in the Poems* (Princeton: Princeton University Press, 1978), p. 223.

21. I suspect that Pope had recognized the irony by 1733 when he wrote his half-mocking and half-affectionate "Prologue, For the Benefit of Mr. Dennis."

22. Marianne Thormählen, *"The Waste Land": A Fragmentary Wholeness* (Lund: C. W. K. Gleerup, 1978), p. 86; and David Spurr, *Conflicts in Consciousness: T. S. Eliot's Poetry and Criticism* (Urbana: University of Illinois Press, 1984), p. 23. Calvin Bedient offers the most thorough discussion of the whole question, and he arrives at the conclusion that there is a dominant voice (*He Do The Police in Different Voices: "The Waste Land" and its Protagonist* [Chicago: University of Chicago Press, 1986], pp. 72–77).

23. I take it that the dominant speaker is speaking in just about the whole of the final two sections as well as in these earlier lines and passages: lines 1–7, 18, 19–20, 37–41, 60–69, 115–16, 118, 120, 124–25, 135–38, and 173–214.

24. C. K. Stead, "Eliot and the English Poetic Tradition," in *The Literary Criticism of T. S. Eliot,* ed. David Newton de-Molina (London: Athlone Press, 1977), p. 204.

25. *The Oxford Book of Modern Verse, 1892–1935,* ed. W. B. Yeats (Oxford: Clarendon Press, 1936), p. xxii.

26. Irvin Ehrenpreis, *Dr Swift,* vol. 2 of *Swift: The Man, His Works and the Age* (London: Methuen, 1967), 2:279–80.

27. Smith, *"The Waste Land,"* p. 39.

28. T. E. Hulme, *Speculations: Essays on Humanism and the Philosophy of Art,* ed. Herbert Read (1924; reprint, London: Kegan Paul, Trench, Trubner and Co., 1936), p. 121.

29. I use "Renaissance" to mean the English Renaissance. "Medieval" should really be "late medieval," but then I would run into problems when discussing Skelton's late position within the late medieval tradition.

30. John Skelton, *The "Bibliotheca Historica" of Diodorus Siculus,* translated by John Skelton, ed F. M. Salter and H. L. R. Edwards, 2 vols., Early English Text Society 233, 239 (1956–57), 2:xxxiii.

31. Gordon, *John Skelton, Poet Laureate,* p. 45.

32. Spearing, *Medieval to Renaissance,* p. 229; Brownlow, "Skelton's Allegorical Denunciation," p. 137.

33. F. R. Leavis, *New Bearings in English Poetry: A Study of the Contemporary Situation* (1932; reprint, London: Chatto and Windus, 1954), p. 195.

34. Louis Menand, *Discovering Modernism: T. S. Eliot and His Context* (Oxford: Oxford University Press, 1987), p. 5. Some of the other critics who have remarked on Eliot's romanticism are: Graham Hough, who argues that his poetry "represents the extreme limits of the romantic method" (*Image and Experience: Studies in a Literary Revolution* [London: Duckworth, 1960], p. 31); C. K. Stead, who maintains that the tradition in which Eliot belongs "whatever it takes over from French writers, runs unbroken from the Romantics" (*The New Poetic* [London: Hutchinson University Library, 1964], p. 191); Frank Kermode (*Romantic Image* [London: Routledge and Kegan Paul, 1957], p. 163); A. D. Moody (*Thomas Stearns Eliot, Poet* [Cambridge: Cambridge University Press, 1979], pp. 107–9); Edward Lobb (*T. S. Eliot and the Romantic Critical Tradition* [London: Routledge and Kegan Paul, 1981], pp. 60– 62); and David Spurr (*Conflicts in Consciousness,* p. 29).

35. M. H. Abrams, *The Mirror and the Lamp: Romantic Theory and the Critical Tradition* (1953; reprint, New York: Norton, 1958), p. 25.

36. A. J. Smith (*John Donne: The Critical Heritage* [London: Routledge and Kegan Paul, 1975], p. 27) writes that the modern criticism of Donne "is incomparably the most illuminating body of commentary on Donne's poetry. But it doesn't break with earlier attitudes in the way that Coleridge broke with eighteenth-century critics."

37. E. R. Curtius, *European Literature and the Latin Middle Ages,* trans. Willard R. Trask (London: Routledge and Kegan Paul, 1953), pp. 348–50.

38. T. S. Eliot, "Last Words," *The Criterion* 18 (1939): 271.

Chapter 2. Youth and Age

1. For the most detailed attempt to equate Magnificence with Wolsey, see *Magnyfycence,* ed. Paula Neuss (Manchester: Manchester University Press, 1980), pp. 33–

42. My emphasis on the youthful folly of the prince inclines toward seeing him more as Henry than as Wolsey.

2. Parrot's complaint, "Besy, besy, besy, and besynes agayne" (57) echoes Fancy's boast, "Bysy, bysy, and ever bysy" (1039), and the danger of excess is the main burden of *Speke Parrot's* final invective and of Liberty's repeated use of "too" (2090–98).

3. H. L. R. Edwards points out that when the poem was written "Jane must have been at least twenty—was, more probably, twenty-two or three" (*Skelton: The Life and Times of an Early Tudor Poet* [London: Jonathan Cape, 1949], p. 109). Fish regards Jane in the poem as a child (*John Skelton's Poetry,* p. 103).

4. Heiserman, *Skelton and Satire,* p. 185.

5. The phrase occurs in the third prose paragraph, unnumbered by Scattergood.

6. Nathaniel Owen Wallace, "The Responsibilities of Madness: John Skelton, 'Speke, Parrot,' and Homeopathic Satire," *Studies in Philology* 52 (1985): 60.

7. *Oxford Dictionary of Proverbs,* 3d ed., rev. F. P. Wilson (Oxford: Clarendon Press, 1970).

8. *Epigrammes* 90:18, in *Ben Jonson,* ed. C. H. Herford, Percy Simpson, and Evelyn Simpson, 11 vols. (Oxford: Clarendon Press, 1925–52), 8:57.

9. Morris notes this childishness (*Genius of Sense,* pp. 277–78).

10. Donald T. Siebert's suggestion that the "consistent attitude of Pope towards the duncers is one of laughter" is a useful antidote to oversolemn readings, but overstated ("Cibber and Satan: *The Dunciad* and Civilization," *Eighteenth-Century Studies* 10 [1976–77]: 208–9).

11. Parts of the passage were added in 1735.

12. James Sutherland does not mention the connection in his volume of the Twickenham edition but does in *English Satire* (Cambridge: Cambridge University Press, 1958), p. 62.

13. Rebecca Ferguson discusses the emphasis on arresting development in the fourth book (*The Unbalanced Mind: Pope and the Rule of Passion* [Brighton: Harvester Press, 1986], pp. 170–86).

14. Colley Cibber, *An Apology for His Life* (London: J. M. Dent, 1914, Everyman), p. 14. Pope may have forgotten that Cibber used the quotation, as Ricardus Aristarchus praises the modesty of his "not taking the commendation" (*Poems* 5:258).

15. *A Letter from Mr. Cibber to Mr. Pope* (1742), in *Pope: The Critical Heritage,* ed. John Barnard (London: Routledge and Kegan Paul, 1973), p. 337.

16. Kinney speculates that Skelton's anti-Wolsey poems may have been circulated among an orthodox Catholic faction "to aid their cause" (*Priest as Poet,* p. 193).

17. Frank Stack, *Pope and Horace: Studies in Imitation* (Cambridge: Cambridge University Press, 1985), p. 126.

18. Arthur Waugh, "The New Poetry," *Quarterly Review,* October 1916, and an unsigned review from *Literary World,* 5 July 1917, both in *T. S. Eliot: The Critical Heritage,* ed. Michael Grant, 2 vols. (London: Routledge and Kegan Paul, 1982), 1:69, 74.

19. Preface to the quarto edition of Pope's letters (1737), *Corr.* 1:xxxvii.

20. *The Letters of Abelard and Heloise,* trans. Betty Radice (Harmondsworth: Penguin, 1974), p. 16, 25.

21. *Satire* 2.1.32–34, in *Horace: Satires, Epistles, Ars Poetica,* trans. H. Rushton Fairclough (Loeb Classical Library, 1947).

22. *Prose Works of Jonathan Swift,* ed. Herbert Davis, 14 vols. (Oxford: Basil Blackwell, 1939–68), 1:1–2.

23. Ibid. 12:117.

24. Another interesting example from this period of Swift's life is the 1730 poem *A Libel on Doctor Delany.* Swift contrasts his own experience with the inexperience of the younger man.

> But I, in *Politicks* grown old,
> Whose thoughts are of a diff'rent Mold,
> Who, from my Soul, sincerely hate
> Both *Kings* and *Ministers of State* . . .

(171–74)

Swift: Poetical Works, ed. Herbert Davis (London: Oxford University Press, 1967). Irvin Ehrenpreis suggests that this poem may have encouraged Pope to write his Horatian poems (*Dean Swift* [Cambridge: Harvard University Press, 1983], vol. 3 of *Swift: The Man, His Works and the Age,* 3:650).

25. *The Complete Works of George Gascoigne,* ed. John W. Cunliffe, 2 vols. (Cambridge: Cambridge University Press, 1910), 2:149.

26. Horace, *Satire* 2.1.34; *Epistle* 1.1.1–11.

27. Ennius, *Satire,* 21, in *Remains of Old Latin,* trans. E. H. Warmington, 4 vols. (Loeb Classical Library, 1953–57), 1:390–91. Juvenal, *Satire* 1:24–25, 11:203. The friend in 13 is also aged (13:16–19) and so too is the main speaker of 3 (3:26–28), all in *Juvenal and Persius,* trans. G. G. Ramsay (Loeb Classical Library, 1930).

28. Gascoigne, *Works* 2:136, 2:139.

29. *Eclogue* 1:142, 160, in *Barclay's "Eclogues,"* ed. Beatrice White, Early English Text Society 175 (1928). Fish draws attention to something of the relationship between *Collyn Cloute* and the first eclogue (*John Skelton's Poetry,* pp. 201–2).

30. Barclay, *Eclogue* 4:387, 5:9. Minalcas's age is somewhat ambiguous. See 4:366, "For thought and study my youth appereth olde."

31. John Peter, *Complaint and Satire in Early English Literature* (Oxford: Clarendon Press, 1956), p. 107.

32. *Epigrammes in the oldest cut and newest fashion* (1599), week 3, epigram 8, in E. A. J. Honigmann, *John Weever: A Biography of a Literary Associate of Shakespeare and Jonson. Together with a Photographic Facsimile of Weever's "Epigrammes," 1599* (Manchester: Manchester University Press, 1987). Peter notes this in *Complaint and Satire,* p. 117.

33. *The Scourge of Vilanie,* "Proemium in librum secundum," line 6, and *Certaine Satyres* 2:1–2, in *The Poems of John Marston,* ed. Arnold Davenport (Liverpool: Liverpool University Press, 1961).

34. *Satyre* 1:1, 106–12, in *Donne: The Poetical Works,* ed. Herbert J. C. Grierson (1929; reprint, London: Oxford University Press, 1971).

35. *Virgidemiarum* 4.1.166–75, in *The Collected Poems of Joseph Hall,* ed. Arnold Davenport (Liverpool: Liverpool University Press, 1949).

36. Alvin Kernan, *The Cankered Muse: Satire of the English Renaissance* (New Haven: Yale University Press, 1969), p. 45. Jonson is a more mature and less violent figure in his *Epigrammes,* but though there are satiric poems in the collection, *Epigrammes* as a whole is not satire. Moreover, the second poem implies that he has had to grow up to produce this kind of book.

37. *Satyr* [*Timon*], lines 1–2, in *The Poems of John Wilmot, Earl of Rochester,* ed. Keith Walker (Oxford: Basil Blackwell, 1984).

38. *Absalom and Achitophel,* lines 1–4, in *The Poems of John Dryden,* ed. James Kinsley, 4 vols. (Oxford: Clarendon Press, 1958). In the elegy to Oldham, Dryden makes the point that satire does not need the qualities which age gives a poet (15).

39. *London: A Poem,* line 256, in *Samuel Johnson: The Complete English Poems,* ed. J. D. Fleeman (Harmondsworth: Penguin, 1971).

40. Juvenal, *Satire* 3.26.124–25; Johnson, *London,* 42.

41. In the *Apology* for *The Rosciad,* Churchill characterizes himself as "a bard just bursting from the shell" (14), in *The Collected Poetical Works of Charles Churchill,* ed. Douglas Grant (Oxford: Clarendon Press, 1956). In *English Bards and Scotch Reviewers,* Byron describes himself as the "least thinking of a thoughtless throng," and goes on to imagine how "every brother rake will smile to see / That miracle, a moralist in me" (689, 699–700), in *Byron: Poetical Works,* ed. Frederick Page and corrected by John Jump (1945; reprint, London: Oxford University Press, 1970). Finally, Roy Campbell in *The Georgiad* is a toreador who loves to take his victims "on the run," in *The Collected Poems of Roy Campbell* (London: Bodley Head, 1949), p. 217.

42. Gulliver goes to Cambridge at fourteen, stays three years (seventeen years old); is apprenticed to John Bates for four years (twenty-one years old); studies at Leyden for two-and-a-half years (twenty-three-and-a-half years old); spends three-and-a-half years on the Swallow (twenty-seven years old); is a doctor in Old Jewry for two years (twenty-nine years old); a ship's surgeon for six (thirty-five years old); and stays at home for another three before setting off on his great series of voyages at the age of about thirty-eight, in 1699 (*Prose Works* 11:19–20). He returns after sixteen-and-a-half years in 1715, at the age of about fifty-four or fifty-five (Ibid., 288). He publishes his *Voyages* in 1726, by which time he must have been sixty-five or sixty-six.

43. Edward Young, *Epistle to Mr. Pope,* 2.13; *Love of Fame,* 2.281–82. In *The Complete Works: Poetry and Prose,* ed. James Nichols, 2 vols. (1854; reprint, Hildesheim: Georg Olms, 1968).

44. In the tenth, for example, he mentions "Flirtilla, who quarrels with me for being old and ugly," and in the eighteenth, characterizes himself as being "in the cool maturity of life" (*The Rambler,* ed. W. J. Bate and Albrecht B. Strauss, vols. 3–5 of *The Yale Edition of the Works of Samuel Johnson* [New Haven: Yale University Press, 1969], 3:51, 59).

45. "A Woman Homer Sung" and "The Coming of Wisdom with Time," in *The Collected Poems of W. B. Yeats,* 2d ed. (London: Macmillan, 1950).

46. The text of *Speke Parott* is not satisfactory. By the first part I mean lines 1–232, and by the second, the rest of the poem.

47. Brownlow, "Skelton's Allegorical Denunciation," p. 128.

48. Lawton makes the important point that Parrot is usually prevented from speaking by the ladies rather than persuaded to speak by them ("Skelton's Use of *Persona,*" pp. 20–21).

49. Griffin points out how important Pope's personality is in the poem (*Poet in the Poems,* p. 217).

50. This applies, of course, to the version of the 1740s in a way that it cannot to those of the late 1720s. Indeed, Martin Scriblerus's prefatory essay to *The Dunciad Variorum* (1729) makes reference to the author's age of forty, a time "when his faculties were in full vigour and perfection" (*Poems* 5:53).

51. John Hervey, *A Letter to Mr. C-b-r* (1742), William Shenstone to William Jago (March 1742), in Barnard, *Pope: Critical Heritage,* p. 252, 333.

52. Howard Erskine-Hill, *Pope: "The Dunciad"* (London: Edward Arnold, 1972), pp. 61–62.

53. Helen Williams contrasts the two poems: "in *The Waste Land* the loss of natural vitality is not dependent on old age; it is part of the blight of youth" (*T. S. Eliot: "The Waste Land"* [1968; reprint, London: Edward Arnold, 1973], p. 23). Philip R. Headings, on the other hand, sees Gerontion as an appropriate speaker

(*T. S. Eliot,* rev. ed. [Boston: G. K. Hall, 1982], p. 83). Finally, Michael H. Levenson argues that Eliot in 1922 may well have regarded himself, like London, as "a little bookkeeper grown old" (*A Geneology of Modernism: A Study of Literary Doctrine, 1908–1922* [Cambridge: Cambridge University Press, 1984], p. 166).

54. *Prothalamion,* lines 5–10, in *Spenser's Minor Poems,* ed. Ernest de Selincourt (Oxford: Clarendon Press, 1910).

55. Jessie L. Weston, *From Ritual to Romance* (1920; reprint, New York: Peter Smith, 1941), p. 112.

56. Ibid., pp. 45–58.

57. Eliot's note to line 216 connects Ferdinand and the Phoenician sailor.

Chapter 3. Intimations of Mortality

1. It is tempting, because of the congruence of ages, to see Lil as a kind of distorted version of Eliot himself—like her, he was, it seems, prematurely "antique."

2. Robert S. Kinsman, "Skelton's *Collyn Cloute:* the Mask of Vox Populi," in *Essays Critical and Historical Dedicated to Lily B. Campbell* (Berkeley: University of California Press, 1950), p. 17.

3. C. S. Lewis, *English Literature in the Sixteenth Century, Excluding Drama* (Oxford: Clarendon Press, 1954), p. 138. Fish regards the poem as demonstrating experience meeting innocence (*John Skelton's Poetry,* p. 120).

4. Heiserman, *Skelton and Satire,* p. 178.

5. Aristotle, *The "Art" of Rhetoric,* trans. John Henry Freese (Loeb Classical Library, 1926), p. 253.

6. Fish notes the pun, (*John Skelton's Poetry,* p. 146). The whole stanza has distinct sexual overtones. After the mention of a maid, Parrot warns "ware ryot" (99–100), and the character Riot in *The Bowge of Courte* has "no pleasure but in harlotrye" (347). Then, someone calls "mete, for Parrot" (102), and he brings attention to the double meaning of "mete" here (food and female flesh) by noting how he has grown "dyvers of language" (103). The last line puns on *meet* and *meat,* a pun that is also used in *Magnyfycence* (2264).

7. *The Canterbury Tales,* 1(A): 3876–82, in *The Complete Works of Geoffrey Chaucer,* ed. F. N. Robinson (1933; reprint, Oxford: Oxford University Press, 1966).

8. Ibid. 4(E): 1465–66, 1831–35, and 1946–49.

9. Ibid. 3(D): 198–200.

10. Horace, *Epistle* 1.1.1.

11. Frank Stack does not remark on this, though the rest of his discussion of the poem is excellent and I follow him on a number of points (*Pope and Horace,* pp. 78–96).

12. Hugh Kenner talks of Tiresias's "fastidious impersonality" (*The Invisible Poet: T. S. Eliot* [London: Methuen, 1960], p. 145).

13. James E. Miller's reading goes against mine; he thinks that Tiresias sees the scene "more from a female than a male point of view" (*T. S. Eliot's Personal Waste Land: Exorcism of the Demons* [University Park: Pennsylvania State University Press, 1977], p. 100).

14. Anne Wright uses the phrase "coping mechanism" for Tiresias (*Literature of Crisis,* p. 198).

15. Marston, *Certaine Satyres* 3: 15–18.

16. Tony Tanner writes, "the verse, enacting the very movements of a poised discriminating mind, celebrates a *possible* order, even while it is often describing an

actual disorder" ("Reason and the Grotesque: Pope's *Dunciad*," in *Essential Articles for the Study of Alexander Pope*, ed. Maynard Mack, rev. and enl. [Hamden: Archon, 1968], p. 827).

17. Griffin describes *The Dunciad* as "perhaps more completely self-revelatory than any of the Horatian poems" (*Poet in the Poems*, p. 217).

18. Pope's secret attraction toward the infantile has often been remarked, most notably perhaps by Emrys Jones ("Pope and Dulness," in *Pope: Recent Essays by Several Hands* ed. Maynard Mack and James A. Winn [Hamden: Archon, 1980], pp. 641–42).

19. Pope's sickness need not, I think, be assumed to have obliterated the sexual side of his character. Details of the sickness are given in Mack, *Alexander Pope*, p. 802.

20. In Barnard, *Pope: The Critical Heritage*, p. 271.

21. Ibid., p. 337.

22. Pope uses "person" in this sense in *Sober Advice*.

> Could you directly go to her Person go,
> Stays will obstruct above, and Hoops below,

> (*Serm.* 1.2.130–31)

The genital significance of the word, which is already clear here, becomes unmistakable a few lines later when "person" is reduced to "thing," Pope's recurring euphemism in the poem (136).

23. Michael Seidel discusses this etymology (*Satiric Inheritance: Rabelais to Sterne* [Princeton: Princeton University Press, 1979], pp. 6–10). See also, Kernan, *Cankered Muse*, pp. 54–57.

24. The lines look back ironically to the messianic strain in Dryden's poetry and, particularly, to the triumphant ending of *Absalom and Achitophel*.

> Henceforth a series of new time began,
> The mighty years in long Procession ran:

> (1028–29)

Dryden himself, of course, is drawing upon a tradition that goes back to Vergil and to the Old Testament prophets.

25. "Quando ver venit meum? / quando fiam uti chelidon?" (*Catullus, Tibullus and "Pervigilium Veneris,"* trans. F. W. Cornish (Loeb Classical Library, 1931, pp. 360–62).

26. Peter Ackroyd, *T. S. Eliot* (1984; reprint, London: Abacus, 1985), pp. 116–17.

27. Elois Knapp Hay suggests that the final line answers the Sibyl's opening (*T. S. Eliot's Negative Way* [Cambridge: Harvard University Press, 1982], p. 68).

28. Maurice Pollet, *John Skelton: Poet of Tudor England*, trans. John Warrington (London: J. M. Dent, 1971), p. 187.

29. Kinney, *Priest as Poet*, p. 24.

30. A. F. Pollard, *Wolsey* (London: Longmans, Green and Co., 1929), p. 363.

31. George Orwell, "The Lion and the Unicorn," in *The Collected Essays, Journalism and Letters of George Orwell*, ed. Sonia Orwell and Ian Angus, 4 vols. (Harmondsworth: Penguin, 1970), 2:98.

32. Curtius, *European Literature and the Latin Middle Ages*, p. 98.

33. Leavis, *New Bearings in English Poetry*, p. 13.

Chapter 4. Massed Ranks

1. *Virgidemiarum,* in Hall, *Collected Poems,* 6:76. The profuseness of the Skeltonic has often been noted. H. L. R. Edwards describes it as "based solidly on amplification" (*Skelton,* p. 26), while L. J. Lloyd talks of Skelton's "fatal prolixity" (*John Skelton: A Sketch of his Life and Writings* [Oxford: Basil Blackwell, 1938], p. 46).

2. See, for example:

> To cease me semeth best,
> And of this tale to rest,
> And for to leve this letter,
> Bicause it is no better:

(Skelton, *Elynour Rummynge,* 235–38)

3. A. D. Nuttall notes the way that the poem contains a tension between, "on the one hand, the cool, minimising, 'gentlemanly' style and, on the other, a Miltonic/Lucretian grandeur" (*Pope's "Essay on Man"* [London: Allen and Unwin, 1984], p. 62).

4.
> Oh blindness to the future! kindly giv'n
> That each may fill the circle mark'd by Heav'n;
> Who sees with equal eye, as God of all,
> A hero perish, or a sparrow fall,
> Atoms or systems into ruin hurl'd,
> And now a bubble burst, and now a world.

(Pope, *Essay on Man* 1:85–90)

5. Dennis Todd makes some comparisons between the imagery of the preface and that of *The Dunciad* ("The 'Blunted Arms' of Dulness: The Problem of Power in *The Dunciad,*" *Studies in Philology* 79 [1982]: 195–202).

6. Cited by John D. Margolis, *T. S. Eliot's Intellectual Development: 1922–1939* (Chicago: University of Chicago Press, 1972), p. 10.

7. For a discussion of the allusion to Satan's journey and of other Miltonic echoes, see Aubrey Williams, *Pope's "Dunciad": A Study of its Meaning* (London: Methuen, 1955), p. 138.

8. Spurr, *Conflicts in Consciousness,* p. xviii.

9. "Stanzas," lines 70–84, in *Arnold: The Complete Poems,* ed. Kenneth Allott and Miriam Allott, 2d ed. (London: Longman, 1979); *The Letters of Matthew Arnold and Arthur Hugh Clough,* ed. Howard Foster Lowry (1932; reprint, New York: Russell and Russell, 1968), p. 65, 97.

10.
> Ah! two desires Toss about
> The poet's feverish blood.
> One drives him to the world without,
> And one to solitude.

(Arnold, "Stanzas," 93–96)

11. Menand, *Discovering Modernism,* p. 8.

12. *Egoist* 5 (1918): 69. Cited by Margolis, *T. S. Eliot's Intellectual Development,* p. 21.

13. Prologue, lines 222–24, in William Langland, *"Piers Plowman": An Edition of the C-text,* ed. Derek Pearsall (Berkeley: University of California Press, 1979).

14. Fame dismisses one set of suitors with,

"Fy on yow," quod she, "evrychon!
Ye masty swyn, ye ydel wrechches,
Ful of roten, slow techches!

(*House of Fame,* in *Chaucer, Complete Works,* 1776–78)

Chaucer's denial of seeking fame occurs in lines 1871–77.

15. *House of Fame,* in Chaucer, *Complete Works,* lines 1259–62.

16. Brownlow, "Skelton's Allegorical Denunciation," pp. 128–31.

17. Ibid., p. 131.

18. See, for example, the first poem of *Agaynste a Comely Coystrowne.*

19. Donne, *Satyre* 4:18–19. For Marvell, see "Flecknoe, an Irish Priest at Rome," lines 19–36, in *Andrew Marvell: The Complete Poems,* ed. Elizabeth Story Donno (Harmondsworth: Penguin, 1972).

20. Rochester, *Satyre* [*Timon*], line 35; and *Tunbridge Wells: A Satyre,* lines 35–38.

21. Mack's view that the speaker of the poem is simply a persona would work against my reading ("The Muse of Satire," *Yale Review* 41 [1950–51]: 80–92), but I take it that Mack was deliberately overstating his case in the early 1950s in order to defend Pope from even more exaggerated personal readings.

22. Horace has, in the text Pope gives, only *"pueri, patresque severi"* (109).

23. The phrase "th'ignoble crowd" is from *Annus Mirabilis* (999). For an account of Dryden and crowds that focuses chiefly on *Absalom and Achitophel,* see Bernard N. Schilling, *Dryden and the Conservative Myth: A Reading of "Absalom and Achitophel"* (New Haven: Yale University Press, 1961), pp. 167–74.

24. *The Medall,* in Dryden, *Poems,* line 92.

25. *Absalom and Achitophel,* 533–34. Dryden's catalog of rebels is a passage of curiously diluted mock-heroic, with a specific sense of neither place nor time.

26. A vivid passage (though still less concrete than many in *The Dunciad*) is in *Astraea Redux,* in Dryden, *Poems,* lines 276–79.

Methinks I see those crowds on *Dovers* Strand
Who in their hast to welcome you to Land
Choak'd up the Beach with their still growing store,
And made a wilder Torrent on the Shore.

27. *The Temple of Fame,* lines 298 and 318, and lines 342, 356, 378.

28. *House of Fame,* in Chaucer, *Complete Works,* lines 1606, 1657, 1690, 1727, 1771, 1811, and lines 1823–24.

29. Rochester, "A Session of the Poets," lines 1–4.

30. Matthew Arnold, *Culture and Anarchy,* ed. J. Dover Wilson (1932; reprint, Cambridge: Cambridge University Press, 1960), pp. 80–81.

31. "The Function of Criticism at the Present Time," in *Matthew Arnold's Essays in Criticism: First and Second Series,* introd. G. K. Chesterton (London: J. M. Dent, 1964), p. 24.

32. The phrase is George T. Wright's, in *The Poet in the Poem: The Personae of Eliot, Yeats and Pound* (Berkeley: University of California Press, 1962), p. 61.

33. Bedient, *He Do The Police,* p. 9.

34. Bedient gives the line to Marie (ibid., p. 27).

35. Ibid., p. 10.

36. Although John Chalker places Parrot among the newly learned ("The Literary Seriousness of John Skelton's *Speke, Parrot,*" *Neophilologus* 44 [1960]: 44), there is the

important difference that Parrot has learned to speak all languages "aptlye," while they have not.

37. Heiserman sees the ignorance of Parrot's readers as central to the development of the poem. Parrot's allegorical method is conventional, but he lacks an audience intelligent enough to follow it, so he must speak out plain (*Skelton and Satire,* pp. 185–86).

38. Scattergood does not print the glosses, but they can be found in *John Skelton: Poems,* ed. Robert S. Kinsman (Oxford: Clarendon Press, 1969).

39. See, for example, the rubrics to lines 32–33 and to lines 47–49.

40. The Twickenham edition's method of referring readers back to the A text for notes which appear in both A and B is, as the editor recognizes, rather inconvenient for readers (*Poems* 5 : 250). Herbert Davis very helpfully prints the 1743 text without addition or omission in *Pope: Poetical Works,* ed. Herbert Davis, introd. Pat Rogers (1966; reprint, Oxford: Oxford University Press, 1978).

41. Erskine-Hill, *Pope: "The Dunciad,"* p. 9. Reuben Brower sees mock-epic more as a "blending of the heroic with other literary styles and non-literary idioms" (*Alexander Pope: The Poetry of Allusion* [London: Oxford University Press, 1959], p. 13; see also pp. 324–25).

42. See, for example:

> Players are just such judges of what is *right*, as Taylors are of what is *graceful*. And in this view it will be but fair to allow, that most of our Author's faults are less to be ascribed to his wrong judgment as a Poet, than to his right judgment as a Player. (*Prose* 2 : 16).

Pope famously parodies their praise in the line, "The Last and greatest Art, the Art to blot" (*Epistle* 2.1.281).

43. Pope may have remembered that Jonson applies "frippery" to Poet-Ape in his epigram 56.

44. Swift's bee says:

> *I visit, indeed, all the Flowers and Blossoms of the Field and the Garden, but whatever I collect from thence, enriches my self, without the least Injury to their Beauty, their Smell, or their Taste.* (*Prose Works* 1 : 149)

In *Ion,* Plato compares lyric poets to Bacchic maidens:

> And the soul of the lyric poet does the same, as they themselves say; for they tell us that they bring songs from honeyed fountains, culling them out of the gardens and dells of the Muses: they, like the bees, winging their way from flower to flower. (*The Dialogues of Plato,* trans. B. Jowett, 4th. ed., 4 vols. (Oxford: Clarendon Press, 1953), 1 : 108.

45. Eric Partridge gives one eighteenth-century meaning of "bug" as "an inciter, esp. to homosexuality" (*A Dictionary of Slang and Unconventional English,* ed. Paul Beale [1937; reprint, London and Boston: Routledge and Kegan Paul, 1984]). Pope clearly uses the word in this sense in the portrait of Sporus (*Arbuthnot,* line 309). Here, it seems to be simply a "low" word.

46. Aubrey Williams provides an invaluable account of the theme of language in *The Dunciad,* particularly in the fourth book (*Pope's "Dunciad,"* pp. 104–30).

Chapter 5. The Citadel

1. See, for example, J. W. H. Atkins, *English Literary Criticism: The Medieval Phase* (1943; reprint, London: Methuen, 1952), pp. 175–76; and Fish, *John Skelton's Poetry*, pp. 30–35.

2. Curtius, *European Literature in the Latin Middle Ages*, pp. 83–85.

3. Barclay, *Eclogue* 1:913–15.

4. See, Robin Skelton, "The Master Poet: John Skelton as Conscious Craftsman," *Mosaic* 6 (1972–73): 74; Gordon, *John Skelton, Poet Laureate*, p. 63; Nelson, *John Skelton, Laureate*, p. 217.

5. *The Complete Works of Sir Philip Sidney*, ed. Albert Feuillerat, 4 vols. (Cambridge: Cambridge University Press, 1923), 3:3. My overall approach to the *Defence* is indebted to Dorothy Connell (*Sir Philip Sidney: The Maker's Mind* [Oxford: Clarendon Press, 1977], pp. 1–8, 34–51).

6. Sidney, *Works* 3:6.

7. Sir John Davies, for example, links the oracles with the devil in "Nosce Teipsum" (lines 83–84), in *The Poems of Sir John Davies*, ed. Robert Krueger (Oxford: Clarendon Press, 1975).

8. Sidney, *Works* 3:7

9. Ibid. 3:9, 19.

10. Herford, Simpson, and Simpson, *Ben Jonson* 8:637, 644

11. Ibid. 1:50, 151, 138.

12. Ibid. 8:565–66, 627. Although much of the material in *Discoveries* is not original, it still represents Jonson's outlook.

13. Ibid. 8:568.

14. Jonson, "Ode to himselfe," lines 51–52, *in Ben Jonson* 8.

15.

> the argument
> Held me a while, misdoubting his intent
> That he would ruin (for I saw him strong)
> The sacred truths to fable and old song,
> (So Samson groped the temple's posts in spite)
> The world o'erwhelming to revenge his sight.
> Yet as I read, soon growing less severe,
> I liked his project, the success did fear;

("On Mr Milton's 'Paradise Lost,'" in Marvell, *Poems*, lines 5–12)

16. Austin Warren notes the inconsistency (*Alexander Pope as Critic and Humanist* [1929; reprint, Gloucester, Mass.: Peter Smith, 1963], p. 31).

17. "To the Pious Memory of the Accomplisht Young LADY Mrs Anne Killigrew," line 57, and preface to *Religio Laici*, in Dryden, *Poems*, p. 311.

18. Louis Bredvold comments on this (*The Intellectual Milieu of John Dryden: Studies in Some Aspects of Seventeenth-Century Thought* [Ann Arbor: University of Michigan Press, 1934], pp. 12–15).

19. Preface to *Religio Laici*, in Dryden, *Poems*, p. 311, 302.

20. *Essays of John Dryden*, ed. W. P. Ker, 2 vols. (Oxford: Clarendon Press, 1900), 1:27, 104.

21. Preface to the *Fables*, in Dryden, *Poems*, p. 1446.

22.

poetic numbers came
Spontaneously, and clothed in priestly robe
My sprit, thus singled out, as it might seem,
For holy services: great hopes were mine;
My own voice cheered me, and, far more, the mind's
Internal echo of the imperfect sound;
To both I listened, drawing from them both
A cheerful confidence in things to come.

(Wordsworth, *The Prelude* (1805–6) 1:60–68, in *"The Prelude": A Parallel Text*, ed. J. C.
Maxwell [Harmondsworth: Penguin, 1971]).

23. *The Letters of John Keats*, ed. Hyder Edward Rollins, 2 vols. (Cambridge: Harvard University Press, 1958), 1:374.

24. "The Function of Criticism at the Present Time," "Thomas Gray," and preface to the first series of *Essays in Criticism*, in *Matthew Arnold's Essays in Criticism*, p. 20, 279, 4.

25. F. W. Bateson, "Criticism's Lost Leader," in Newton-de Molina, *The Literary Criticism of T. S. Eliot*, p. 3.

26. Roger Sharrock writes that the "qualities of impersonality, mystery, and authority, in combination with the display of reason and learning, are the ingredients of success" ("Eliot's Tone," in Newton-de Molina, *The Literary Criticism of T. S. Eliot*, p. 174).

27. Brian Lee notes this device in relation to "Tradition and the Individual Talent" (*Theory and Personality: The Significance of T. S. Eliot's Criticism* [London: Athlone Press, 1979], pp. 51–52).

28. Denis Donoghue connects the idea of tradition with "ecclesiastical dogma" ("Eliot and the *Criterion*," in Newton-de Molina, *The Literary Criticism of T. S. Eliot*, p. 32).

29. Fish suggests that Occupation is poetry (*John Skelton's Poetry*, p. 234).

30. Griffin writes that "correcting the self, like correcting a poem, was for Pope a matter of editing, rearranging, polishing, adjusting, and, in some cases, reinventing" (*Poet in the Poems*, p. 32).

31. The most recent and detailed commentator on this is Stack (*Pope and Horace*, p. 278).

32. Maynard Mack, *The Garden and the City* (Toronto: Toronto University Press, 1969), p. 100.

33. Henry St. John, Viscount Bolingbroke, *Letters on the Spirit of Patriotism and on the Idea of a Patriot King*, ed. A. Hassall (Oxford: Clarendon Press, 1926), pp. 7–8.

34. Lee argues that "Tradition and the Individual Talent" should be given a full reading which takes account of its personal meanings (*Theory and Personality*, p. 30).

35. John Butt writes that Pope is the "most allusive of our poets" (*Poems* 4:xliv), while Edmund Wilson argues that the school of Eliot and Pound "depends on literary quotation and reference to an unprecedented degree," and that "in 'The Waste Land,' he carries his tendency to what one must suppose its extreme possible limits" (*Axel's Castle: A Study in the Imaginative Literature of 1870–1930* [1931; reprint, London: Fontana, 1984], p. 93).

36. G. K. Hunter discusses the way that Milton transforms some of his materials from Homer and Vergil (*"Paradise Lost"* [London: Allen and Unwin, 1980], pp. 117–20).

37. See Griffin, *Poet in the Poems*, pp. 24–26.

38. It is another odd coincidence that none of the three poems is the result of

entirely independent work. Eliot handed *The Waste Land* over to Pound for pruning; Pope leaned first on Swift, later on Warburton; and *Speke Parott* has been reassembled by Skelton's nineteenth-century editor.

39. *Paradise Lost* 7:31, in *Milton: Poems,* ed. B. A. Wright (London: J. M. Dent, 1956).

40. B. Rajan, *"Paradise Lost" and the Seventeenth-Century Reader* (1947; reprint, London: Chatto and Windus, 1962), p. 18.

41. John Traugott makes the point well: "all ironists begin as snobs, for irony is a trope whose rhetorical effect depends upon the audience's wish to ally themselves with the elite speaker" (*"A Tale of a Tub,"* in *Focus: Swift,* ed. C. J. Rawson [London: Sphere, 1971], p. 84).

42. Swift, *Prose Works* 2:195–96.

43. All the pamphlets connected with the hoax that are printed in the appendix of the second volume of Swift's *Prose Works* recognize the irony.

44. D. H. Lawrence, *Fantasia of the Unconscious and Psychoanalysis of the Unconscious* (London: Heinemann, 1961), p. 5, 83.

45. Chalker, "The Literary Seriousness of Skelton's *Speke Parott,*" p. 40; Brownlow, "Skelton's Allegorical Denunciation," p. 137; Pollet, *John Skelton,* p. 121; Fish, *John Skelton's Poetry,* p. 145; Spearing, *Medieval to Renaissance,* p. 265.

46. Scattergood's translation. The Latin is "Vix tua percipient, qui tua teque legent."

47. Angus Calder, *T. S. Eliot* (Brighton: Harvester Press, 1987), p. 75.

48. Calder suggests, for example, that Pope's assumption of a reader's acquaintance with the popular comedy *The Plain Dealer* and recognition of the common nicknames Bavius and Maevius imply the "confident belief" he outlines (ibid., p. 74).

49. *Spectator* 370, in *The Spectator,* ed. Donald F. Bond, 5 vols. (Oxford: Clarendon Press, 1965), 3:393; *Craftsman* 20; the quotation from Gay is cited by John Fuller (*John Gay: Dramatic Works,* ed. John Fuller, 2 vols. [Oxford: Clarendon Press, 1983], 1:46).

50. Pliny, *Natural History,* trans H. Rackham, 10 vols. (Loeb Classical Library, 1938, 1:7. The quotation means "to give novelty to what is old, brilliance to the commonplace, light to the obscure, attraction to the stale" (1:11).

51. Watts to the countess of Herford, 15 June 1938 (Barnard, *Pope: The Critical Heritage,* p. 247); Swift to Pope, 16 July 1728 (*ibid.,* p. 217); *Lives of the Poets* (ibid., p. 478).

52. See *An Essay on "The Dunciad"* (1728), in Barnard, *Pope: The Critical Heritage,* pp. 214–16.

53. Williams, *Pope's "Dunciad,"* p. 149. Although Williams is speaking specifically of the theological allusions, the phrase can apply to the classical allusions as well.

54. See, Ronald Bush, *T. S. Eliot: A Study in Character and Style* (Oxford: Oxford University Press, 1983), pp. 56–58.

55. Susan Schibanoff, "Taking Jane's Cue: *Phyllyp Sparowe* as a Primer for Women Readers," *PMLA* 101 (1986): 843.

Chapter 6. Breaches in the Wall

1. Graham Hough, "The Poet as Critic," in de Molina, *The Literary Criticism of T. S. Eliot,* p. 55.

2. Kinsman's translation of "Hic lege Flaccum et obserua plantatum diabolum" (*John Skelton: Poems,* p. 162).

3. Brownlow, "Skelton's Allegorical Denunciation," p. 128.

4. Preserved Smith, *Erasmus: A Study of his Life, Ideals and Place in History* (1932; reprint, New York: Frederick Unger, 1962), p. 169.

5. Brower makes the point that "however much Pope owes to literature of the past, he owes more to his own past" (*The Poetry of Allusion*, p. 346).

6. Kernan, *The Cankered Muse*, p. 89.

7. Schilling, *Dryden and the Conservative Myth*, p. 295.

8. "To Matthew Prior Esq.: Upon the Roman Satirists," in *The Critical Works of John Dennis*, ed. Edward Niles Hooker, 2 vols. (Baltimore: Johns Hopkins Press, 1943), 2:218–19.

9. Fish argues that Parrot betrays at once "a wish to be detached and be involved" (*John Skelton's Poetry*, p. 138).

10. Prologue to *Eneydos,* and letter to Prince Henry, in *Skelton: The Critical Heritage,* ed. Anthony S. G. Edwards (London: Routledge and Kegan Paul, 1981), pp. 43–44.

11. G. R. Owst, *Literature and the Pulpit in Medieval England: A Neglected Chapter in the History of English Letters and the English People* (Cambridge: Cambridge University Press, 1933), p. 233.

12. Nelson, *John Skelton, Laureate,* pp. 236–37.

13. Thomas R. Edwards writes of the "struggle between tonal dignity and conceptual ugliness" ("Light and Nature: A Reading of *The Dunciad*," in Mack, *Essential Articles,* p. 770).

14. Griffin emphasizes this (*Poet in the Poems,* pp. 220–21).

15. Dennis, *Critical Works* 1:396–97.

16. The modern critic closest to Dennis is James Reeves. He, too, makes the accusation of hypocrisy but unfortunately mars a real case by intemperate argument (*The Reputation and Writings of Alexander Pope* [London: Heinemann, 1976], p. 243).

17. *Johnson, Life of Pope,* in Barnard, *Pope: The Critical Heritage,* p. 502.

18. Jones, "Pope and Dulness," pp. 633–42.

19. I have rather different conflicts in mind from Spurr's conflict between the intellect and the imagination (*Conflicts in Consciousness,* p. xii).

20. Ward writes that the "prophetic ambitions" of *The Waste Land* are "compromised . . . by the erratic individual note of spleen and anguish" (*Between Two Worlds,* p. 70).

21. Bernard Bergonzi, *The Myth of Modernism and Twentieth-Century Literature* (Brighton: Harvester Press, 1986), p. 92.

22. Lewis, *English Literature in the Sixteenth Century,* p. 142; Nelson, *John Skelton, Laureate,* p. 184.

23. Stephen Spender, *Eliot* (Glasgow: Fontana, 1975), p. 106.

24. The phrase is F. W. Brownlow's ("The Boke Compiled by Maister Skelton, Poet Laureate, Called Speake Parrot," *English Literary Renaissance* 1 [1971]: 7–8).

25. Lewis, *English Literature in the Sixteenth Century,* p. 140.

26. Daniel Defoe, *Legion's Memorial,* in *The Shortest Way with the Dissenters and Other Pamphlets* (Oxford: Basil Blackwell, 1927), p. 112.

Epilogue

1. Hough, *Image and Experience,* p. 3.

2. Donne, *Of the Progresse of the Soule,* lines 45–48.

3. Christopher Marlowe, *Doctor Faustus,* ed. Roma Gill (London: Ernest Benn, 1965), 2.1.176.

4. Wordsworth, *Prelude* (1850), 6:605–6.

5. *Epipsychidion,* lines 164–73, in *Shelley: Poetical Works,* ed. Thomas Hutchinson, corrected G. M. Matthews (1943; reprint, London: Oxford University Press, 1970).

Works Cited

Abrams, M. H. *The Mirror and the Lamp: Romantic Theory and the Critical Tradition.* 1953. Reprint. New York: Norton, 1958.

Ackroyd, Peter. *T. S. Eliot.* 1984. Reprint. London: Abacus, 1985.

Aristotle. *The "Art" of Rhetoric.* Translated by John Henry Freese. Loeb Classical Library, 1926.

Arnold, Matthew. *Arnold: The Complete Poems.* Edited by Kenneth Allott and Miriam Allott. 2d ed. London and New York: Longman, 1979.

———. *Culture and Anarchy.* Edited by J. Dover Wilson. 1932. Reprint. Cambridge: Cambridge University Press, 1960.

———. *The Letters of Matthew Arnold and Arthur Hugh Clough.* Edited by Howard Foster Lowry. 1932. Reprint. New York: Russell and Russell, 1968.

———. *Matthew Arnold's Essays in Criticism: First and Second Series.* Introduced by G. K. Chesterton. London: J. M. Dent, 1964.

Atkins, J. W. H. *English Literary Criticism: The Medieval Phase.* 1943. Reprint. London: Methuen, 1952.

Barclay, Alexander. *Barclay's "Eclogues."* Edited by Beatrice White. Early English Text Society, o.s. 175, 1928.

Barnard, John, ed. *Pope: The Critical Heritage.* London: Routledge and Kegan Paul, 1973.

Bateson, F. W. "Criticism's Lost Leader." In *The Literary Criticism of T. S. Eliot,* edited by David Newton-de Molina, 1–19. London: Athlone Press, 1977.

Bedient, Calvin. *He Do The Police in Different Voices: "The Waste Land" and its Protagonist.* Chicago: University of Chicago Press, 1986.

Bergonzi, Bernard. *The Myth of Modernism and Twentieth-Century Literature.* Brighton: Harvester Press, 1986.

Bredvold, Louis. *The Intellectual Milieu of John Dryden: Studies in Some Aspects of Seventeenth-Century Thought.* Ann Arbor: University of Michigan Press, 1934

Brooks-Davies, Douglas. *Pope's "Dunciad" and the Queen of Night: A Study in Emotional Jacobitism.* Manchester: Manchester University Press, 1985.

Brower, Reuben. *Alexander Pope: The Poetry of Allusion.* London: Oxford University Press, 1959.

Brownlow, F. W. "The Boke Compiled by Maister Skelton, Poet Laureate, Called Speake Parrot," *English Literary Renaissance* 1 (1971): 3–26.

———. "*Speke, Parrot:* Skelton's Allegorical Denunciation of Cardinal Wolsey." *Studies in Philology* 65 (1968): 124–39.

Bush, Ronald. *T. S. Eliot: A Study in Character and Style.* Oxford: Oxford University Press, 1983.

Byron, Lord. *Byron: Poetical Works*. Edited by Frederick Page, and corrected by John Jump. 1945. Reprint. London: Oxford University Press, 1970.

Calder, Angus. *T. S. Eliot*. Brighton: Harvester Press, 1987

Campbell, Roy. *The Collected Poems of Roy Campbell*. London: Bodley Head, 1949.

Catullus. *Catullus, Tibullus and "Pervigilium Veneris."* Translated by F. W. Cornish. Loeb Classical Library, 1931.

Chalker, John. "The Literary Seriousness of John Skelton's *Speke, Parrot.*" *Neophilologus* 44 (1960): 39–47.

Chaucer, Geoffrey. *The Complete Works of Geoffrey Chaucer*. Edited by F. N. Robinson. 1933. Reprint. Oxford: Oxford University Press, 1966.

Churchill, Charles. *The Collected Poetical Works of Charles Churchill*. Edited by Douglas Grant. Oxford: Clarendon Press, 1956.

Cibber, Colley. *An Apology for His Life*. London: J. M. Dent, Everyman's Library, 1914.

Connell, Dorothy. *Sir Philip Sidney: The Maker's Mind*. Oxford: Clarendon Press, 1977.

The Craftsman. Edited by Caleb Danvers (pseud.). 14 vols. Collected edition. London; 1731 and 1737.

Cunningham, J. S. "Pope, Eliot and 'The Mind of Europe.'" In *"The Waste Land" in Different Voices,* edited by A. D. Moody, 67–86. London: Edward Arnold, 1974.

Curtius, E. R. *European Literature and the Latin Middle Ages*. Translated by Willard R. Trask. London: Routledge and Kegan Paul, 1953.

Defoe, Daniel. *"The Shortest Way with the Dissenters" and Other Pamphlets*. Oxford: Basil Blackwell, 1927.

Dennis, John. *The Critical Works of John Dennis*. Edited by Edward Niles Hooker. 2 vols. Baltimore: Johns Hopkins University Press, 1943.

Donne, John. *Donne: The Poetical Works*. Edited by Herbert J. C. Grierson. 1929. Reprint. London: Oxford University Press, 1971.

Donoghue, Denis. "Eliot and the *Criterion*." In *The Literary Criticism of T. S. Eliot,* edited by David Newton-de Molina, 20–41. London: Athlone Press, 1977.

Dryden, John. *Essays of John Dryden*. Edited by W. P. Ker. 2 vols. Oxford: Clarendon Press, 1900.

———. *The Poems of John Dryden*. Edited by James Kinsley. 4 vols. Oxford: Clarendon Press, 1958.

Edwards, Anthony S. G., ed. *Skelton: The Critical Heritage*. London: Routledge and Kegan Paul, 1981.

Edwards, H. L. R. *Skelton: The Life and Times of an Early Tudor Poet*. London: Jonathan Cape, 1949.

Edwards, Thomas R. "Light and Nature: A Reading of *The Dunciad*." In *Pope: Recent Essays by Several Hands,* edited by Maynard Mack and James A. Winn, 768–89. Hamden: Archon, 1980.

Ehrenpreis, Irvin. *Dean Swift*. Vol. 3 of *Swift: The Man, His Works and the Age*. Cambridge: Harvard University Press, 1983.

———. *Dr. Swift*. Vol. 2 of *Swift: The Man, His Works and the Age*. London: Methuen, 1967.

Eliot, T. S. *After Strange Gods: A Primer of Modern Heresy.* London: Faber and Faber, 1934.

———. "Last Words." *The Criterion* 18 (1939): 269–75.

———. *Selected Essays.* 1932. Reprint. London: Faber and Faber, 1951.

———. *The Complete Poems and Plays of T. S. Eliot.* London: Faber and Faber, 1969.

———. *The Sacred Wood.* 1920. Reprint. London: Methuen, 1928.

———. *The Use of Poetry and the Use of Criticism.* 1933. Reprint. London: Faber and Faber, 1964.

———. *"The Waste Land": A Facsimile and Transcript of the Original Drafts, Including the Annotations of Ezra Pound.* Edited by Valerie Eliot. London: Faber and Faber, 1971.

———. *"To Criticize the Critic" and Other Writings.* London: Faber and Faber, 1965.

Erskine-Hill, Howard. *Pope: "The Dunciad."* London: Edward Arnold, 1972.

Ferguson, Rebecca. *The Unbalanced Mind: Pope and the Rule of Passion.* Brighton: Harvester Press, 1986.

Fish, S. E. *John Skelton's Poetry.* New Haven: Yale University Press, 1965.

Gascoigne, George. *The Complete Works of George Gascoigne.* Edited by John W. Cunliffe. 2 vols. Cambridge: Cambridge University Press, 1910.

Gay, John. *John Gay: Dramatic Works.* Edited by John Fuller. 2 vols. Oxford: Clarendon Press, 1983.

Gordon, Ian. *John Skelton: Poet Laureate.* Melbourne: Melbourne University Press, 1943.

Grant, Michael, ed. *T. S. Eliot: The Critical Heritage.* 2 vols. London: Routledge and Kegan Paul, 1982.

Griffin, Dustin H. *Alexander Pope: The Poet in the Poems.* Princeton: Princeton University Press, 1978.

Griffin, Robert. "Pope and the Prophets." In *Modern Critical Views: Alexander Pope,* edited by Harold Bloom, 133–44. New York: Chelsea House, 1986.

Hall, Joseph. *The Collected Poems of Joseph Hall.* Edited by Arnold Davenport. Liverpool: Liverpool University Press, 1949.

Hay, Eloise Knapp. *T. S. Eliot's Negative Way.* Cambridge: Harvard University Press, 1982.

Headings, Philip R. *T. S. Eliot.* Rev. ed. Boston: G. K. Hall, 1982.

Heiserman, A. R. *Skelton and Satire.* Chicago: University of Chicago Press, 1961.

Honigmann, E. A. J. *John Weever: A Biography of a Literary Associate of Shakespeare and Jonson, Together with a Photographic Facsimile of Weever's "Epigrammes," 1699.* Manchester: Manchester University Press, 1987.

Horace. *Horace: Satires, Epistles, "Ars Poetica."* Translated by H. Rushton Fairclough. Loeb Classical Library, 1947.

Hough, Graham. *Image and Experience: Studies in a Literary Revolution.* London: Duckworth, 1960.

———. "The Poet as Critic." *The Literary Criticism of T. S. Eliot,* edited by David Newton de-Molina, 42–63. London: Athlone Press, 1977.

Hulme, T. E. *Speculations: Essays on Humanism and the Philosophy of Art.* Edited by Herbert Read. 1924. Reprint. London: Kegan Paul, Trench, Trubner and Co., 1936.

Hunter, G. K. *"Paradise Lost."* London: Allen and Unwin, 1980.

Johnson, Samuel. *Johnson on Shakespeare*. Edited by Arthur Sherbo. Vols. 8–9 of *The Yale Edition of the Works of Samuel Johnson*. New Haven: Yale University Press, 1968.

———. *The Rambler*. Edited by W. J. Bate and Albrecht B. Strauss. Vols. 3–5 of *The Yale Edition of the Works of Samuel Johnson*. New Haven: Yale University Press, 1969.

———. *Samuel Johnson: The Complete English Poems*. Edited by J. D. Fleeman. Harmondsworth: Penguin, 1971.

Jones, Emrys. "Pope and Dulness." In *Pope: Recent Essays by Several Hands*, edited by Maynard Mack and James A. Winn, 633–52. Hamden: Archon, 1980.

Jonson, Ben. *Ben Jonson*. Edited by C. H. Herford, Percy Simpson, and Evelyn Simpson. 11 vols. Oxford: Clarendon Press, 1925–52.

Juvenal. *Juvenal and Persius*. Translated by G. G. Ramsay, Loeb Classical Library, 1930.

Keats, John. *The Letters of John Keats*. Edited by Hyder Edward Rollins. 2 vols. Cambridge: Harvard University Press, 1958.

Kenner, Hugh. *The Invisible Poet: T. S. Eliot*. London: Methuen, 1960.

Kermode, Frank. *Romantic Image*. London: Routledge and Kegan Paul, 1957.

Kernan, Alvin. *The Cankered Muse: Satire of the English Renaissance*. New Haven: Yale University Press, 1959.

Kinney, Arthur F. *John Skelton: Priest as Poet*. Chapel Hill: University of North Carolina Press, 1987.

Kinsman, Robert S. "Skelton's *Collyn Cloute*: The Mask of *Vox Populi*." In *Essays Critical and Historical Dedicated to Lily B. Campbell*, 17–33. Berkeley: University of California Press, 1950.

Langland, William *"Piers Plowman": An Edition of the C-text*. Edited by Derek Pearsall. Berkeley: University of California Press, 1979.

Lawrence, D. H. *Fantasia of the Unconscious and Psychoanalysis of the Unconscious*. London: Heinemann, 1961.

Lawton, David. "Skelton's Use of *Persona*." *Essays in Criticism* 30 (1980): 9–28.

Leavis, F. R. *New Bearings in English Poetry: A Study of the Contemporary Situation*. 1932. Reprint. London: Chatto and Windus, 1954.

Lee, Brian. *Theory and Personality: The Significance of T. S. Eliot's Criticism*. London: Athlone Press, 1979.

Lees, Francis Noel. "Noah and *The Waste Land*." *Critical Quarterly* 23 (Spring 1980): 80.

The Letters of Abelard and Heloise. Translated by Betty Radice. Harmondsworth: Penguin, 1974.

Levenson, Michael H. *A Geneology of Modernism: A Study of Literary Doctrine, 1908–1922*. Cambridge: Cambridge University Press, 1984.

Lewis, C. S. *English Literature in the Sixteenth Century, Excluding Drama*. Oxford: Clarendon Press, 1954.

Lloyd, L. J. *John Skelton: A Sketch of his Life and Writings*. Oxford: Basil Blackwell, 1938.

Lobb, Edward. *T. S. Eliot and the Romantic Critical Tradition*. London: Routledge and Kegan Paul, 1981.

Mack, Maynard. *Alexander Pope: A Life*. New Haven: Yale University Press, 1985.

————, ed. *Essential Articles for the Study of Alexander Pope*. Rev. and enl. Hamden: Archon, 1968.

————. *The Garden and the City*. Toronto: Toronto University Press, 1969.

————. "The Muse of Satire." *Yale Review* 41 (1950–51): 80–92.

Mack, Maynard, and James A. Winn, eds. *Pope: Recent Essays by Several Hands*. Hamden: Archon, 1980.

Margolis, John D. *T. S. Eliot's Intellectual Development, 1922–1939*. Chicago: University of Chicago Press, 1972.

Marlowe, Christopher. *Doctor Faustus*. Edited by Roma Gill. London: Ernest Benn, 1965.

Marston, John. *The Poems of John Marston*. Edited by Arnold Davenport. Liverpool: Liverpool University Press, 1961.

Marvell, Andrew. *Andrew Marvell: The Complete Poems*. Edited by Elizabeth Story Donno. Harmondsworth: Penguin, 1972.

Menand, Louis. *Discovering Modernism: T. S. Eliot and His Context*. Oxford: Oxford University Press, 1987.

Miller, James E. *T. S. Eliot's Personal Waste Land: Exorcism of the Demons*. University Park: Pennsylvania State University Press, 1977.

Milton, John. *Milton: Poems*. Edited by B. A. Wright. London: J. M. Dent, 1956.

Moody, A. D. *Thomas Stearns Eliot, Poet*. Cambridge: Cambridge University Press, 1979.

Morris, David B. *Alexander Pope: The Genius of Sense*. Cambridge: Harvard University Press, 1984.

Newton-de Molina, David, ed. *The Literary Criticism of T. S. Eliot*. London: Athlone Press, 1977.

Nuttall, A. D. *Pope's "Essay on Man."* London: Allen and Unwin, 1984.

Orwell, George. *The Collected Essays, Journalism and Letters of George Orwell*. Edited by Sonia Orwell and Ian Angus. 4 vols. Harmondsworth: Penguin, 1970.

Owst, G. R. *Literature and the Pulpit in Medieval England: A Neglected Chapter in the History of English Letters and the English People*. Cambridge: Cambridge University Press, 1933.

The Oxford Book of Modern Verse, 1892–1935. Edited by W. B. Yeats. Oxford: Clarendon Press, 1936.

The Oxford Dictionary of Proverbs. Revised by F. P. Wilson. 3d ed. Oxford: Clarendon Press, 1970.

Partridge, Eric. *A Dictionary of Slang and Unconventional English*. Edited by Paul Beale. 1937. Reprint. London and Boston: Routledge and Kegan Paul, 1984.

Peter, John. *Complaint and Satire in Early English Literature*. Oxford: Clarendon Press, 1956.

Plato. *The Dialogues of Plato*. Translated by B. Jowett, 4th ed. 4 vols. Oxford: Clarendon Press, 1953.

Pliny. *Natural History*. Translated H. Rackham. 10 vols. Loeb Classical Library, 1938.

Pollard, A. F. *Wolsey*. London: Longmans, Green and Co., 1929.

Pollet, Maurice. *John Skelton: Poet of Tudor England*. Translated by John Warrington. London: J. M. Dent, 1971.

Pope, Alexander. *Pope: Poetical Works.* Edited by Herbert Davis. 1966. Reprint. Oxford: Oxford University Press, 1978.

———. *The Correspondence of Alexander Pope.* Edited by George Sherburn. 5 vols. Oxford: Clarendon Press, 1956.

———. *The Prose Works of Alexander Pope.* Edited by Norman Ault and Rosemary Cowler. 2 vols. Oxford: Basil Blackwell, 1936 and 1986.

———. *The Twickenham Edition of the Poems of Alexander Pope.* Edited by John Butt and others. 11 vols. London: Methuen, 1939–69.

Pound, Ezra. *Selected Poems by Ezra Pound.* Edited by T. S. Eliot. 1928. Reprint. London: Faber and Faber, 1948.

Rajan, B. *"Paradise Lost" and the Seventeenth-Century Reader.* 1947. Reprint. London: Chatto and Windus, 1962.

Reeves, James. *The Reputation and Writings of Alexander Pope.* London: Heinemann, 1976.

Remains of Old Latin. Translated by E. H. Warmington. 4 vols. Loeb Classical Library, 1953–57.

Schibanoff, Susan. "Taking Jane's Cue: *Phyllyp Sparowe* as a Primer for Women Readers." *PMLA* 101 (1986): 832–47.

Schilling, Bernard N. *Dryden and the Conservative Myth: A Reading of "Absalom and Achitophel."* New Haven: Yale University Press, 1961.

Seidel, Michael. *Satiric Inheritance: Rabelais to Sterne.* Princeton: Princeton University Press, 1979.

Sharrock, Roger. "Eliot's Tone." In *The Literary Criticism of T. S. Eliot,* edited by David Newton-de Molina, 160–83. London: Athlone Press, 1977.

Shelley, P. B. *Shelley: Poetical Works.* Edited by Thomas Hutchinson, and corrected by G. M. Matthews. 1943. Reprint. London: Oxford University Press, 1970.

Sidney, Philip. *The Complete Works of Sir Philip Sidney.* Edited by Albert Feuillerat. 4 vols. Cambridge: Cambridge University Press, 1923.

Siebert, Donald T. "Cibber and Satan: *The Dunciad* and Civilization." *Eighteenth-Century Studies* 10 (1976–77): 203–21.

Skelton, John. *John Skelton: Poems.* Edited by Robert S. Kinsman. Oxford: Clarendon Press, 1969.

———. *John Skelton: The Complete English Poems.* Edited by John Scattergood. Harmondsworth: Penguin, 1983.

———. *Magnyfycence.* Edited by Paula Neuss. Manchester: Manchester University Press, 1980.

———. *The "Bibliotheca Historica" of Diodorus Siculus, Translated by John Skelton.* Edited by F. M. Salter and H. L. R. Edwards. 2 vols. Early English Text Society, o.s. 233, 239 (1956–57).

Skelton, Robin. "The Master Poet: John Skelton as Conscious Craftsman." *Mosaic* 6 (1972–73): 67–92.

Smith, A. J. *John Donne: The Critical Heritage.* London: Routledge and Kegan Paul, 1975.

Smith, Grover. *"The Waste Land."* London: Allen and Unwin, 1983.

Smith, Preserved. *Erasmus: A Study of his Life, Ideals and Place in History.* 1932. Reprint. New York: Frederick Unger, 1962.

Spacks, Patricia Meyer. *An Argument of Images*. Cambridge: Harvard University Press, 1971.

Spearing, A. C. *Medieval to Renaissance in English Poetry*. Cambridge: Cambridge University Press, 1985.

The Spectator. Edited by Donald F. Bond, 5 vols. Oxford: Clarendon Press, 1965.

Spence, Joseph. *Anecdotes, Observations and Characters of Books and Men Collected from the Conversation of Mr. Pope and Other Eminent Persons of his Time*. Edited by Samuel Weller Singer. London: Centaur, 1964.

Spender, Stephen. *Eliot*. Glasgow: Fontana, 1975

Spenser, Edmund. *Spenser's Minor Poems*. Edited by Ernest de Selincourt. Oxford: Clarendon Press, 1910.

Spurr, David. *Conflicts in Consciousness: T. S. Eliot's Poetry and Criticism*. Urbana: University of Illinois Press, 1984.

St. John, Henry, Viscount Bolingbroke. *Letters on the Spirit of Patriotism and on the Idea of a Patriot King*. Edited by A. Hassall. Oxford: Clarendon Press, 1926.

Stack, Frank. *Pope and Horace: Studies in Imitation*. Cambridge: Cambridge University Press, 1985.

Stead, C. K. "Eliot and the English Poetic Tradition." In *The Literary Criticism of T. S. Eliot*, edited by David Newton de-Molina, 184–206. London: Athlone Press, 1977.

———. *The New Poetic*. London: Hutchinson University Library, 1964.

Sutherland, James. *English Satire*. Cambridge: Cambridge University Press, 1958.

Swift, Jonathan. *Prose Works of Jonathan Swift*. Edited by Herbert Davis. 14 vols. Oxford: Basil Blackwell, 1939–68.

———. *Swift: Poetical Works*. Edited by Herbert Davis. London: Oxford University Press, 1967.

Tanner, Tony. "Reason and the Grotesque: Pope's *Dunciad*." In *Essential Articles for the Study of Alexander Pope*, edited by Maynard Mack, 825–44. Hamden: Archon, 1980.

Thormählen, Marianne. *"The Waste Land": A Fragmentary Wholeness*. Lund: C. W. K. Gleerup, 1978.

Todd, Dennis. "The 'Blunted Arms' of Dulness: The Problem of Power in *The Dunciad*." *Studies in Philology* 79 (1982): 177–204.

Traugott, John. *"A Tale of a Tub."* In *Focus: Swift*, edited by C. J. Rawson. London: Sphere, 1971.

Wallace, Nathaniel Owen. "The Responsibilities of Madness: John Skelton, 'Speke, Parrot,' and Homeopathic Satire." *Studies in Philology* 52 (1985): 60–80.

Ward, David. *T. S. Eliot, Between Two Worlds: A Reading of T. S. Eliot's Poetry and Plays*. London: Routledge and Kegan Paul, 1973.

Warren, Austin. *Alexander Pope as Critic and Humanist*. 1929. Reprint. Gloucester, Mass.: Peter Smith, 1963

Weston, Jessie L. *From Ritual to Romance*. 1920. Reprint. New York: Peter Smith, 1941.

Williams, Aubrey. *Pope's "Dunciad": A Study of its Meaning*. London: Methuen, 1955.

Williams, Helen. *T. S. Eliot: "The Waste Land."* 1968. Reprint. London: Edward Arnold, 1973.

Wilmot, John, Earl of Rochester. *The Poems of John Wilmot, Earl of Rochester.* Edited by Keith Walker. Oxford: Basil Blackwell, 1984.

Wilson, Edmund. *Axel's Castle: A Study in the Imaginative Literature of 1870–1930.* 1931. Reprint. London: Fontana, 1984.

Wordsworth, William *"The Prelude": A Parallel Text.* Edited by J. C. Maxwell. Harmondsworth: Penguin, 1971.

Wright, Anne. *Literature of Crisis, 1910–1922: "Howards End." "Heartbreak House," "Women in Love" and "The Waste Land."* London: Macmillan, 1984.

Wright, George T. *The Poet in the Poem: The Personae of Eliot, Yeats and Pound.* Berkeley: University of California Press, 1962.

Yeats, W. B. *The Collected Poems of W. B. Yeats.* 2d ed. London: Macmillan, 1950.

Young, Edward. *Edward Young: The Complete Works, Poetry and Prose.* Edited by James Nichols. 2 vols. 1854. Reprint. Hildesheim: Georg Olms, 1968.